Exam Ref MS-101
Microsoft 365
Mobility and Security
Second Edition

Brian Svidergol
Bob Clements
Charles Pluta

Exam Ref MS-101 Microsoft 365 Mobility and Security, Second Edition

Published with the authorization of Microsoft Corporation by:
Pearson Education, Inc.

ISBN-13: 978-0-13-747177-5
ISBN-10: 0-13-747177-7

Library of Congress Control Number: 2021944465

1 2021

TRADEMARKS

WARNING AND DISCLAIMER

SPECIAL SALES

For information about buying this title in bulk quantities, or for special sales opportunities (which may include electronic versions; custom cover designs; and content particular to your business, training goals, marketing focus, or branding interests), please contact our corporate sales department at corpsales@pearsoned.com or (800) 382-3419.

For government sales inquiries, please contact governmentsales@pearsoned.com.

For questions about sales outside the U.S., please contact intlcs@pearson.com.

EDITOR-IN-CHIEF
Brett Bartow

EXECUTIVE EDITOR
Loretta Yates

DEVELOPMENT EDITOR
Rick Kughen

SPONSORING EDITOR
Charvi Arora

MANAGING EDITOR
Sandra Schroeder

SENIOR PROJECT EDITOR
Tracey Croom

COPY EDITOR
Rick Kughen

INDEXER
Valerie Haynes Perry

PROOFREADER
Scout Festa

TECHNICAL EDITOR
Boyd Nolan

EDITORIAL ASSISTANT
Cindy Teeters

COVER DESIGNER
Twist Creative, Seattle

COMPOSITOR
Danielle Foster

Contents at a glance

Contents

Chapter 2   **Implement Microsoft 365 security and threat management**   **81**

Chapter 3   **Manage Microsoft 365 governance and compliance**   **147**

Acknowledgments

I would like to thank my wife, Jennifer, for being supportive and putting up with the odd hours getting this book finished. To Elias Mereb and Brian Svidergol, thank you for the years of friendship, conferences, dinners, and everything else. And to my friends and colleagues Ed Gale, Joshua Waddell, and Aaron Lines, thank you for your friendship, mentorship, and advice the last couple of years. Finally, to all the IT professionals and readers of this book, thank you for taking the time to read, explore, learn, test, and "play around" with these technologies while you are learning. Keep it up, and good luck!

About the Authors

BRIAN SVIDERGOL designs and builds infrastructure, cloud, and hybrid solutions. He holds many industry certifications, including Microsoft Certified Solutions Expert (MCSE) – Cloud Platform and Infrastructure. Brian is the author of several books covering everything from on-premises infrastructure technologies to hybrid cloud environments. He has extensive real-world experience from startup organizations to large Fortune 500 companies on design, implementation, and migration projects.

BOB CLEMENTS specializes in enterprise device management. He holds industry certifications relating to client manageability and administration for Windows, Mac, and Linux. Bob has an extensive background in designing, implementing, and supporting device-management solutions for private- and public-sector companies. In his free time, he enjoys spending time with his family, writing, and exploring new technologies.

CHARLES PLUTA is a technical consultant and Microsoft Certified Trainer who has authored several certification exams, lab guides, and learner guides for various technology vendors. As a technical consultant, Charles has assisted small, medium, and large organizations in deploying and maintaining their IT infrastructure. He is also a speaker, staff member, or trainer at several large industry conferences every year. Charles has a degree in computer networking and holds over 25 industry certifications. He makes it a point to leave the United States to travel to a different country once every year. When not working on training or traveling, he plays pool in Augusta, Georgia.

Introduction

The MS-101 exam focuses on common tasks and concepts that an administrator needs to understand to plan, migrate to, deploy, and manage Microsoft 365 services. A majority of these services are included as part of the Enterprise Mobility + Security suite, with some optional compliance add-ons.

As an enterprise administrator responsible for the Microsoft 365 services in your organization, you will need to understand identities, security, policies, and industry and regulatory compliance as they relate to the organization to be successful.

This book assumes you already have a working knowledge of some Microsoft 365 services, including Exchange, SharePoint, Teams, or Windows 10. To complete some of the step-by-step guides, or to use some of the features that are outlined, you'll also need a supported device, or even a virtual machine, to be able to join and manage from your tenant.

This book covers every major topic area found on the exam, but it does not cover every exam question. Only the Microsoft exam team has access to the exam questions, and Microsoft regularly adds new questions to the exam, making it impossible to cover specific questions. You should consider this book a supplement to your relevant real-world experience and other study materials. If you encounter a topic in this book that you do not feel completely comfortable with, use the "Need more review?" links you'll find in the text to find more information and take the time to research and study the topic. Great information is also available on MSDN, on TechNet, and in blogs and forums.

Organization of this book

This book is organized by the "Skills measured" list published for the exam. The "Skills measured" list is available for each exam on the Microsoft Learn website: *http://aka.ms/examlist*. Each chapter in this book corresponds to a major topic area in the list, and the technical tasks in each topic area determine a chapter's organization. If an exam covers six major topic areas, for example, the book will contain six chapters.

Preparing for the exam

Microsoft certification exams are a great way to build your résumé and let the world know about your level of expertise. Certification exams validate your on-the-job experience and product knowledge. Although there is no substitute for on-the-job experience, preparation through study and hands-on practice can help you prepare for the exam. This book is *not* designed to teach you new skills.

We recommend that you augment your exam preparation plan by using a combination of available study materials and courses. For example, you might use the Exam Ref and another study guide for your "at home" preparation and take a Microsoft Official Curriculum course for the classroom experience. Choose the combination that you think works best for you. Learn more about available classroom training and find free online courses and live events at *http://microsoft.com/learn*. Microsoft Official Practice Tests are available for many exams at *http://aka.ms/practicetests*.

Note that this Exam Ref is based on publicly available information about the exam and the authors' experience. To safeguard the integrity of the exam, authors do not have access to the live exam.

Microsoft certifications

Microsoft certifications distinguish you by proving your command of a broad set of skills and experience with current Microsoft products and technologies. The exams and corresponding certifications are developed to validate your mastery of critical competencies as you design and develop, or implement and support, solutions with Microsoft products and technologies both on-premises and in the cloud. Certification brings a variety of benefits to the individual and to employers and organizations.

> **NEED MORE REVIEW?**   **ALL MICROSOFT CERTIFICATIONS**
>
> For information about Microsoft certifications, including a full list of available certifications, go to *http://www.microsoft.com/learn*.

Quick access to online references

Throughout this book are addresses to webpages that the author has recommended you visit for more information. Some of these links can be very long and painstaking to type, so we've shortened them for you to make them easier to visit. We've also compiled them into a single list that readers of the print edition can refer to while they read.

Download the list at *https://MicrosoftPressStore.com/ExamRefMS1012e/downloads*.

The URLs are organized by chapter and heading. Every time you come across a URL in the book, find the hyperlink in the list to go directly to the webpage.

Errata, updates & book support

We've made every effort to ensure the accuracy of this book and its companion content. You can access updates to this book—in the form of a list of submitted errata and their related corrections—at:

MicrosoftPressStore.com/ExamRefMS1012e/errata

If you discover an error that is not already listed, please submit it to us at the same page.

For additional book support and information, please visit *MicrosoftPressStore.com/Support*.

Please note that product support for Microsoft software and hardware is not offered through the previous addresses. For help with Microsoft software or hardware, go to *http://support.microsoft.com*.

Stay in touch

Let's keep the conversation going! We're on Twitter: *http://twitter.com/MicrosoftPress*.

CHAPTER 1

Implement modern device services

This chapter covers cloud-based services within Microsoft 365 that are designed to deploy, secure, and manage devices in the enterprise. Throughout this book, you will work with various Microsoft technologies that are included in the Enterprise Mobility + Security (EMS) licensing suite. A majority of services are administered through the Microsoft Endpoint Manager admin center, but there are other portals such as the Azure Portal and the Microsoft Store for Business portal. Along the way there will be several walkthroughs and examples that illustrate how to manage these tools. For these demonstrations we do recommend that you follow along in your own lab. Here are a few links to help get you started:

- **Enterprise Mobility + Security 90-day trial (includes Azure Active Directory Premium P2)** *https://www.microsoft.com/cloud-platform/enterprise-mobility-security-trial*
- **Office 365 Business Premium 30-day trial** *https://products.office.com/business/office-365-business-premium*

Skills in this chapter:

- 1.1: Plan device management
- 1.2: Manage device compliance
- 1.3: Plan for apps
- 1.4: Plan Windows 10 deployment
- 1.5 Enroll devices

Skill 1.1: Plan device management

Device management is one of the core services provided by Microsoft Intune that is managed through the Microsoft Endpoint Manager admin center. Device management requires that the Microsoft Endpoint Manager be configured, and that the appropriate licenses are available in the tenant. You will assign these licenses to users, which in turn can use the devices that are enrolled in the tenant. After the devices are enrolled, you can manage and monitor the devices from the Microsoft Endpoint Manager admin center.

This skill covers how to:
- Plan device monitoring
- Plan Microsoft Endpoint Manager implementation
- Plan for configuration profiles

Plan device monitoring

This skill section reviews device, or *endpoint*, monitoring options available through Microsoft 365 Defender. These offerings enable organizations to monitor the health and compliance of the devices and apps in their environment. The two primary tools for monitoring endpoints are provided through the Microsoft 365 security center and the Microsoft Endpoint Manager admin center.

The Microsoft 365 security center is a one-stop shop that brings Defender for Endpoint, Defender for Office 365, Microsoft 365 Defender, and other tools together into one interface. From the security center, you can perform many monitoring actions:

- **View your Microsoft Secure Score** The Secure Score gives you recommended improvement actions based on the current configuration of your environment.
- **View device compliance** Determine the number, type, and names of devices that are compliant, noncompliant, in a grace period, or not evaluated.
- **View devices at risk** Display the number of devices and their risk level based on the current configuration.
- **View devices with active malware** Track the security events and enforce configuration, compliance, and remediation through Intune device management.

To enable Microsoft 365 Defender, you must have either the *global administrator* or *security administrator* Azure Active Directory role. When you enable Microsoft 365 Defender, there are tenant settings that must be configured, including:

- **Data storage location** The primary location of business for the organization where data residency will apply.
- **Data retention** The default retention period is six months, but can be changed.
- **Preview features** Preview features are enabled by default.

The Microsoft Endpoint Manager admin center provides an all-in-one admin center for device enrollment, device and configuration compliance, endpoint security, and other reporting capabilities. The built-in reports are categorized into four focus areas.

- **Operational** Targeted and action-oriented data
- **Organizations** High-level summary reviews for an organization
- **Historical** Displays patterns and trends over a period of time
- **Specialist** Enables you to use the underlying data to create your own custom reports

Figure 1-1 shows the default home page of the Microsoft Endpoint Manager admin center with healthy and active device status reports.

> **NOTE** To review the logs used as part of reporting, you must have either the *global administrator* or *Intune service administrator* role, or have the *Intune administrator* role with read permissions.

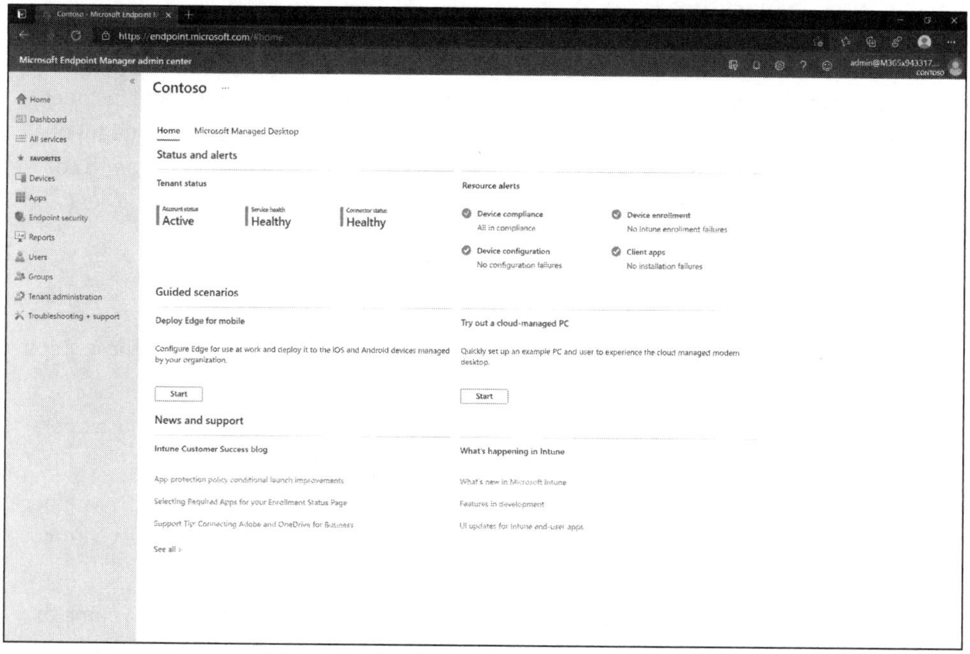

FIGURE 1-1 Microsoft Endpoint Manager admin center

Plan Microsoft Endpoint Manager implementation

Microsoft offers a combination of endpoint solutions that are managed through the Microsoft Endpoint Manager admin center. These offerings have changed over the years, with heavy investments in cloud services and integration with Azure. The introduction of Windows 10 has also influenced the way you manage devices with a set of native mobile device management (MDM) protocols within the operating system, eliminating the need to install another agent on your endpoints. Which solution to choose depends on your organization's deployment goals and objectives. The two primary device-management solutions provided by Microsoft are:

- **Microsoft Intune**   This solution works best for customers who require modern management capabilities for Windows 10 devices, but also need to limit their on-premises server infrastructure. Microsoft Intune is a cloud-based management solution that does not require additional server infrastructure. Platform support for Intune includes management capabilities for Windows 10 and macOS. You also have access to features like Autopilot, which can help reduce traditional operating system deployment requirements.

- **Co-management between Microsoft Intune and ConfigMgr**   This solution bridges Microsoft Intune and ConfigMgr, enabling customers to co-manage devices based on their requirements. ConfigMgr is an on-premises management solution that includes additional platform support, such as Windows Server. It also includes a unique set of technologies, such as task sequences and image deployment. Environments with co-management can take workloads for their Windows 10 devices and mobile devices and move them to the cloud, while still supporting traditional infrastructure.

Set up Intune

There are several steps required to set up Intune before you can manage devices. These steps are as follows:

1. **Understand supported configurations**   These include the supported device operating system, network requirements, and commercial versus sovereign cloud.

2. **Create a subscription**   Add Intune to your tenant, taking into consideration whether you have a Microsoft Online Services account, an Enterprise Agreement, or a volume licensing agreement.

3. **Configure a custom domain name**   Configure a custom or vanity domain name to use with your tenant. It is recommended to do this before adding user accounts to simplify account management.

4. **Add users and groups**   Add individual users and groups to Intune. Alternatively, connect to Active Directory with Intune for synchronization.

5. **Assign licenses**   Associate purchased Intune or Enterprise Mobility + Security licenses with user accounts.

6. **Set the MDM authority**   This applies only to tenants with a service release earlier than 1911. Tenants running 1911 or later are automatically configured to Intune.

7. **Assign apps**   Apps can be assigned to groups for automatic or optional installation.

8. **Configure devices**   Configure the profiles that manages device settings and features.

9. **Customize the portals**   Add your company branding to the various portals.

10. **Enable device enrollment**   Enable certain devices to be enrolled for management by Intune.

11. **Configure app policies**   Configure specific app protection policies for apps protected by Intune.

EXAM TIP

Some exam items require you to understand the order of steps to configure a solution. For example, licenses and the MDM authority must be configured before you can configure device enrollment.

NEED MORE REVIEW?   **SETTING UP MICROSOFT INTUNE**

For a more detailed step by step for setting up Intune, visit *https://docs.microsoft.com/en-us/mem/intune/fundamentals/setup-steps*.

Assign licenses

You can assign Intune licenses to users from both the Microsoft Endpoint Manager admin center and the Azure portal within Azure Active Directory. To assign a license from the admin center, follow these steps:

1. Log in to the Microsoft Endpoint Manager admin center at *https://endpoint.microsoft.com*.
2. Click **Users**.
3. Click **All Users**, then click the user for whom you want to change license assignments.
4. Click **Licenses**, and then click **Assignments**.
5. Select the **Microsoft Intune** check box and click **Save**. (The location of the check box varies depending on the type of license you purchased.)

Figure 1-2 shows the Microsoft Intune license enabled as part of the Enterprise Mobility + Security E5 license suite. Each licensed user can access and use the services defined in their profiles for up to 15 managed devices.

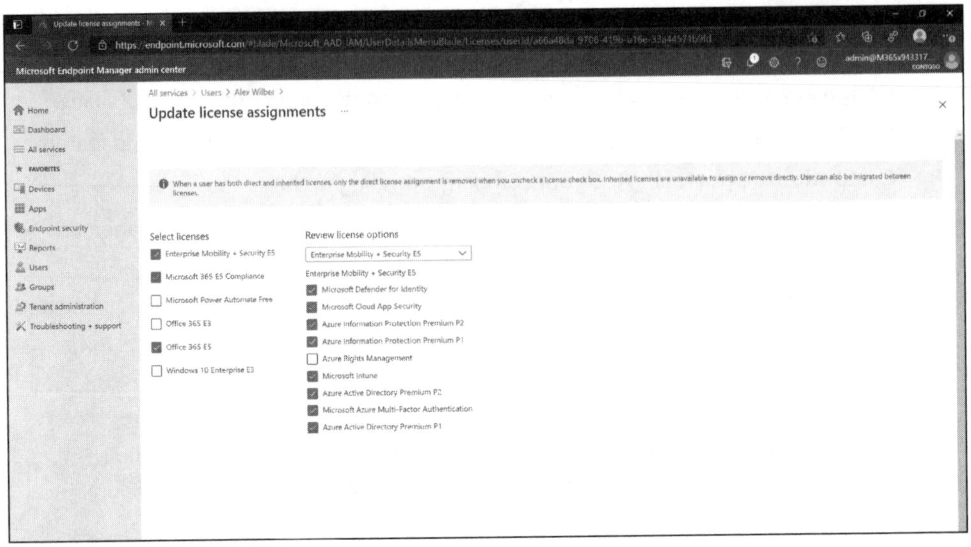

FIGURE 1-2   Assign licenses to users.

Plan for configuration profiles

In this section, you'll review the available settings for configuration profiles. Configuration profiles define the settings that you wish to implement on the devices that are managed. For example, you can customize the browser settings on Windows clients or prevent access to Bluetooth on mobile devices. Configuration profiles are built to define these settings per platform. The supported platforms from the Microsoft Endpoint Manager admin center are:

- Android device administrator
- Android Enterprise
- iOS/iPad OS
- macOS
- Windows 10 and later

After you select the platform to define a profile for, you must select a profile type. The types of profiles vary depending on the platform you selected. For macOS and Windows device types, the options are either Settings Catalog or Templates. The Settings Catalog is a list of all available settings for the selected operating system. For Windows, that equates thousands of settings.

Templates are commonly used tools that need configuration. For example, there are templates for endpoint protection, VPN and Wi-Fi configuration, certificates, device features, and more.

> **NEED MORE REVIEW?**   **SETTING UP MICROSOFT INTUNE**
>
> For more information on applying the settings of a configuration profile, visit
> *https://docs.microsoft.com/en-us/mem/intune/configuration/device-profiles.*

You create a configuration profile from the Microsoft Endpoint Manger admin center. To create a configuration profile, perform the following steps:

1. Log in to the Microsoft Endpoint Manager admin center at *https://endpoint.microsoft.com/*.
2. Click **Devices**.
3. Click **Configuration Profiles**.
4. Click **Create Profile**.
5. In the Platform drop-down menu, select an operating system—in this example, **Windows 10 and Later**.
6. In the **Profile** type drop-down menu, select a profile—in this example, **Templates**.
7. In the list of available templates, click **Wi-Fi**.
8. Click **Create**.
9. On the **Basics** tab, type a name for the profile, such as **Required-Wi-Fi**.
10. Click **Next**.
11. In the **Wi-Fi Type** drop-down menu, select **Basic**.
12. Complete the configuration settings for the Wi-Fi network the device will connect to.

    Figure 1-3 illustrates automatically connecting to a Wi-Fi network named *ContosoWifi* that has WPA2 security and a pre-shared key of *Secure123!*.

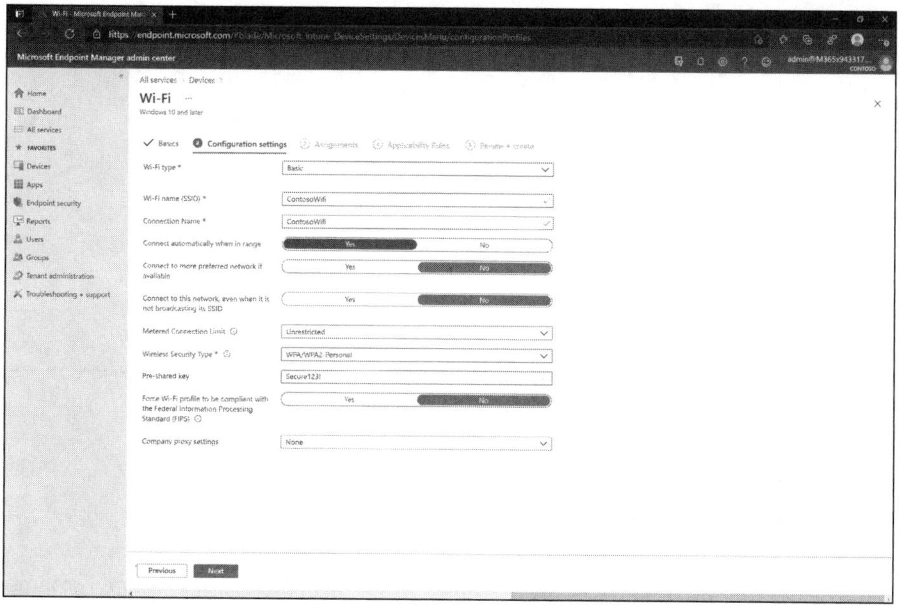

FIGURE 1-3   Wi-Fi configuration profile settings

13. Click **Next**.

14. On the **Assignments** tab, click **Add All Devices**. Alternatively, select the groups of devices that the profile should apply to.

15. Click **Next**.

16. On the **Applicability Rules** tab, leave the defaults blank. Alternatively, add rule filters to specify when this configuration profile should be applied.

17. Click **Next**, and then click **Create**.

    The configuration rule is created and added to the devices you selected.

After you create the profile, you can see its status on a per-device and per-user level. Note, however, that it might take a few minutes for the profile to deploy and be applied on the devices, depending on the number of devices and their connection type. Figure 1-4 shows the status of the newly created profile being applied to a Windows 10 device.

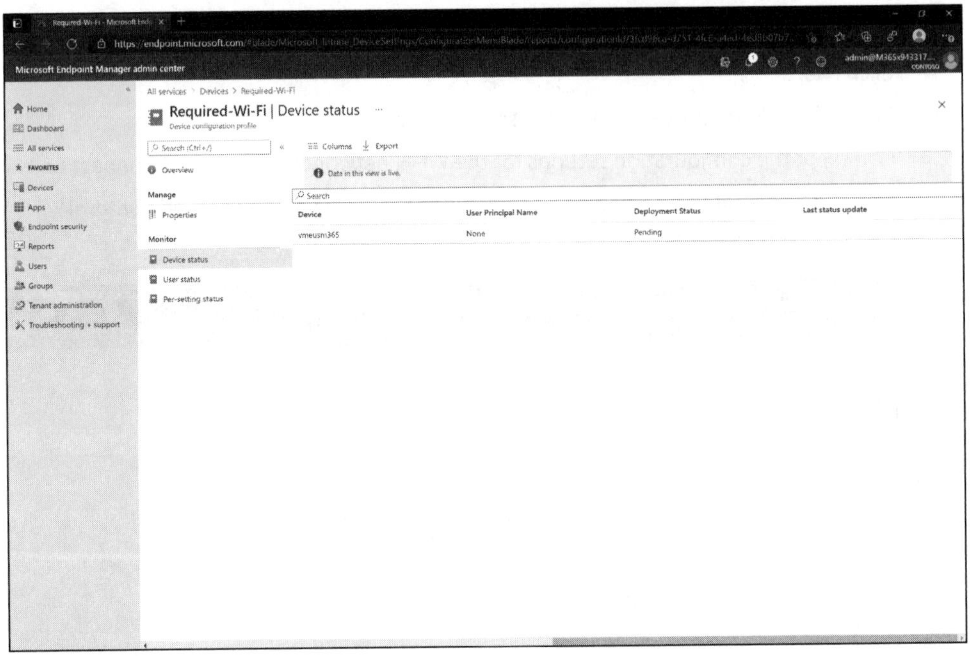

FIGURE 1-4   Pending profile deployment

Skill 1.2: Manage device compliance

Device compliance is the practice of ensuring that the devices accessing your environment meet a distinct set of requirements, often defined by the IT and cybersecurity teams in your organization. For the purposes of this exam, device compliance is also referred to as a feature in Microsoft Intune. This feature is provided to aid administrators in defining their compliance requirements and using them to delegate access to data and services. As an administrator, it is your job to understand the use cases for device compliance and how to implement them.

The compliance policies that you define make up the connective tissue for several other actions in the platform. For example, the compliance status of a device can be leveraged as a determining factor for granting access to Exchange Online. This is accomplished using conditional access policies, another key feature covered in this chapter. Conditional access policies are a different type of policy, managed within Azure Active Directory (Azure AD), for allowing and denying access to data and services.

> **This skill covers how to:**
> - Plan for device compliance
> - Plan for attack surface reduction
> - Configure security baselines
> - Configure device-compliance policy

Plan for device compliance

This skill section covers planning considerations for device compliance. This includes topics such as prerequisites before implementation, compliance workflows, and possible use cases for your organization. Later in this chapter, you will work with conditional access policies. One of the dependencies for conditional access is the compliance status of the end-user device. The MS-101 exam presents scenarios dealing with Intune enrollment, device compliance, and conditional access. As you prepare, take time to work with these technologies in the Azure portal and see what the dependencies are.

Understand the prerequisites for device compliance

Before you get started creating device-compliance policies, there are some technical prerequisites to plan for. Throughout this book you will see some trending prerequisites for each of the cloud technologies, particularly around the required subscriptions. Keep an eye out for these for the exam and take some extra time to understand which features are included with the various subscription models.

These are the prerequisites for device compliance:

- **Subscriptions**   Device-compliance technology relies on Azure AD and Microsoft Intune. The device must be enrolled in Intune to receive a compliance policy, and the compliance flag is written to Azure AD for other features, such as conditional access. At a minimum you need a standalone Intune subscription and an Azure AD Premium P1 subscription. The higher-tiered subscriptions, such as Azure AD Premium P2, do not include additional capabilities focused on device compliance.
- **Platform support**   Device-compliance policies support a wide range of platforms. (For clarification, the term *platform* refers to the operating system, not the physical hardware.)

Platform support is an important prerequisite if you are planning to manage devices that are not supported. At the time of this writing, the following platforms are supported:

- Android
- Android Enterprise
- iOS
- macOS
- Windows 8.1
- Windows 10
- **Enrollment** Devices cannot report compliance until they are enrolled in Microsoft Intune.

> *NEED MORE REVIEW?* **CHOOSING A SUBSCRIPTION**
>
> For more information about the different editions of Azure AD and their corresponding subscription tier, visit *https://azure.microsoft.com/en-us/pricing/details/active-directory/*. For more information about subscriptions pertaining to Microsoft Intune, visit *https://www.microsoft.com/en-us/cloud-platform/microsoft-intune-pricing*.

Understand the process flow for device compliance

Device compliance and conditional access are both policy-based technologies. You configure the policy to address your needs, and then assign that policy to the desired resources in Microsoft Intune. Devices will evaluate the policy and report back whether they meet the requirements or not. The compliance state is then written to the device object in Azure AD as a custom attribute. The state of that attribute will determine whether the device is approved to access data and services. This is where conditional access enters the picture, which is covered in more detail later in this chapter.

Figure 1-5 illustrates the device-compliance flow. In this example, we are using the default configuration for device compliance. As an administrator, you have a few options to change this flow to meet your needs.

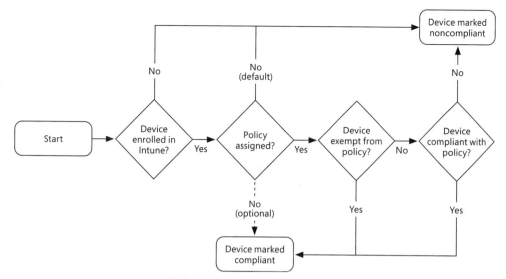

FIGURE 1-5   Device-compliance process flow

These next few items address controls that are available to administrators to alter the device-compliance flow.

- **Intune enrollment**   Devices that are not enrolled in Intune cannot receive device-compliance policies. This also applies to devices that are Azure AD joined. This was covered earlier in the prerequisites section. In this context, it can also be used to prevent compliance policies from applying to unmanaged devices.

- **Policy assignment**   In the compliance policy settings for Microsoft Intune, you have the option to mark devices as compliant if they do not have a policy assigned. By default, all devices without an assigned policy are marked as noncompliant. But you do have the option to change this behavior, making all devices compliant by default. This is represented by the dashed line between the policy assigned and the device marked compliant in the illustration, also marked as optional.

- **Device exemption**   Device exemption is another control you can configure. This is accomplished in the policy settings by defining which device platforms the compliance policy is scoped for. If your compliance policy includes all platforms except iOS, then iOS devices will be exempt from running that policy.

EXAM TIP

As you prepare for this exam, spend time looking at each of the device-compliance options in the Intune portal. Be aware of the settings from both a portal and PowerShell perspective.

Determine use cases for device compliance

In this section, you are going to look at some potential use cases for device compliance. First, understand that compliance policies contain a series of rules that you define. These rules determine whether a device is compliant. Compliance policies can help to remediate certain conditions, but in most cases the device will be quarantined, and remediation will be left up to the user. For example, suppose you have a device-compliance policy that has a security rule that requires a password before unlocking a device. If a device is noncompliant with this policy, the user will be prompted to set a password on their noncompliant device.

Users with devices that are marked as noncompliant will receive notifications about the conflicting rules. As an administrator, you can also create a conditional access policy to block these devices until they are remediated. See Table 1-1 for a series of compliance policies and corresponding sample use cases.

TABLE 1-1 Device compliance use cases

Platform	Setting(s)	Sample Use Case
Windows 10	Minimum OS version Valid operating system builds	Windows 10 devices that are not running the latest cumulative update are marked as noncompliant. Windows 10 devices running a supported release are still valid while upgrades are rolling out.
macOS	Require system integrity protection	macOS devices that do not have system integrity protection enabled are marked as noncompliant.
Android	Rooted devices Encryption of data storage on device	Android devices that are rooted are marked as noncompliant. Android devices that do not have data storage encryption enabled are marked as noncompliant.
iOS	Jailbroken devices Minimum OS version Restricted apps	iOS devices that are jailbroken are marked as noncompliant. iOS devices that are not running the latest major release of iOS are marked as noncompliant. iOS devices that have the Dropbox app installed are marked as noncompliant.

Design conditional access policies

In this skill section, you will review the design aspects of conditional access policies. As you prepare for these skills, plan to spend time working in the Azure portal and following along to review the interface and controls for conditional access.

This section began by covering what device compliance means from a cloud-management perspective. Now you will see how device compliance is used to establish access requirements for data and services in your organization.

DESIGN FOR THE PROTECTION OF DATA AND SERVICES USING CONDITIONAL ACCESS POLICIES

There are a variety of policy settings available for conditional access, and a mixture of configurations that you can implement. Let's first look at the Conditional Access Policies blade in the

Azure portal. This will help set the stage for conditional access policies and introduce you to some key terms. Figure 1-6 shows the New Conditional Access Policy blade. Let's drill down and take a closer look at each of the available options.

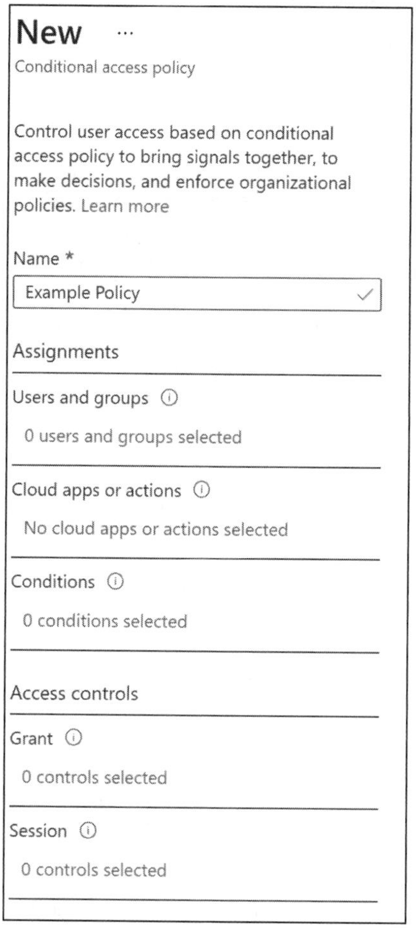

New ⋯

Conditional access policy

Control user access based on conditional access policy to bring signals together, to make decisions, and enforce organizational policies. Learn more

Name *

| Example Policy   ✓ |

Assignments
_____

Users and groups ⓘ

  0 users and groups selected
_____

Cloud apps or actions ⓘ

  No cloud apps or actions selected
_____

Conditions ⓘ

  0 conditions selected
_____

Access controls
_____

Grant ⓘ

  0 controls selected
_____

Session ⓘ

  0 controls selected
_____

FIGURE 1-6   Conditional access policy creation

- **Assignments**   These define the scope, criteria, and conditions of the policy you are deploying. The New Conditional Access Policy blade contains three assignment categories:
  - **Users and Groups**   These define who will receive the policy. You can either include or exclude users and groups. Although the New Conditional Access Policy blade does not prevent you from proceeding, all conditional access policies require a user and group assignment before they can be applied. For includes, you can select all users or specific users and groups. For example, if you have a group that contains only your marketing team, you can select that as an option. For excludes, you can select all guest users (defined by the userType attribute), specific directory roles (such as application developer), or specific users or groups.

- **Cloud Apps or Actions**   These define the services that users will access for productivity. You have the choice to include or exclude services on a predefined list of supported cloud apps. For includes, you can select all cloud apps or specific apps, such as Microsoft Teams. For excludes, you can select specific apps.
- **Conditions**   These define when a policy is applied. See Table 1-2 for a breakdown of each condition, the available options, and some sample use cases.

TABLE 1-2   Conditional access options

Condition	Description	Options	Sample Use Case
Sign-in risk	Azure AD determines a user's sign-in risk based on a configurable policy under Azure AD Identity Protection.	High, medium, low, or no risk	Enforce MFA policy for users who are flagged with a medium sign-in risk.
Device platforms	Azure AD retrieves the operating system of the joined device, but the information is not verified. This should be combined with a Microsoft Intune enrollment and device-compliance policy.	Android, iOS, Windows Phone, Windows, macOS	Enforce an app restriction policy on iOS and Android devices only.
Locations	Locations are used to define trusted network locations. Trusted network locations are configured in Azure AD under Named Locations.	Trusted locations	Block access to Exchange Online from the San Francisco office with an IP subnet of 10.20.11.0/22
Client apps (preview)	Set conditional restrictions based on specific client apps.	Browsers, mobile apps, and desktop clients	Restrict access to mobile apps unless the device is marked as compliant.
Device state (preview)	Exclude corporate or trusted devices from conditional access restrictions.	Hybrid Azure AD joined devices, devices marked as compliant	Enforce restrictions to Office 365 Exchange Online for noncompliant devices.

- **Access Controls**   These define additional requirements for granting or denying access, along with session controls for limiting the experience within cloud apps. The following options are available from the Access Controls section:
  - **Grant**   This enables you to block access based on the conditions that you defined under the Assignments section. Alternatively, you can choose to grant access and enforce additional requirements. For example, you can require MFA or only grant access to devices that are marked as compliant through device-compliance policies.
  - **Session**   This enables you to limit the experience within certain cloud apps. At the time of this writing, Exchange Online and SharePoint Online are the only cloud apps that support app enforced restrictions. Enabling this feature adds real-time monitoring and control capabilities to these apps.

Now that you have spent some time exploring the interface, let's look at how a conditional access policy is constructed. The policy is made up of two parts: the condition and the access control. You can also look at these in the following context: *when this happens* (condition), *then do this* (access control). For the exam you should be familiar with this formula and how it corresponds to conditional access restrictions. See Table 1-3 for a few examples on how conditional access policies are assembled.

TABLE 1-3   Conditions and access controls

When This Happens (Condition)	Then Do This (Access Control)
Windows and macOS device owners are accessing SharePoint Online from an untrusted network. Additional security requirements are needed.	Grant access to SharePoint Online for Windows and macOS devices. Require multi-factor authentication and a compliant device when accessed from an untrusted network.
The sales team is accessing Exchange Online from their iOS and Android devices. These devices must be compliant before access is granted.	Grant access to Exchange Online for the sales group. Require all sales team device owners to be enrolled in Intune and marked as compliant.
All users are accessing Microsoft Teams from trusted and untrusted networks. Users that are on an untrusted network need additional security requirements.	Grant access to Microsoft Teams for all users. Require multi-factor authentication when accessed from an untrusted network.
BYOD devices are accessing Exchange Online from their browser. Access needs to be restricted to approved apps.	Grant access to Exchange Online for all users. Restrict access to trusted client apps only.

The following list covers prerequisites that you must be familiar with. Some of these are firm requirements and others are strategic questions to help prepare you for designing policies.

- **Subscriptions**   The basic capabilities of conditional access are available with an Azure AD premium subscription. There are additional capabilities, however, that will not be available until you upgrade your subscription. These include the following:

  - **Azure AD Premium P1**   The P1 subscription provides you with the basic capabilities of conditional access policies.

  - **Azure AD Premium P2**   The P2 subscription enables Identity Protection, which is required if you want to leverage sign-in risk. Sign-in risk is a capability that determines whether a user sign-in is malicious and measures the risk level. This can be leveraged as part of your policy conditions.

  - **Microsoft Intune**   Intune can be purchased standalone or through an Enterprise Mobility + Security E3 or E5 subscription. Policy definitions that require a compliant device depend on the device being enrolled in Intune.

> *NEED MORE REVIEW?*   **SUBSCRIPTION DETAILS**
>
> For more information about Azure AD subscriptions, visit *https://azure.microsoft.com/ pricing/details/active-directory/.* For more information about Microsoft Intune subscriptions, visit *https://www.microsoft.com/cloud-platform/microsoft-intune-pricing.*

- **Permissions**   Before you can start creating and managing conditional access policies, you will need the appropriate permissions assigned to your account. Conditional access administrator is a predefined role that that enables the necessary privileges.

- **Requirements to be delivered** What requirements do you have for device compliance and conditional access? This is something you should start defining from the beginning. Determine whether your goal is something straightforward (such as enforcing multi-factor authentication for users) or something more advanced (such as restricting access to SharePoint Online from Windows devices when they are connected to an untrusted network).

- **Device management** What kind of device-management solution are you using today? The full capabilities of conditional access have dependencies on Microsoft Intune, but if you are using ConfigMgr, you can enable co-management and start leveraging conditional access policies sooner.

- **Device platforms** What types of devices and operating systems do you need to support? Conditional access policies support a variety of operating systems. At the time of this writing, the only current outliers are devices running Linux. Consider the devices in your environment and what types of restrictions you need to enforce.

- **Email requirements** What are your access requirements around email? Email is often used as one of the first services for enforcing conditional access restrictions. If your goal is to enable access restrictions for Exchange Online, then selecting the cloud app from the default list of assignments is straightforward, and is something you will look at later in this chapter. If your goal is to enable access restrictions for an on-premises Exchange server, you must plan for additional prerequisites, such as installing and configuring the on-premises Exchange connector.

DESIGN DEVICE-BASED AND APP-BASED CONDITIONAL ACCESS POLICIES

First, understand that a conditional access policy can contain any mixture of options, including device-based and app-based restrictions. The distinction between device-based and app-based restrictions is relative to the controls that you select and how you structure your policies. That said, device-based and app-based policies can have different requirements and can operate independently of each other if you choose.

Let's look at a few examples:

- **Device-based** This first policy focuses on device-based controls. Here, the policy requires multi-factor authentication on untrusted networks for iOS devices. The policy is assigned to all users. In this example we have not defined any app-based restrictions, keeping the focus on the platform and network.

- **App-based** This second policy focuses on app-based controls. Here, the policy requires approved client apps when accessing Exchange Online. This policy is assigned to all users. In this example we have not defined any device-based restrictions, keeping the focus on application controls.

- **Mixed** This third policy includes a mixture of controls. Here, the policy requires all platforms to be enrolled in Intune and marked compliant before they can access Exchange Online from approved client apps. In this example we are specifying device-based restrictions and app-based restrictions to accomplish the desired result.

At this stage you should have a good understanding of the differences between device-based and app-based policies. Next, let's examine the individual controls related to each policy type. The following items are focused on device-based policy requirements:

- **Azure AD joined**   This requirement is available as both a condition and an access control item. When you are defining a condition, you have the option to exclude devices that are Azure AD joined. This is available through the Device State blade. You could use this in a scenario where you are locking down access, but want to ignore Azure AD–joined devices. Alternatively, when you are defining the controls for granting access, you have the option to require Azure AD–joined devices. This is available through the Grant blade for access control and can be used as one of many required controls before enabling access to cloud apps.

- **Device compliance**   This requirement is available as both a condition and an access control item, similar to the Azure AD–joined requirement mentioned in the previous bullet. Devices must be enrolled in Microsoft Intune and be marked as compliant for this requirement to work. When you are defining a condition, you have the option to exclude devices that are marked as compliant. This is available through the Device State blade. This could be used in a scenario where you are locking down access but want to ignore enrolled devices that are compliant. Alternatively, when you are defining the controls for granting access, you have the option to require enrolled and compliant devices. This is available through the Grant blade for access control and can be used as one of many required controls before enabling access to cloud apps.

- **Device enrollment**   This requirement is not directly defined through a conditional access policy but is a prerequisite for identifying device compliance.

- **Device platforms**   This requirement is available as a condition item. When you are defining a condition, you have the option to include or exclude the following operating systems: Android, iOS, Windows Phone, Windows, and macOS. This is available through the Device Platforms blade. It could be used in a scenario where you are restricting access to a cloud app and want to exclude certain platforms.

Next, let's examine app-based requirements. We introduced session controls earlier in this skill section, which enable you to limit the experience within cloud apps. Two of the requirements we are going to cover are enabled using session controls. The following items are focused on app-based policy requirements.

- **Use app-enforced restrictions**   This requirement is available as an access control item. When you are defining access controls, you have the option to enable app-enforced restrictions. This is defined on the Session blade. It could be used in a scenario where you need to provide limited access to Office 365 Exchange Online or SharePoint Online for noncompliant devices.

- **Use conditional access app control**   This requirement is available as an access control item. When you are defining access controls, you have the option to enable conditional access app control. This is defined on the Session blade. It could be used in a scenario where you need to monitor and control application access in real time. Access and session policies can then be configured through the Cloud App Security portal, enabling granular control over user access.

- **Available policies** These include access, activity, app discovery, app permission, cloud discovery anomaly detection, files, and session policies. Some of these are designed for monitoring and alerting, while others have automated actions that can be enabled.

- **Require approved client app** This requirement is available as an access control item. When you are defining access controls, you have the option to enable the requirement for approved client apps. This is defined on the Grant blade. It can be used in a scenario where you need to ensure services are accessed only from approved client applications.

> *NOTE* **APPROVED CLIENT APPS**
>
> Enabling the requirement for approved client apps will prevent users from accessing services from native or third-party apps that Microsoft has not approved. For a list of approved client apps, visit *https://docs.microsoft.com/azure/active-directory/conditional-access/technical-reference#approved-client-app-requirement*.

Plan for attack surface reduction

Reducing the attack surface is a method of reducing the number of vulnerabilities and threats the organization might be exposed to by using these devices. This section covers how to reduce the attack surface by using Intune to increase endpoint security. After you enroll Windows 10 (or later) devices in Intune, you can use endpoint security policies and Windows Defender's antivirus software to configure device security settings and mitigate attacks.

> *NOTE* To use security policies in Intune to reduce the attack surface, you must be using Windows 10 or later as the device operating system, and the Windows Defender antivirus software must be the primary antivirus software on the device.

Endpoint security profiles

To reduce the attack surface of a device, you can use endpoint security profiles in Intune. When creating a new profile, the supported operating system is Windows 10 or later. The available profile settings are as follows:

- **App and Browser Isolation** Isolating processes and applications on the device can prevent known and zero-day attacks. You can manage these settings with Windows Defender Application Guard with Defender for Endpoint by identifying the apps, websites, or networks that should be trusted.

- **Device Control**   This setting enables you to configure security settings for removable media on the device.

- **Attack Surface Reduction Rules**   This setting configures the available options in the Defender for Endpoint software on the device. This can include configuring rules and actions to take for downloaded executable files or suspicious scripts.

- **Exploit Protection**   This helps protect against malware that has been identified to use known exploits for the selected platform or device to prevent the malware from spreading.

- **Web Protection (Microsoft Edge Legacy)**   This setting enables you to protect against harmful websites that are phishing, using known exploits, distributing malware, and more.

- **Application Control**   These settings enable you to block unsigned scripts or installation files and restrict applications that can access the system kernel.

Configure endpoint security profiles

To create a policy that uses one of these available profile settings, follow these steps.

1. Log in to the Microsoft Endpoint Manager admin center at *https://endpoint.microsoft.com*.
2. Click **Endpoint Security**.
3. Under **Manage**, click **Attack Surface Reduction**.
4. Click **Create Policy**.
5. Select the platform and desired profile type. For this example, select **Device Control**.
6. Click **Create**.
7. On the **Basics** tab, type a name for the policy — for example, **DeviceControlPolicy** — and click **Next**.
8. On the **Configuration Settings** tab, configure the desired policy. For example, set *Block Removable Storage* and *Block Bluetooth Connections* to **Yes**. (See Figure 1-7.) Then click **Next**. Figure 1-7 shows these settings being configured.
9. On the **Scope Tags** tab, select any desired scope tags. For this example, leave the default (blank) settings as is and click **Next**.

   Scope tags enable you to filter the policy to specific tags.
10. On the **Assignments** tab, configure the included or excluded groups that the policy should apply to. For this example, click **Add All Devices** and then click **Next**.
11. On the **Review + Create** tab, click **Create**.

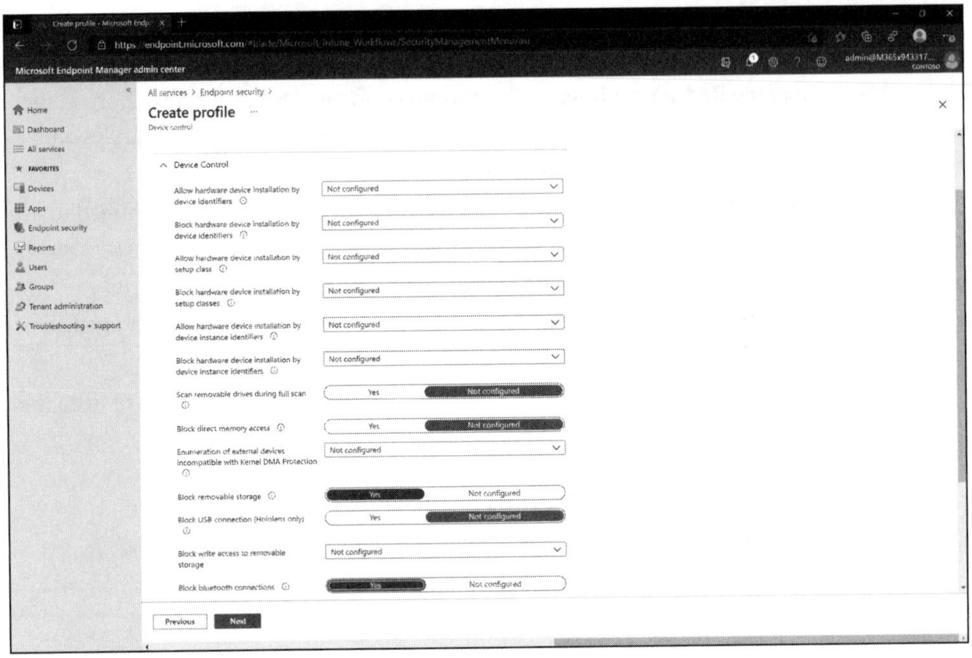

FIGURE 1-7 Endpoint security policy

Similar to the configuration profile you created in skill section 1.1, the endpoint security policy you create here will apply to the users or devices that you assigned it to in step 10.

After you create the policy, you can view its assignment status and properties by selecting it. Figure 1-8 displays the configured policy in the Microsoft Endpoint Manager admin center.

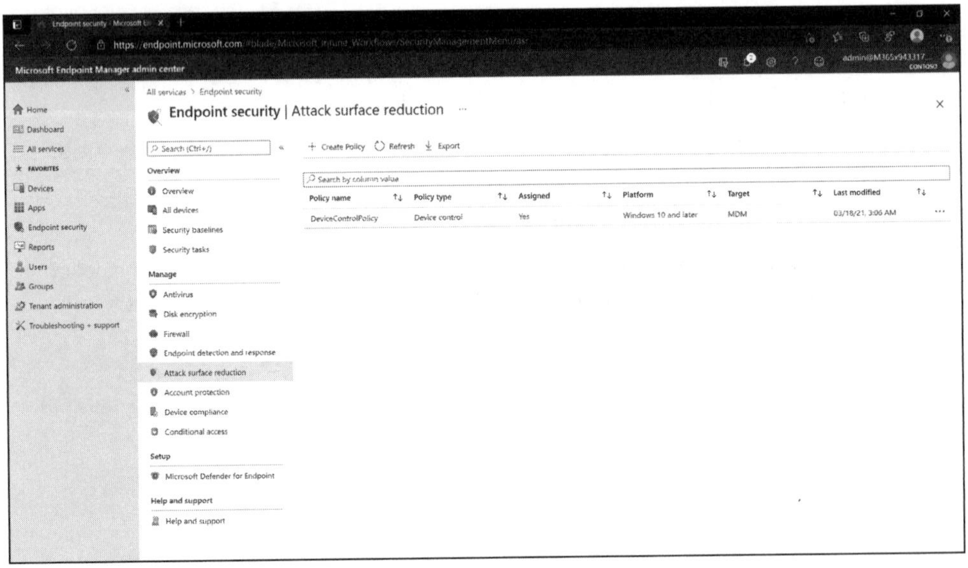

FIGURE 1-8 Configured and assigned endpoint security policy

Configure security baselines

This section introduces security baselines and how to configure them for Windows 10 devices that are managed by Intune. Security baselines provide a default configuration of settings or policies that are applied to a group of users or devices. For example, you can automatically assign a set of security policies for a publicly accessible kiosk machine. A different set of policies, or a baseline, can be configured for mobile devices carried by sales staff. The settings you configure for these devices might span multiple individual policies and are combined to create a baseline.

There are three types of security baseline instances that can be created and managed with Intune:

- **MDM security baseline** This baseline enables you to configure any of the thousands of various settings that are available in Windows 10.
- **Microsoft Defender for Endpoint baseline** This baseline is used specifically with Defender for Endpoint and configures the various settings included with Defender.
- **Microsoft Edge baseline** This baseline configures settings that relate specifically to the Microsoft Edge web browser.

Baselines can and will change over time with the introduction of new features for the platform you are targeting or as best practices evolve. When one of these things happen, a new version is introduced to the baseline. You can also choose to change the version of a baseline on your own without the need to create a new profile.

Creating multiple versions or having multiple instances of a baseline can cause conflicts in settings. As your organization grows, or you simply have more baselines to manage, be aware of the conflicts that can arise by having different baselines for different devices.

You configure security baselines in the Microsoft Endpoint Manager admin center. Follow these steps:

1. Log in to the Microsoft Endpoint Manager admin center at *https://endpoint.microsoft.com*.
2. Click **Endpoint Security**, and then click **Security Baselines**.
3. Click the desired baseline instance to create a policy for — for example, **Microsoft Edge Baseline**.
4. Click **Create Profile**.
5. On the **Basics** tab, type a name for the policy — for example, **BrowserBaseline** — and then click **Next**.
6. On the **Configuration Settings** tab, configure the desired settings for the Microsoft Edge browser. For example, set the **Enable Saving Passwords to the Password Manager** setting to **Enabled**. Then click **Next**.
7. On the **Scope Tags** tab, set any filters based on scope tags to apply the profile to. Then click **Next**.

8. On the **Assignments** tab, select the devices or users to apply the baseline to. For example, click **Add All Devices**. Then click **Next**.

9. Click **Create**. Figure 1-9 shows the configured baseline policy with the Microsoft Edge settings defined.

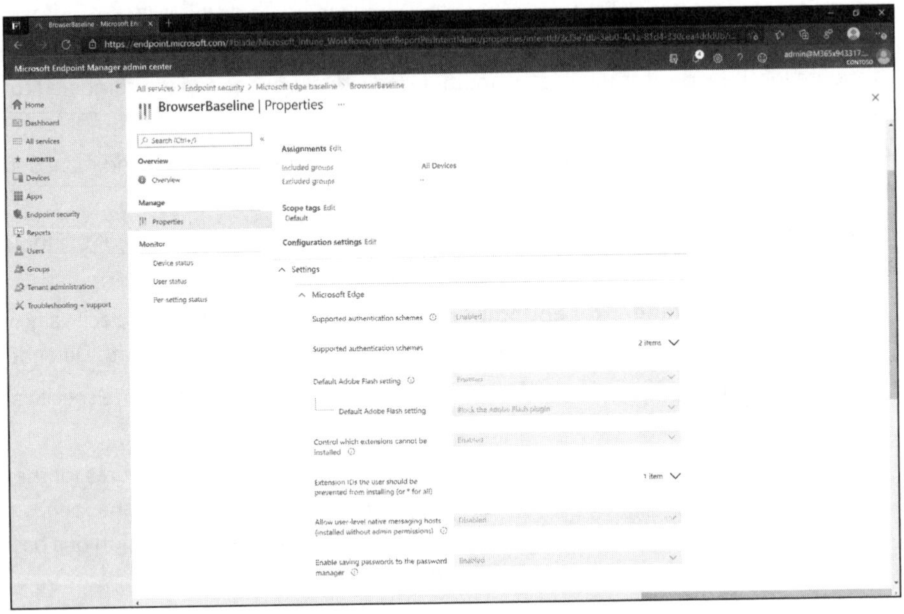

FIGURE 1-9 Security baseline for Microsoft Edge

Configure device-compliance policy

This section covers the creation process for device-compliance policies in Microsoft Intune. The examples cover common use cases for device compliance. Like the other policies and profiles you have explored so far, there are various options and configurations for administrators to work with. These include the ability to connect with third-party vendor solutions to enhance the native capabilities.

> **NOTE** As you navigate through the portal, remember that conditional access policies can leverage compliance status for restricting access to data and services.

Navigate and configure device-compliance settings

When you access the Device Compliance blade for the first time, the first thing you might notice is the number of options available compared to the conditional access interface. The core functions are split into three groups: manage, monitor, and setup.

1. Log in to the Microsoft Endpoint Manager admin center at *https://endpoint.azure.com/*.

2. Click **Devices**, and then click **Compliance Policies**.

3. Click **Create Policy**.

4. Select the desired platform for the policy to apply to, and then click **Create**.

5. On the **Basics** tab, provide a name for the policy, such as **CompliancePolicy**, and then click **Next**.

6. On the **Compliance Settings** tab, select the settings required for the device to be considered compliant, and then click **Next**. For example, choose **Require** for the **Require BitLocker** setting. Figure 1-10 shows the compliance settings to configure for Windows 10 device health.

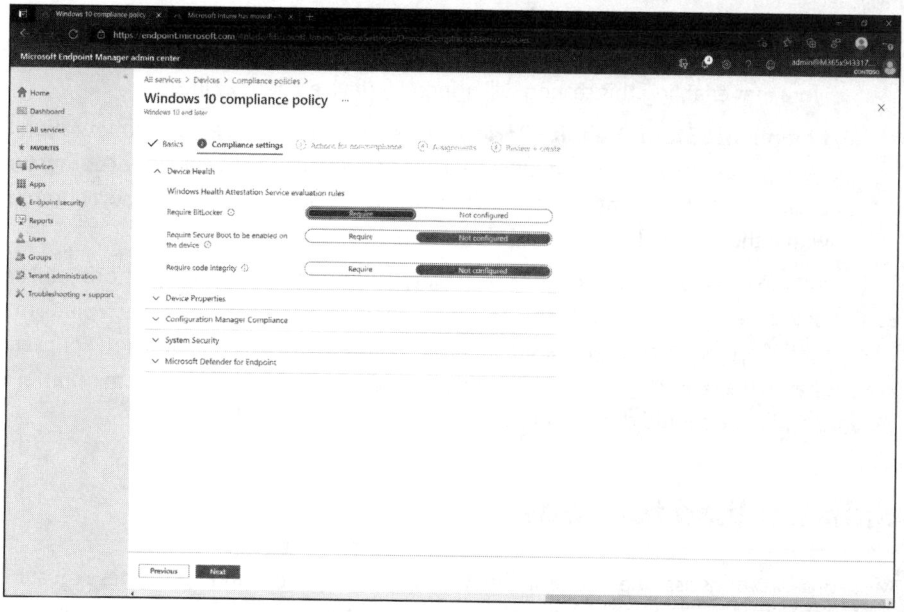

FIGURE 1-10 Device-compliance policies

7. On the **Actions for Noncompliance** tab, select the action(s) to take if the device does not meet the settings defined on the previous tab, and then click **Next**.

   For example, you can choose to send an email notification to the end user and other recipients or retire the device after a set period of time.

8. On the **Assignments** tab, add the users or groups that you want the policy to apply to. For example, click **Add All Users**. Then click **Next**.

9. Review your settings and then click **Create**.

Device compliance includes several built-in reports for administrators to review and export as needed. This includes an overview dashboard, providing a high-level look at overall compliance and areas of interest. Later in this section you will look at monitoring in more detail.

When you first begin working with device compliance, there are some configurations that you should review. In the **Compliance Policies** blade, click **Compliance Policy Settings**. There are three controls on this blade that you should explore before you begin creating policies.

- **Mark Devices with No Compliance Policy Assigned As [Compliant | Not Compliant]** The default configuration for this setting is Not Compliant. In many cases, this will be the desired setting, because you will want to have some understanding of the device state before granting it access to services. For example, consider a scenario in which you assign a conditional access policy that requires devices to be compliant to access Exchange Online.

- **Enhanced Jailbreak Detection [Enabled | Disabled]** The default configuration for this setting is Disabled. Enabling this feature requires iOS devices to evaluate and report their jailbreak status more frequently in conjunction with leveraging location services. Note that enabling this setting will affect the device's battery life.

- **Compliance Status Validity Period (Days) [1–120]** The default configuration for this setting is 30 days. This value determines the frequency with which devices must report back their device-compliance status to Intune. If a device does not report compliance within the required timeframe, it will be marked as noncompliant.

Each compliance policy you create is associated with a specific device platform, unlike conditional access policies, which enable you to select multiple platforms. Each platform has its own set of options. Some will be similar across platforms, but others will not. For example, macOS has a rule requiring system integrity protection, which is exclusive to this platform. Based on this, you should design your policies on a per-platform basis.

Skill 1.3: Plan for apps

Most organizations assume responsibility for a range of devices and apps. These must be maintained and supported to ensure that employees are productive, are successful, and have a healthy work-life balance.

There are common factors that organizations must consider when planning for devices:

- The physical hardware and generation of that hardware
- The operating system and version
- Peripherals such as display adapters or printers

For apps, planning considerations may include:

- Line-of-business (LOB) applications
- Preferred publishers
- Licensing
- Version control

As you plan for devices and apps, you must also consider how these planning considerations will be distributed, configured, and supported.

For the MS-101 exam, planning for devices and apps is focused on testing your knowledge of the Microsoft 365 ecosystem and how these technologies solve different problems. This chapter focuses on device management and security. This includes a deep dive into device co-management and a look at device profiles and security with Microsoft Intune. App deployment, management of apps, and app security will also be covered.

> **This skill covers how to:**
> - Create and configure Microsoft Store for Business
> - Plan app deployment
> - Plan for mobile application management

Create and configure Microsoft Store for Business

The method in which applications are delivered to users and devices has evolved over the years. For traditional Win32 applications, some organizations may still have help desk staff who manage and install these apps manually. Others may be leveraging features like ConfigMgr's application model, which offers a custom-tailored self-service method for employees to install traditional Win32 applications.

Another self-service app experience is available through the Microsoft Store. This service was introduced in Windows 8 as a standalone application that was installed with the operating system. At that time, it was referred to as the Windows Store. As with many other app store platforms, consumers can navigate the store and install apps that Microsoft had approved for publication. The apps in the Microsoft Store are not packaged in the traditional Win32 format. Instead, they are packaged using the Universal Windows Platform (UWP).

Enterprise and education customers have access to the Microsoft Store for Business (MSfB) or Microsoft Store for Education (MSfE), respectively. For this exam, we will focus on the MSfB, but the two stores provide parallel offerings. Administrators also have the option to configure a private store, enabling them to purchase apps in bulk, assign licenses, and deliver apps using self-service or direct assignment. This design has evolved with Windows 10 and is the focus here.

Plan for Microsoft Store for Business prerequisites

The MSfB is designed for organizations that want to take a modern approach to managing their application portfolio. Managing and delivering apps using this solution provides IT administrators with several capabilities. Table 1-4 contains a list of core features included with the MSfB.

TABLE 1-4 Microsoft Store for Business features

Feature	Description
Scaling flexibility	The MSfB is a cloud-based technology, providing a robust and reliable infrastructure for hosting and distributing apps across different geolocations and org sizes. Customers that already have Azure AD, Office 365, and Windows 10 deployed can enable an end-to-end app-management solution using the MSfB. Customers that have an on-premises management solution can enable integration with the MSfB and begin modernizing their apps.
Purchasing and licensing	Administrators can procure apps and licensing in volume. Licenses can be assigned and reclaimed.
Private store	Administrators can enable a private store for their organization. This store can be customized with managed apps and collections, providing users with a tailored experience. The private store can be accessed from the Microsoft Store app on Windows 10 devices or from a web browser.
App distribution	Apps acquired through the MSfB can be distributed to users in multiple ways. For example, apps can be: Assigned to users or groups and made available through the private store for download and installation Distributed using ConfigMgr or third-party management solutions, or during image deployment Distributed offline without connecting to the MSfB using the Deployment Image Servicing and Management (DISM) command-line tool or provisioning packages
Line-of-business apps	Administrators can add LOB apps to the private store for management and distribution.
App updates	Apps that are purchased and managed online can receive automatic updates through the MSfB.

As you begin planning for MSfB, there are a few prerequisites that you should be familiar with. First, you must understand the difference between the two available licensing models: online-licensed apps and offline-licensed apps. Which licensing model you choose can dictate which prerequisites you need to address.

- **Online-licensed apps**   Apps purchased using the online licensing model require users to connect to the Microsoft Store service to acquire the app and corresponding license. Licenses are maintained using the user's Azure AD identity. This is the default license model, and it will be the primary option if your users have Azure AD accounts and if access to the Microsoft Store is enabled.

- **Offline-licensed apps**   Apps purchased using the offline licensing model do not require connectivity to the Microsoft Store. Instead, administrators can download their purchased apps and licenses for deployment within their internal network. Not all apps support offline licensing. It is up to the independent software vendor (ISV) to opt in for this option in the development center by selecting the *Disconnected (Offline) Licensing setting* during submission. Offline-licensed apps can be deployed at imaging time using a provisioning package or distributed to systems using a management solution such as ConfigMgr.

Next, let's cover the baseline prerequisites for setting up MSfB. These are items you must plan for before you begin your implementation. Take note of the items that mention online and offline licensing requirements. These will differ slightly depending on which licensing model you choose.

- **Microsoft Store for Business account** A global administrator must visit *https://businessstore.microsoft.com* and sign in to activate the private store.
- **Azure AD accounts for admins** Administrators tasked with acquiring apps, distributing apps, and manage licensing need an Azure AD account. These requirements are the same for both online and offline licensing.
- **Azure AD accounts for users** An Azure AD account is required for users who access the MSfB to download and install online-licensed apps. Users do not require an Azure AD account for offline-licensed apps.
- **Platform support** Users accessing the MSfB must do so from a supported PC or mobile device. This includes Windows 10, version 1511, or later.
- **Browser support** Administrators managing the MSfB must do so from a supported browser. MSfB is compatible with Internet Explorer 10 or later and current versions of Microsoft Edge, Chrome, or Firefox.

Set up the private store

The private store is designed to help organizations deliver a unified experience to their employees when browsing and installing apps. This feature enables administrators to customize their own private Microsoft Store and manage app purchasing and distribution. From a user-experience perspective, this includes the ability to adjust app visibility in the store based on user or group membership, along with grouping and sorting apps to your liking. Figure 1-11 shows an example of the Contoso Electronics private store. In this section, we will walk through the process of setting up a private store for MSfB.

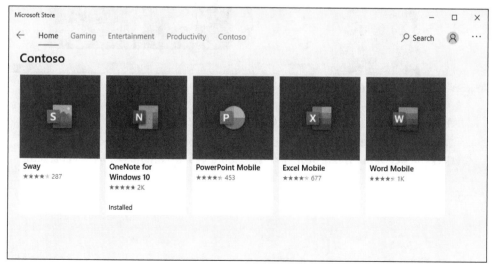

FIGURE 1-11 Contoso private store

For the following example, suppose you are an admin for Contoso Electronics. You have been tasked with creating a private store for your organization. Follow these steps to set up the private store:

1. Navigate to the **Microsoft Store For Business** at *https://businessstore.microsoft.com.*

2. Sign in using an Azure AD global administrator account.

   Signing in without a global administrator account will only give you access to browse the standard Microsoft Store For Business.

3. In the menu bar at the top of the page, click the **Private Store** option. (See Figure 1-12.)

   If this option is not visible, maximize your browser window. Alternatively, locate the collapse menu button in the upper-left corner, click it, and select **Private Store** from the navigation menu.

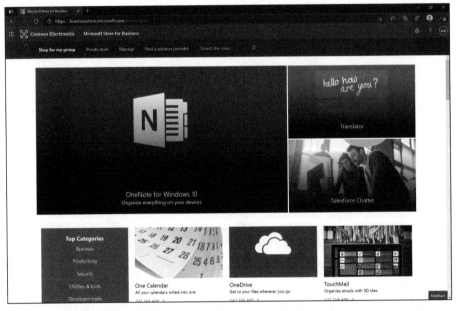

FIGURE 1-12 Microsoft Store for Business portal

A Microsoft Store for Business consent form opens.

4. The first time you try to manage the private store, you will be prompted to activate it. Click the **Activate Private Store** link (see Figure 1-13) to continue with the initial setup.

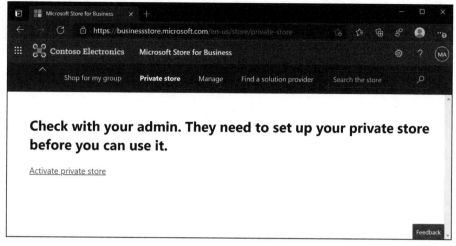

FIGURE 1-13 Microsoft Store for Business activation screen

The private store has now been created and is associated with your Azure AD tenant. Once this happens and the store becomes available, you can access the Manage menu, which contains several administrative options, which you will review in more detail in the next section.

At the time of this writing, if you click the Private Store option after accepting the consent form, you will see text that states: *Check with your admin. They need to set up your private store before you can use it.* This can be a bit confusing because the store has already been created. It turns out that before you can access the private store and see apps, you must accept a service agreement. You can do this by adding an app to your inventory.

Continuing with the Contoso Electronics scenario, register a free copy of the OneNote app to trigger and accept the pending service agreement.

1. In the menu bar at the top of the page, type **OneNote** in the search box and press **Enter**.

   If the search box is not visible, maximize your browser window. Alternatively, locate the collapse menu button in the upper-left corner, click it, and enter your search term in the navigation menu.

2. In the search results, locate and click the free **Microsoft OneNote** app.

3. On the OneNote shop page, click **Get the App**.

4. Review the Microsoft Store for Business and Education Services Agreement, select the check box to accept the agreement, and click **Accept**. (See Figure 1-14.) This agreement is required to start using the private store.

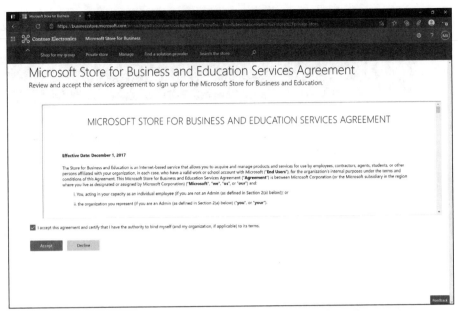

FIGURE 1-14 Microsoft Store for Business and Education Services Agreement

5. On the **Thanks for Your Order** page, click **Close**. This confirms that the app has been purchased and added to your app inventory.

> **NOTE GET NEW APPS**
>
> It may take as long as 24 hours for new apps you add to your inventory to become visible in the private store. In the preceding example, the OneNote app was visible in the private store within 5 minutes. This is worth noting if you are troubleshooting why a recently added app has not appeared in the private store yet.

At the conclusion of this scenario, the Private Store option on the menu bar will be replaced with the name of your organization (taken from your Azure tenant). When you click your organization name, you should see the OneNote app listed in your app inventory. At this stage, you can open the Microsoft Store on a compatible Windows 10 device, sign in with your Azure AD credentials, and access your organization's private store.

> **REAL WORLD ONLY SHOW THE PRIVATE STORE**
>
> The private store can provide organizations with an end-to-end app-management solution. In some environments, once the private store is deployed, you might need to hide the default Microsoft Store. You can achieve this using group policy with the following setting: Only Display The Private Store within the Microsoft Store. For more information on configuring this policy setting, visit *https://docs.microsoft.com/microsoft-store/manage-access-to-private-store#show-private-store-only-using-group-policy*.

Configure Microsoft Store for Business

The management portal for MSfB contains several pages for app administration, licensing, and account management. Among these pages are a few controls to customize the private store. This section will introduce you to the portal and walk through each of the available menu options.

Figure 1-15 shows the MSfB management portal. To access this portal, you click the Manage button along the top of the screen. In this figure you see a navigation menu in the left pane, and the Overview page open on the right. The navigation menu contains the administrative controls for managing your organization's MSfB experience. Let's take a closer look at the available options in the navigation menu.

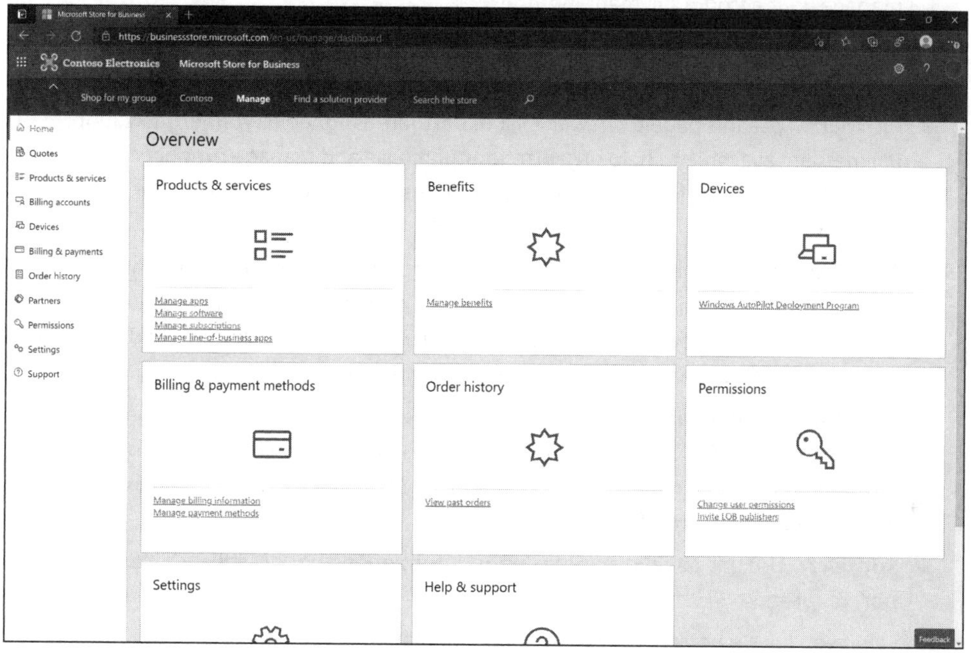

FIGURE 1-15   Microsoft Store for Business management portal

- **Home**   This directs you to a page that provides an overview dashboard with summary information for various items such as license availability and recent purchases. The overview also includes drill-down objects to other management options such as settings and permissions.

- **Quotes**   Use this page to view and interact with quotes that have been assigned to your organization for apps and other solutions. This page will be blank unless you have a partner that has sent you a quote.

- **Products & Services**   Use this page to view your app inventory, benefits information, and new LOB apps. App inventory will include all registered apps for your organization along with drill-down details and customization options for each app. Benefits information is tied to your Microsoft agreement. LOB apps are any newly registered LOB apps assigned to your organization.

- **Benefits** Use this page to view account profile information, status information for your Microsoft agreements, connected tenants that you established with the Microsoft Products and Services Agreement (MSPA), and review requests that require admin approval.

- **Devices** Use this page to manage your Windows AutoPilot deployments. AutoPilot is a technology that enables administrators to reduce traditional imaging needs by configuring automated system setup and configuration with Azure AD, Intune, Office 365, and MSfB.

- **Billing & Payments** Use this page to view invoices assigned to your organization and manage your account payment methods.

- **Order History** Use this page to view your order history and order details for software and subscriptions purchased by your organization.

- **Partners** Use this page to view the list of partners assigned to your organization. Partners are available to help organizations purchase and manage products and services. You can search for partner details by navigating to the Find a Solution Provider menu option.

- **Permissions** Use this page to view and manage the role-based access controls for your organization. This includes roles for admin, purchaser, basic purchaser, and device guard signer. Once your private store is active, it is important to review the default options and define the roles according to your business needs.

- **Settings** Use this page to view and manage the core settings for your organization's store experience. This includes shopping controls based on role-based access, distribution settings, and connectivity to your preferred MDM solution, device guard policies, and notification controls for invoices.

- **Support** Use this page to access support information about MSfB and opening support requests.

Now that you have a better understanding of the management portal, let's look at some customization controls for the private store. There are two primary locations that contain settings pertaining to the private store. The first is the private store itself, which is listed in the menu bar as the name of your organization. In this example, the private store is called Contoso Electronics. Click this link to access the store interface, shown in Figure 1-16.

This page enables administrators to customize the store interface for their employees. The changes you make here will be visible to employees when they access your organization's private store. Available options include the ability to create new collections by clicking the **+Add Collection** button. You can also remove collections and assign apps to collections by clicking the more options icon (•••) next to the collection name.

In this example, the default collection, Contoso Electronics, which contains all available apps by default, is hidden. To replace this collection, we created two new collections: Contoso (shown in Figure 1-16) and File Sharing (not shown). These new collections contain a custom list of apps based on our preference.

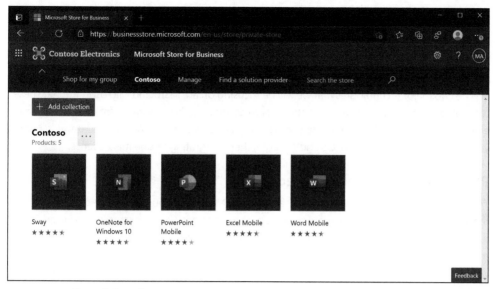

FIGURE 1-16 Microsoft Store for Business private store

To access the second location for customizing the private store, open the **Manage** page, click the **Products & Services** tile, and then click the **Apps & Software** tab. On this page, you will see a list of apps from your inventory, as shown in Figure 1-17.

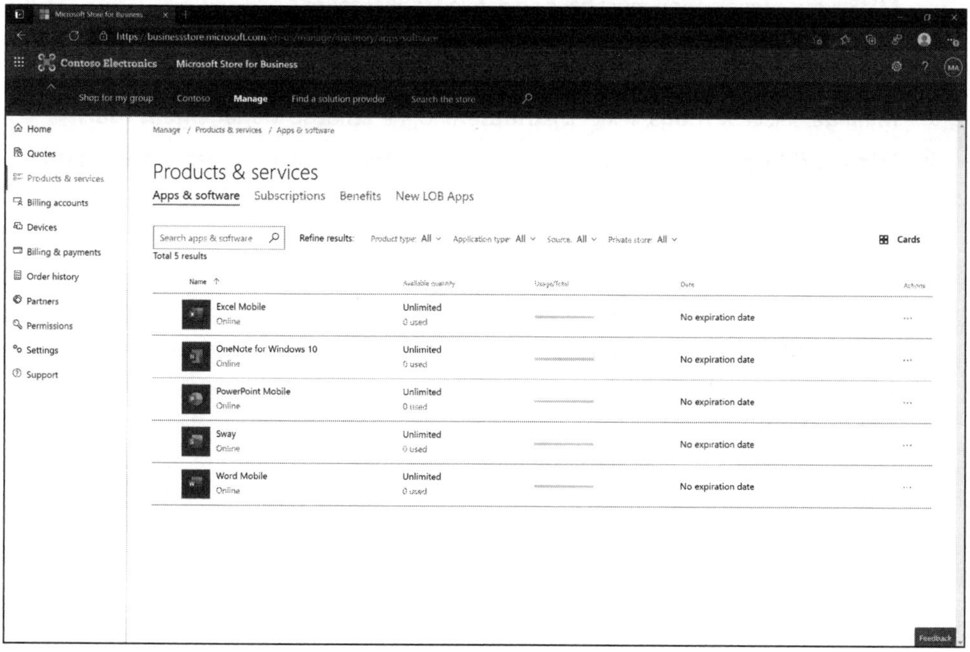

FIGURE 1-17 Private store availability

Plan app deployment

In this section, you will work with app deployment in the cloud. App deployment with Microsoft 365 is centralized around cloud-based management. Traditional solutions for on-premises app deployment are still available, but working with apps in the cloud is the focus for this exam.

The two major technologies that we will be focusing on are MSfB and Microsoft Intune. These technologies can operate independently, but are designed to be integrated for end-to-end coverage. For example, MSfB standalone can offer a suitable solution for Windows 10 devices, but if you need to distribute apps to iOS and Android, then integrating Intune makes sense.

Plan for app deployment prerequisites

There are a few different ways to deploy apps in the Microsoft cloud. The prerequisites for these methods depend on the requirements of the organization. For example, if your organization uses Office 365 but does not have an Intune subscription, you can still use the MSfB to help manage apps on Windows 10 devices. If your organization does have an Intune subscription, you can set up an MSfB account and integrate it with Intune to streamline the management and distribution of your apps across multiple platforms.

Based on the examples described previously, many prerequisites for app deployment are conditional. That said, you should be familiar with each of the available options and in what situations they apply:

- **Microsoft Store for Business Standalone**   If you choose to leverage the benefits of MSfB, your organization must have an active MSfB account.

- **Microsoft Store for Business + Intune**   If you plan to connect your MSfB account with Intune, you must activate Microsoft Intune. You can do this from the Intune portal; choose **Manage**, select **Settings**, select **Distribute**, and then choose **Management Tools**.

- **Microsoft Intune**   If you choose to leverage Intune for app management and distribution, your organization must have an active Intune subscription. This includes setting the MDM authority to Intune in the Azure portal.

- **Device Enrollment**   If you plan to require app installation on devices, those devices must be enrolled with Intune.

- **Supported Platforms**   MSfB supports Windows 10 devices. If you need to support other platforms, such as Android or iOS, you must consider an Intune subscription.

- **Supported App Types**   MSfB supports the conversion of multiple Windows app file formats into APPX bundles for distribution. This conversion process requires an install sequence and capture of the app. Intune has a conversion process that converts the installer to a compatible INTUNEWIN bundle. The Intune solution is in preview at the time of this writing. Both scenarios should be planned for if you have a requirement to deploy Win32 apps.

Plan for app deployment types

This section covers planning considerations for app deployment types. This refers to the various app deployment types that Microsoft Intune supports. In the management portal, administrators have access to a variety of app types that they can deploy to users and devices.

One of the first things to consider when planning your app-management model is file formats. An app's file format can vary by publisher and platform. Variations by publisher exist only for Windows apps, where you have traditional file formats such as EXE and MSI, and newer formats such as APPX and MSIX. This segmentation adds a lot of effort for IT admins that support a variety of apps. Variations by platform includes Android, iOS, and Windows. Modern and mobile apps are all platform-specific and must be considered.

Next, you should know which app-deployment types are available in Intune, and what options they provide. For this, you will open the management portal and look at the client apps.

1. Log in to the Microsoft Endpoint Manager admin center at *https://endpoint.microsoft.com/*.

2. Click **Apps**.

3. On the **Apps** blade, click **All Apps**.

4. On the **All Aps** blade, click **Add**.

5. On the **Add App** blade, review the list of available app types. See Table 1-5 for a breakdown of each app type and its capabilities.

TABLE 1-5 Client app types

Platform	App Type	Notes
Android, iOS, Windows, Managed Google Play	Store app	All store apps require an app store URL that directs the app to the appropriate provider. With MSfB integration, Microsoft Store apps are automatically synchronized with Intune every 24 hours.
Windows 10, macOS	M365 apps, Microsoft Edge v77 and later	Microsoft 365 apps can be bundled as a suite or created as standalone apps. Additional configuration options are available for architecture type, update channel, removal of previous MSI versions, automatic agreement acceptance, and shared computer activation.
macOS	Microsoft Defender for Endpoint	Manage app deployment for macOS when using the Microsoft Defender for Endpoint on an Apple macOS device.
Web link	Other	Web links enable you to create an app that launches a browser to a specific URL, such as your help desk portal.
Built-in app	Other	Built-in apps enable you to quickly distribute curated managed apps, such as Office 365 and Adobe Reader for iOS and Android.
Line-of-business (LOB) app	Other	Line-of-business (LOB) apps enable you to upload in-house apps. Accepted file formats include MSI, MSIX, MSIXBUNDLE, APPX, and APPXBUNDLE.
Windows app (Win32) (preview)	Other	Win32 app enables you to upload a repackaged application using the INTUNEWIN file format. At the time of this writing, this feature is in preview.
Android Enterprise system app	Other	Android Enterprise system apps allow you to enable or disable certain system applications for Android devices that are managed by an enterprise.

Create and deploy apps with Intune

This section walks through the app-creation process in Intune and covers how to deploy those apps to enrolled devices. Intune's app-deployment capabilities continue to evolve, with recent additions including Win32 app support. These are some notable milestones for the product because Win32 app support breaks the barrier from traditional on-premises app management requirements with new cloud capabilities.

MANAGE STORE APPS WITH INTUNE

Before you start working with apps in Intune, remember that you can synchronize Microsoft Store apps. Enabling this capability will simplify the management of Microsoft Store apps and provide you the ability to deploy them using Intune.

1. Navigate to the Microsoft Store for Business at *https://www.microsoft.com/business-store*.

2. Sign in using an Azure AD account with admin access.

3. On the menu bar at the top of the page, click **Manage**.

4. Click **Settings** in the navigation menu on the left.

5. On the **Settings** page, select the **Distribute** tab.

6. On the **Distribute** tab, under **Management Tools**, click **Activate** in the **Action** column for the **Microsoft Intune** and **Microsoft Intune Enrollment** settings , as shown in Figure 1-18.

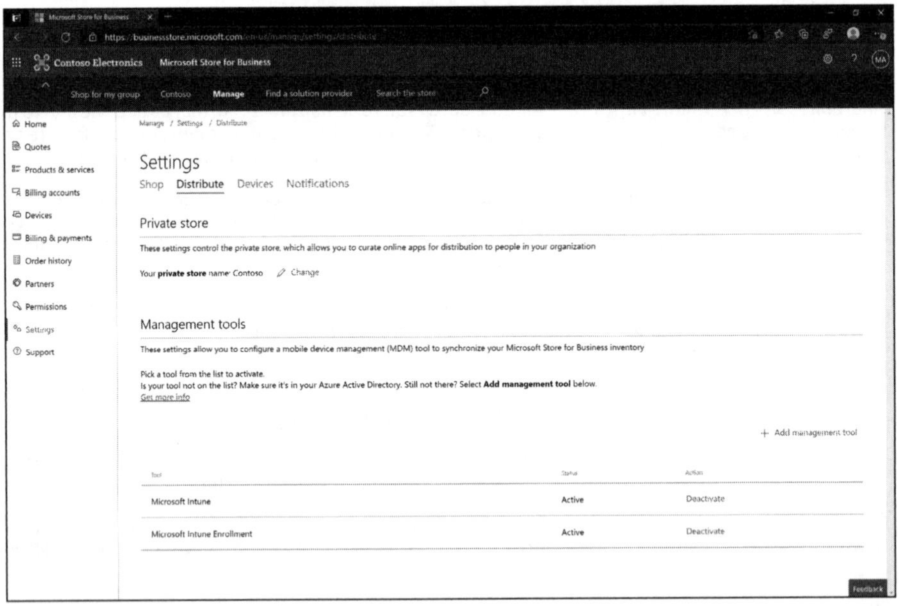

FIGURE 1-18   Microsoft Store for Business management tools

CREATE APPS IN INTUNE

We covered app deployment types earlier in this skill. This is one of the first options that you configure when creating apps in Intune. From there, you can begin adding apps to your Intune library. In this section, you will add an Office 365 app to your Intune app library. This will introduce you to the app-creation process and help you get comfortable with the portal.

1. Log in to the Microsoft Endpoint Manager admin center at *https://endpoint.microsoft.com/*.

2. Click **Apps**, and then click **All Apps**.

3. On the **All Apps** blade, click **Add** in the menu.

4. On the **Add Microsoft 365 Apps** blade, select **Windows 10** under the **Office 365 Suite** app type, and then click **Next**.

5. In the **App Suite Information** tab, fill in the following values and then click **Next**:

   - **Suite Name** Type a name for the app. This name should be unique to prevent conflicts in the company portal. This is a required field.

   - **Suite Description** Type a description for the app. This is a required field.

   - **Publisher** This field is prepopulated for Office 365 apps. For apps where the field is not populated, enter a publisher for the app.

   - **Category** This field is optional. There are nine categories to choose from, and you can select as many as you want. Assigning a category enables users to filter apps more easily. Office 365 apps default to the Productivity category.

   - **Display This as a Featured App in the Company Portal** This toggle specifies whether the app will appear on the main page of the company portal. Set the toggle to **Yes**.

   > **NOTE** The company portal is used by employees to access and install apps. It can be accessed from the Microsoft Store app or by visiting *https://portal.manage.microsoft.com/*.

   - **Information URL** This field is optional. You can enter a web address that contains information about the app. For this example, leave this field blank.

   - **Privacy URL** This field is optional. You can enter a web address that contains privacy information about the app. Leave this field blank.

   - **Developer** This field is optional. It is prepopulated for Office 365 apps.

   - **Owner** This field is optional. It is prepopulated for Office 365 apps.

   - **Notes** This field is optional. Leave this field blank.

   - **Logo** This field is optional. It is prepopulated for Office 365 apps.

6. On the **Configure App Suite** tab, open the **Select Office Apps** drop-down list in the **Configure App Suite** section. You will see a list of all the available products in the Microsoft 365 suite.

7. Select the check box next to each of the following products (see Figure 1-19):

- **Excel**
- **OneDrive**
- **OneNote**
- **Outlook**
- **PowerPoint**
- **Teams**
- **Word**

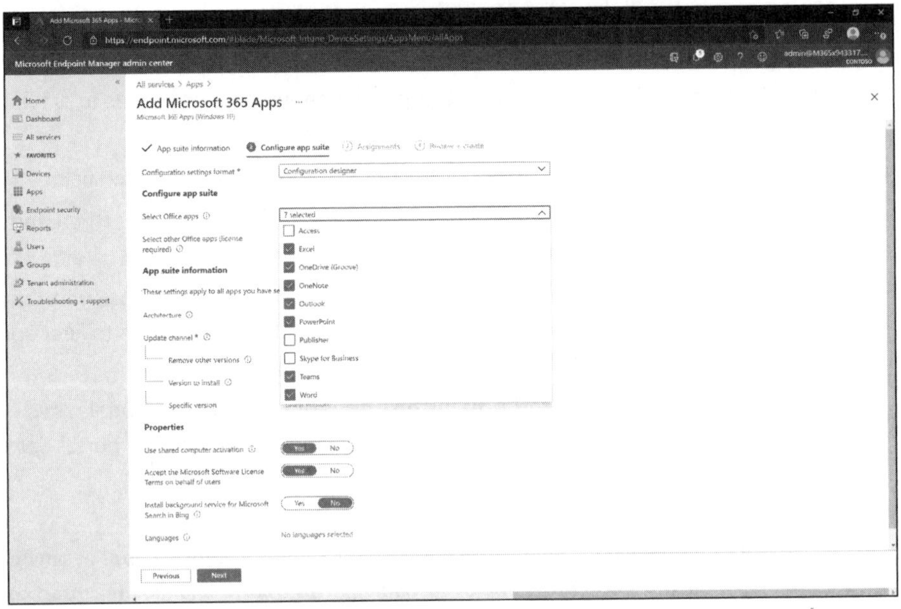

FIGURE 1-19 Office 365 app suite configuration

The **Configure App Suite** tab also includes information pertaining to app metadata, such as the app's name and description. Because this is an Office 365 app, some fields are prepopulated, such as the publisher and app icon.

8. In the **App Suite Information** section of the **Configure App Suite** tab, fill in the following values and leave other values at their default setting. (See Figure 1-20.) Then click **Next**.

- **Architecture**   64-bit
- **Update Channel**   Monthly (Targeted)
- **Remove Other Versions**   Yes
- **Version to Install**   Latest
- **Specific Version**   Latest Version

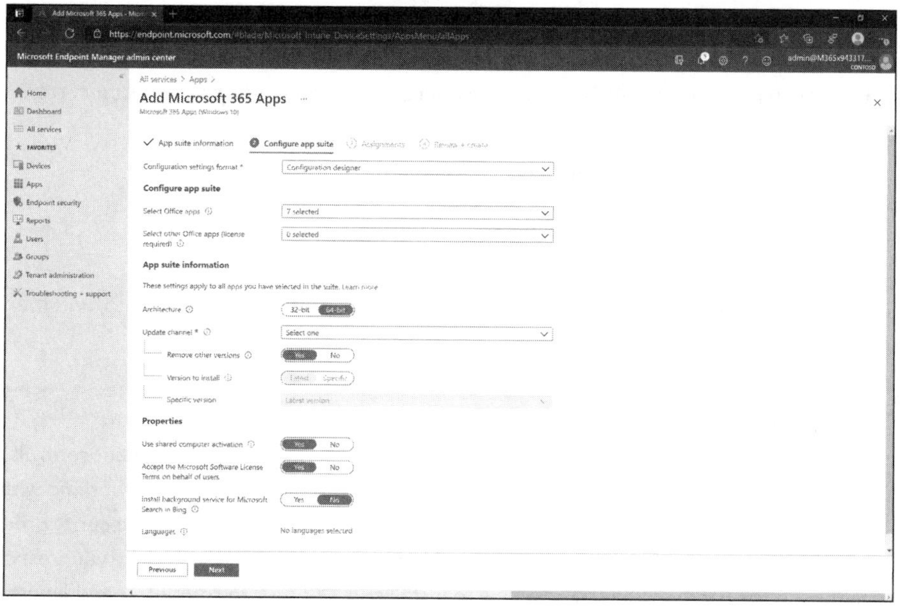

FIGURE 1-20 Office 365 app suite information

9. In the **Properties** section of the **Configure App Suite** tab, fill in the following values, leave the other values at their default setting, and click **Next**. (Refer to Figure 1-20.)

    ■ **Use Shared Computer Activation**   Yes

    ■ **Accept the Microsoft Software License Terms on Behalf of Users**   Yes

    ■ **Languages**   No changes

10. On the **Assignments** tab, choose whether to make the device available to specific users, devices, or groups, and then click **Next**.

11. On the **Review + Create** tab, click **Create**.

With these steps complete, you should have the new Office 365 Suite app listed on the Client Apps – Apps blade alongside the MSfB apps you saw earlier in this skill section.

ASSIGN APPS IN INTUNE

You can assign apps that are present in your Intune app library to groups of users and devices for install or uninstall. When you create a new app assignment, you are given three assignment types to choose from:

■ **Available for enrolled devices**   Makes the app available to devices that are enrolled in Intune.

■ **Required**   Forces the app to install on the targeted group of users or devices.

■ **Uninstall**   Forces the app to be uninstalled from the targeted group of users or devices.

In the following example, you will assign the Office 365 Suite app to various Contoso Electronics groups and configure the app to be required for all devices.

1. Log in to the Microsoft Endpoint Manager admin center at *https://endpoint.microsoft.com/*.

2. Click **Apps** and then click **All Apps**.

3. Locate the **Microsoft 365 apps for Windows 10** app and select it.

4. On the app page, click **Properties**.

5. On the **Properties** page, next to **Assignments**, click **Edit**.

6. On the **Assignments** blade, select the groups to add the assignment to, and then click **Review + Save**.

EXAM TIP

Plan for questions on the exam that will test your knowledge of the assignment controls. Spend time creating groups, adding users and devices to those groups, and working with the include and exclude assignments. A sample scenario might include two security groups and five computers with different membership between the groups. It will be your responsibility to answer questions such as how to install app XYZ on two computers and uninstall app ABC from the other three computers.

Plan for mobile application management

This section covers planning considerations for application management on mobile devices. *Application management* refers to the protection of company data within an application. For example, suppose a user opens an email containing confidential information from their corporate account using Microsoft Outlook for Android. You can use application management to prevent the user from copying data from the email and pasting it into another application. For the exam, you must be comfortable with creating and assigning these policies.

Plan for app protection prerequisites

The capability to manage the data within an application has evolved over the years. Microsoft's solution for this is called *app protection policies*. This is a feature available with Microsoft Intune.

In the past, application management required the management of the device running the app. With app protection policies, the policy is assigned to the user. This alleviates the need for devices to be enrolled in an MDM. Instead, the user signs in to the app with their Azure AD account and the necessary policies get applied.

The following list covers the basic prerequisites for deploying app protection policies in an organization:

- **Azure AD subscription** A basic Azure AD subscription is required to establish Azure AD accounts.

- **Intune subscription**   App protection policies are a capability of Microsoft Intune. You need an Intune subscription to create and manage these policies. In addition, users to whom these policies are assigned require an Intune license.

- **Office 365 subscription**   App protection policies assigned to Office 365 mobile apps require users to have an Office 365 license assigned to their Azure AD account.

- **Azure AD account**   Users must have an Azure AD account.

- **Supported platforms**   App protection policies are supported for iOS, Android, and Windows 10.

- **Security groups**   App protection policies are assigned to Azure AD security groups that contain user objects. You must create the desired groups in Azure AD or synchronize your existing on-premises groups using Azure AD Connect.

- **Supported apps**   App protection policies are not available for all apps. The app must support the Intune SDK features that enable app management.

Configure app protection policies

In this section you will create an app protection policy and assign it to a group of users. A common scenario that you may be presented with is app management for Office 365. These are often the core productivity apps for users, and company data is an important aspect to consider.

In the following example, you are going to create an app protection policy for the Contoso Electronics sales team. These users travel often and use a mixture of corporate and personal mobile devices to access company resources. The app protection policy will control data for each of the core Office 365 mobile apps.

1. Log in to the Microsoft Endpoint Manager admin center at *https://endpoint.microsoft.com/*.

2. Click **Apps**.

3. Under **Policy**, click **App Protection Policies**.

4. On the **App Protection Policies** blade, click **Create Policy**, and then click **Android**.

5. On the **Basics** tab, fill in the following information:

   - **Name**   APP for Android

   - **Description**   APP for Office 365 apps on Android

   - **Platform**   Android

   - **Target To All App Types**   Yes

6. On the **Apps** tab, select the following apps and click **Next**:

   - **Excel**

   - **OneNote**

   - **Outlook**

   - **PowerPoint**

   - **Word**

7. On the **Data Protection** tab (see Figure 1-21), select the following options and click **Next**.

- **Backup Org Data to Android Backup Services**   Block
- **Send Org Data to Other Apps**   Policy Managed Apps
- **Receive Data from Other Apps**   Policy Managed Apps
- **Save Copies of Org Data**   Block
- **Allow User to Save Copies to Selected Services**   OneDrive For Business
- **Restrict Cut, Copy, And Paste Between Other Apps**   Policy Managed Apps
- **Screen Capture and Google Assistant**   Disable
- **Encrypt Org Data**   Require
- **Encrypt Org Data on Enrolled Devices**   Require
- **Sync App with Native Contacts App**   Disable
- **Printing Org Data**   Disable
- **Share Web Content with Policy Managed Browsers**   Require

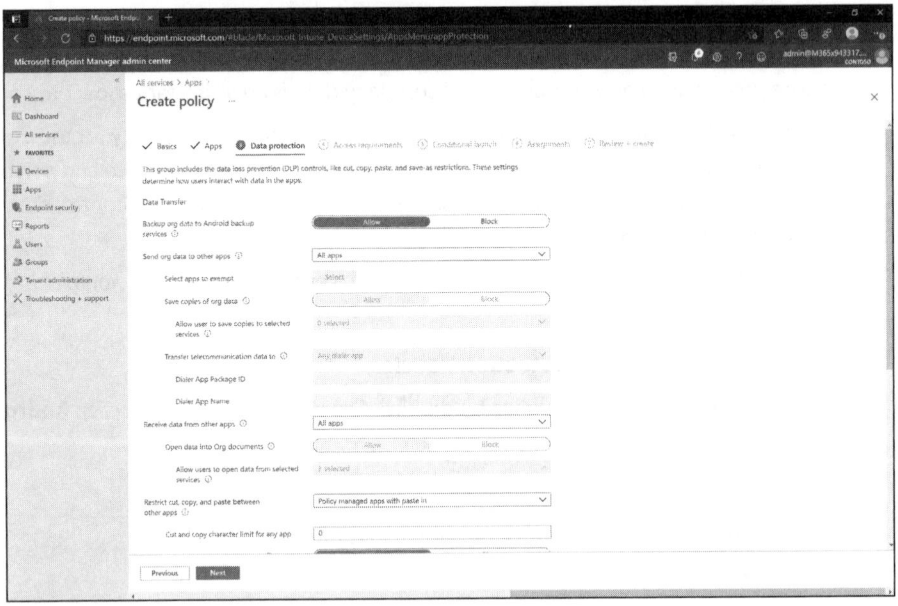

FIGURE 1-21   App protection policy Data Protection tab

8. On the **Access Requirements** tab (see Figure 1-22), select the following options and click **OK**.

- **PIN for Access**   Require
- **PIN Type**   Numeric
- **Simple PIN**   Block

- **Select Minimum PIN Length**   6
- **Fingerprint Instead Of PIN For Access (Android 6.0+)**   Allow
- **Override Fingerprint with PIN After Timeout**   Require
- **Timeout (Minutes of Inactivity)**   30
- **App PIN When Device PIN Is Set**   Require
- **Work or School Account Credentials for Access**   Require
- **Recheck the Access Requirements After (Minutes of Inactivity)**   30

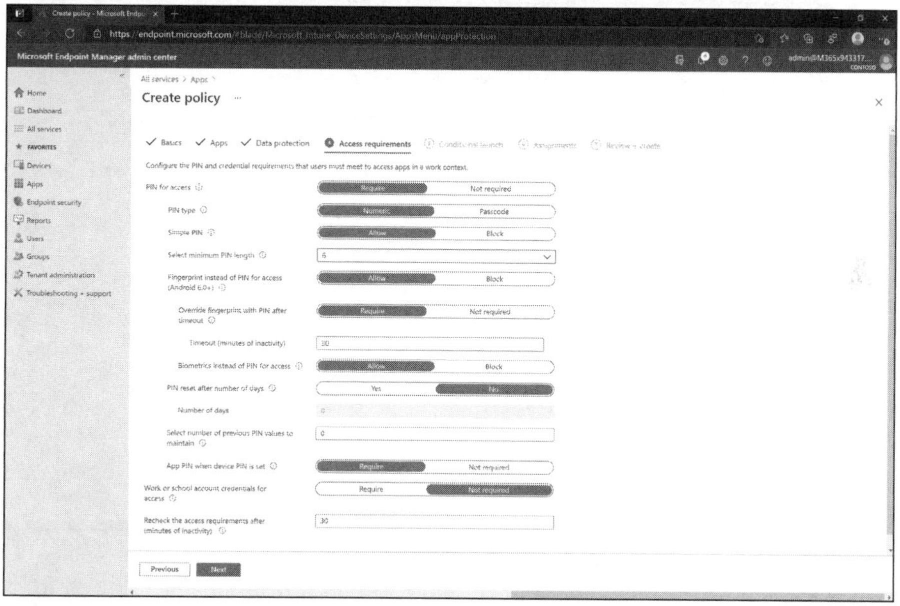

FIGURE 1-22   App protection policy Access Requirements tab

9. On the **Conditional Launch** tab (see Figure 1-23), review the default options and click **OK**.

    Conditional launch enforces periodic checks to ensure that app protection policies are up to date and compliant. There are seven available settings:

    - **Max PIN Attempts**   If a user enters their PIN incorrectly more than the defined number of times, the user can be forced to reset their PIN or the app data can be wiped.
    - **Offline Grace Period**   If the managed app does not check in for a defined period, access to the app can be blocked or the app data can be wiped.
    - **Jailbroken/Rooted Devices**   If the device has been jailbroken or rooted, access to the app can be blocked or the app data can be wiped.
    - **Min OS Version**   If the device OS does not meet the minimum version, the user can be warned, access to the app can be blocked, or the app data can be wiped.

- **Min App Version**   If the app does not meet the minimum version, the user can be warned, access to the app can be blocked, or the app data can be wiped.

- **Min Patch Version**   If the device OS does not meet the minimum patch version, the user can be warned, access to the app can be blocked, or the app data can be wiped.

- **Device Manufacturer(s)**   If the device is not made by the specified manufacturer, access to the app can be blocked or the app data can be wiped.

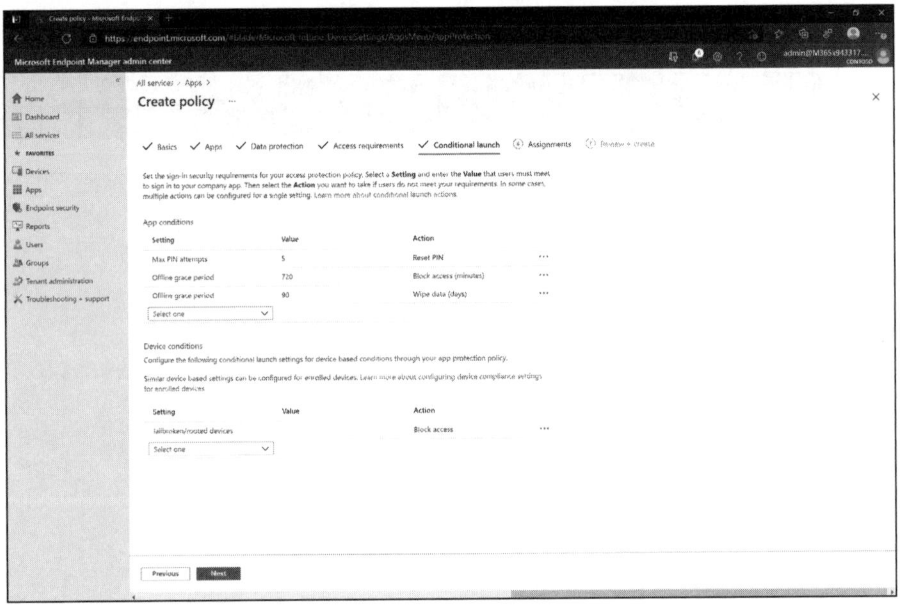

FIGURE 1-23   App protection policy Conditional Launch tab

10. On the **Add a Policy** blade, click **Create**.

11. On the **Client Apps – App Protection Policies** blade, select the **APP for Android** policy.

12. On the **Intune App Protection** blade, under **Manage**, click **Assignments**.

13. On the **Intune App Protection – Assignments** blade, on the Include tab, click **Select Groups to Include**.

14. Select the **Contoso Electronics Sales** group and click **Select**.

After completing these steps, you should have a new app protection policy created and deployed. You can review the check-in information for users that access this app by navigating to the **APP For Android** setting and selecting **Overview**. This tab provides insight into how many users are accessing the associated apps and the check-in count for each app in the policy.

Skill 1.4: Plan Windows 10 deployment

In 2015, Microsoft released Windows 10, an operating system that would completely shift the industry and the way in which enterprises managed and supported Windows. In the past, you could expect a new version of Windows every three to five years, and the support lifecycle for those versions would overlap by a good margin. Organizations had very little pressure to quickly adopt the next major release. They could wait 12 months for major issues to be addressed, and then spend an additional 12 to 18 months testing and deploying the next release of Windows.

Windows 10 has evolved greatly since its introduction. The current version of the popular client operating system is delivered to customers as a service, meaning that instead of waiting three to five years for new features or intermittent service packs, Microsoft deploys a major feature update every six months. These feature updates introduce new capabilities, security enhancements, bug fixes, and much more. In addition, the support lifecycle for Windows 10 releases is shorter than previous versions of Windows. This encourages organizations to stay current with Windows 10.

This skill section covers Windows 10 in depth. This includes planning considerations around Windows as a service (WaaS), a term you should become very familiar with. It walks through the various deployment methods for Windows 10 and looks at the pros and cons for each. It also covers upgrade readiness, a service that helps customers prepare for Windows 10 and maintain compatibility. Finally, it looks at the various security features introduced with Windows 10, which represent one of the major benefits of adopting and staying current with Windows 10.

This skill covers how to:

- Plan for Windows as a service (WaaS)
- Plan the appropriate Windows 10 Enterprise deployment method
- Analyze upgrade readiness for Windows 10
- Evaluate and deploy additional Windows 10 Enterprise security features

---

Plan for Windows as a service (WaaS)

IT organizations that have delivered and supported earlier versions of Windows will experience some significant changes when they adopt Windows 10. Although upgrading to Windows 10 (moving from Windows 7 to Windows 10, for example) shares a lot of similarities with previous upgrades, once your fleet of devices is running Windows 10, you must establish guiding principles for supporting upcoming feature updates, such as hardware, driver, and application compatibility.

This section introduces the core components and services of WaaS. This includes a closer look at servicing channels, which determine your feature update deployment cycle. It also covers Windows Insider for Business. This is a program based on Windows Insider that provides organizations with a centralized approach for testing and providing feedback.

Identify the core components for WaaS

The term *as a service* (*aaS*) reflects a transformation in the way digital services are provided to customers. Some common examples of this model include software as a service (SaaS) and infrastructure as a service (IaaS). Both examples are built on cloud-based technologies. Customers now have the option to purchase Microsoft Office as a subscription (SaaS), providing frequent updates and new capabilities every month. Landing servers in your local data center may not be realistic when you can move those servers to the cloud (IaaS) and reduce on-premises support and maintenance.

With Windows 10, Microsoft introduced Windows as a service (WaaS). The idea behind WaaS is that customers no longer buy a new version of Windows every three to five years. Instead, you purchase Windows 10 and receive frequent updates and features.

Moving Windows to a semi-annual release schedule enabled Microsoft to make some foundational changes in how the operating system would be serviced moving forward. As part of that transformation, the company introduced new components in Windows 10 to support the WaaS model. Each of the following is a key component of WaaS and relates to how you will manage Windows 10.

- **Feature updates** These updates deliver new functionality to the operating system. Feature updates are a core design change in Windows 10 and are a foundation of WaaS. Microsoft delivers these updates twice a year, once in the fall and one in the spring. From a deployment perspective, these updates are designed to be installed in place, over the existing version of Windows 10. Users can expect to retain all their data and applications during the upgrade process. Microsoft has also introduced several tools to help administrators deliver these updates. We will be reviewing each of these tools in this skill section.

- **Quality updates** These updates deliver security and reliability fixes to the operating system. Quality updates redefine the way administrators manage patching for Windows devices. Before Windows 10, Microsoft released a variety of individual updates on "patch Tuesday." In managed environments, administrators could then choose which updates to install. For example, some organizations might only install critical security updates each month or completely miss an important update from a previous month. This resulted in fragmented patch levels and reliability issues. Quality updates help address these problems. They are cumulative, meaning the patch content from the previous month is automatically rolled into the next month's update. They are also condensed, reducing the number of individual updates you need to deploy and manage. For example, instead of six individual security updates for August, you have a single quality update.

- **Servicing channels** Servicing channels are the management controls used to determine which release of Windows 10 is deployed and when. Feature updates can be delivered using management solutions such as ConfigMgr, but they can also be delivered through Windows Update. Administrators must consider how they want to manage these updates and how frequently they want them installed.

- **Deployment rings** Deployment rings are used to roll out Windows 10 feature updates in stages. A ring contains a collection of devices that you determine are ready for the upgrade. You might have a ring for pilot devices and a ring for production. These rings can also directly relate to different management solutions and deployment scenarios such as ConfigMgr with Windows 10 Servicing or Intune with Windows 10 Update Rings.

- **Windows Insider** The Windows Insider program was originally delivered in parallel with the first release of Windows 10. Customers were given the opportunity to join this program and test pre-release features. Participants had access to a feedback mechanism where they could share ideas and bugs. For enterprise customers, Windows Insider for Business was introduced to make enrollment easier.

Plan for servicing channels

We touched briefly on servicing channels in the last section. This section covers servicing channels in detail.

First, it is worth noting that the terminology for servicing channels has changed since their introduction. This was done to help align the update terminology between Windows 10 and Office 365. Earlier naming standards used branch identifiers — for example, Current Branch (CB), Current Branch for Business, and Long-Term Servicing Branch (LTSB). LTSB is still associated with some early editions of Windows Enterprise, but all other components are now referred to as servicing channels.

Servicing channels are broken down into three different types, each delivering a different service. As an administrator, it is your responsibility to identify and deploy the appropriate servicing channel based on the needs of your organization.

- **Insider program** With Windows 10, Microsoft has encouraged customers to start their testing early. Windows Insider delivers a servicing channel that enables customers to enroll their devices and begin testing new features and capabilities before they are released to the general public. This enables business customers to start compatibility testing earlier. Members of the Insider program also have a direct feedback link through the Feedback Hub application. The Insider program supports three deployment rings:

  - **Fast ring** Members of this ring are the first to receive new features and changes. These enhancements are validated on a small population of devices before they become available to the fast ring. Customers should expect possible issues and blockers when enrolled in this ring.

  - **Slow ring** Members of this ring receive Insider builds after members of the fast ring. These builds include updates and fixes for issues identified by fast ring members. There is still a risk that these builds could experience issues, but in general, they are more stable.

  - **Release preview ring** Members of this ring receive a release preview Insider build in advance of general availability. This enables organizations to start piloting the next release of Windows 10 with minimal risk while still having the ability to provide feedback.

- **Semi-annual channel**   After a new feature update is released to the general public, it enters the semi-annual channel. At this point, administrators can begin managing how these updates are delivered to their production devices. There are two deployment rings for this servicing channel.

  - **Semi-annual channel (targeted)**   Newly released updates will enter this deployment ring first. Customers who choose this ring will receive the latest feature update, with the option to defer up to 365 days.

  - **Semi-annual channel**   After a period of time, usually about four months, feature updates are moved to the semi-annual channel deployment ring. This provides organizations with another option for postponing their rollout in addition to the 365-day deferral rules.

- **Long-term servicing channel**   Customers with specialized systems running Windows 10, such as medical equipment or heavy machinery, can leverage the long-term servicing channel to prevent the deployment of feature updates and receive extended support. Unlike with the semi-annual channel, administrators must install the LTSB edition of Windows 10 Enterprise. There is no configuration option to quickly switch between the long-term servicing channel and semi-annual channel. Administrators must re-image devices if they need to make this change. Also, the long-term servicing channel is not designed for systems that are used for productivity or content creation. Devices running Office should not be using the long-term servicing channel.

Each servicing channel also has a different release cadence and support lifecycle. See Table 1-6 for these details.

TABLE 1-6   Servicing channel support

Servicing Channel	New Releases	End of Support
Insider program – fast ring	Weekly	It varies from release to release, but all Insider builds will eventually expire if you do not stay current.
Insider program - slow ring	Monthly	It varies from release to release, but all Insider builds will eventually expire if you do not stay current.
Semi-annual channel	Every six months	Fall releases have 30 months of support. Spring releases have 18 months of support.
Long-term servicing channel	Every two to three years	Up to 10 years of support.

Plan for Windows Insider for Business

Windows Insider delivers pre-release builds of Windows 10 to customers that enroll in the Insider program. Once enrolled, your device will start receiving Insider builds. As a participant, you get to try new features and capabilities before they are released. The Insider build also includes a dedicated channel for reporting issues or general feedback to the Windows development team. Through this program Microsoft can collect real-world data from a vast range of users and devices. This data helps address issues and improve Windows before an update is released to the general public.

After joining the Insider program, you enroll your existing Windows 10 device by navigating to the **Windows Insider Program Settings** page, shown in Figure 1-24. From there, click **Get Started** and enter your account credentials.

FIGURE 1-24   Windows Insider Program Settings page

Windows Insider for Business is the same Insider program that we just reviewed, but with some extra controls to help organizations manage their enrolled users and devices. These controls include:

- **Domain registration**   Customers that are synced with Azure Active Directory (Azure AD) can register their tenant with the Windows Insider program. This enables employees to sign in with their Azure AD credentials.

- **Track feedback**   The feedback submitted through the Feedback Hub is tagged with the corresponding user's Azure AD account. This feedback can then be tracked for internal analysis and data collection.

You can register your domain with the Windows Insider program by following these steps:

1. Navigate to the Windows Insider registration page at *https://insider.windows.com/en-us/register*.

2. Sign in with your Azure AD account and confirm you have access to complete the registration.

   Confirmation is shown at the top of the page under **Register Your Domain with the Windows Insider Program**.

   Your account must meet the following requirements. If these requirements are met, you will see a message prompting you to register your domain, as shown in Figure 1-25.

   ■ Assigned the global administrator role in Azure AD

   ■ Existing participant of the Windows Insider program

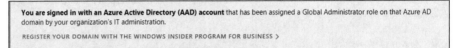

You are signed in with an Azure Active Directory (AAD) account that has been assigned a Global Administrator role on that Azure AD domain by your organization's IT administration.

REGISTER YOUR DOMAIN WITH THE WINDOWS INSIDER PROGRAM FOR BUSINESS >

FIGURE 1-25 Windows Insider for Business sign-in confirmation

3. On the **Manage Insider Preview Builds** page, click the **Register** link.

4. On the **Register** page, review the program agreement, select the check box to accept the terms, and click **Register**.

5. Review the registration results to confirm your organization was successfully registered. (See Figure 1-26.)

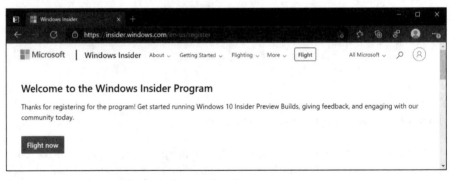

FIGURE 1-26 Windows Insider for Business registration

Plan the appropriate Windows 10 Enterprise deployment method

With Windows 10, deployment methods involve both the initial deployment of the operating system and the deployment of future feature updates. Feature updates in Windows 10 are responsible for upgrading the operating system from one major release to the next. Both scenarios play an important role when you are supporting WaaS. You can use many of the techniques covered in this section to manage new deployments of Windows 10 and support future feature updates.

Windows 10 allows for many of the traditional deployment scenarios that you may already be familiar with. For example, deploying the latest version of Windows during an organization's next major hardware refresh was a common scenario for earlier versions of the operating system. There are new methods available with Windows 10, however — for example, the in-place upgrade, which can help simplify your migration if new hardware is not readily available.

In this section, you will look at a variety of deployment methods available for Windows 10, along with the pros and cons for each method. This includes capabilities available with modern servicing, such as Windows Update for Business. You will also work with task sequences in ConfigMgr as part of the in-place upgrade. Finally, this section covers the traditional methods that are still supported with Windows 10.

Plan for deploying Windows 10 Enterprise

There are two main scenarios associated with Windows 10 deployment. The first scenario involves moving to Windows 10 from an earlier version of the operating system — for example, if your client devices have Windows 8.1 installed, and you are planning a migration to Windows 10. The second scenario involves keeping Windows 10 current with the latest feature updates — for example, your client devices have Windows 10, version 1803 installed, and you are planning to upgrade to Windows 10, version 1809. There are deployment methods for each of these scenarios.

In some cases, a deployment method can be used for both deployments and upgrades, such as the in-place upgrade. Other methods are more specific, such as Windows Update for Business. The first thing you must understand is what options are available and in what scenarios they apply.

- **Traditional methods** This category includes several of the deployment methods used with earlier versions of the Windows operating system. Microsoft has continued to support these methods, and has released compatibility updates for tools such as the Microsoft Deployment Toolkit (MDT) and the Windows Assessment and Deployment Kit (Windows ADK), both of which support traditional imaging and upgrades. Specific deployment methods in this category include the following:

- **Bare metal** This deployment method is for scenarios where new hardware is procured or existing hardware is repurposed. In both situations, a Windows image is installed and configured according to the organization's IT standards. Bare metal deployments occur at most organizations and are commonly leveraged in situations where you must roll out a new version of the operating system or another major application, such as Microsoft Office. It can help consolidate efforts.

- **Refresh** This deployment method is for scenarios where an existing device needs to be wiped and reloaded. In this situation, the existing user state is backed up, the disk is wiped, the latest image is installed, and the user state is restored. Refresh deployments are often seen when a device becomes inoperable and needs to be wiped. This type of deployment can also be used in upgrade scenarios, such as moving from Windows 7 to Windows 10.

- **Replace** This deployment method is similar to the refresh method but includes new hardware as part of the process. For example, suppose a user is running a three-year-old laptop with Windows 8.1 installed. You could back up the user state on this laptop and replace it by restoring the backup to a new laptop running Windows 10.

- **In-place upgrade** This deployment method is for scenarios where an earlier version of Windows (including an earlier version of Windows 10) is installed on a device and you upgrade the device to Windows 10 or to a newer release of Windows 10. This method pertains to upgrading to Windows 10 and staying current. For example, suppose you have a device running Windows 7 and you deploy an in-place upgrade for Windows 10, version 1809. Alternatively, suppose you have a device running Windows 10, version 1803 and you deploy an in-place upgrade for Windows 10, version 1809. Either way, you could use this deployment method. This method retains the applications, settings, and user data on the system. The old version of Windows is moved to a Windows.old folder for a configurable amount of time, which can then be referenced in the event you need to roll back the operating system.

- **Modern servicing** This deployment method is for scenarios where you need to keep current with new releases of Windows 10. Similar to the in-place upgrade, modern servicing can address situations where you are moving from one version of Windows 10 to the next. However, modern servicing technologies are specific to Windows 10, and cannot be used with earlier versions of the operating system. Windows Update for Business (WUfB), Windows Server Update Services (WSUS), and System Center Configuration Manager (ConfigMgr) are all tools that support modern servicing.

Now that you have covered the basic deployment methods for Windows 10, let's take a look at the different deployment formats. Windows 10 is available in two formats:

- **Electronic Software Delivery (ESD)** Available through Windows Update or the Windows 10 Media Creation Tool

- **Windows Imaging Format (WIM)** Available through traditional installation media (ISO)

There are a number of solutions available for each deployment format, with pros and cons for each. See Table 1-7 for a breakdown of these formats.

TABLE 1-7 Modern servicing techniques

Deployment Format	Delivery Solution	Pros	Cons
Electronic Software Delivery (ESD)	Windows Update for Business (WUfB) Windows Server Update Services (WSUS) System Center Configuration Manager (ConfigMgr)	Smallest package size Fastest installation	Limited control to handle pre and post upgrade tasks
Windows Imaging Format (WIM)	System Center Configuration Manager (ConfigMgr) Microsoft Deployment Toolkit (MDT) Third-party management solutions	Full control over the upgrade experience end-to-end	Highest administrative effort Largest package size

The delivery solutions noted in Table 1-7 are described as follows:

- **Windows Update for Business (WUfB)**   WUfB is a series of new policies available to Windows 10 clients. These policies enable administrators to manage the servicing channel and deferral settings for Windows 10 feature updates and quality updates. This service delivers updates to clients through the public Windows Update network using the ESD deployment format. WUfB policies can be configured using a group policy object (GPO) or Intune MDM policy.

- **Windows Server Update Services (WSUS)**   WSUS is an on-premises solution for organizations that need to fully manage the updates that they deploy to their clients. Administrators can synchronize with the Microsoft Update catalog and deploy approved updates for all supported versions of the Windows operating system. This includes feature updates and quality updates for Windows 10.

- **System Center Configuration Manager (ConfigMgr)**   ConfigMgr is an on-premises device-management solution for organizations that need to fully manage the updates that they deploy to their clients. With ConfigMgr, administrators are given the option to use task sequences or software updates (WSUS). With task sequences, you have additional control over the in-place upgrade scenario.

- **Microsoft Deployment Toolkit (MDT)**   MDT is a free deployment tool that enables administrators to support Windows 10 images and in-place upgrades. Similar to ConfigMgr, MDT uses task sequences for image creation and upgrades.

As you prepare to deploy Windows 10 using the in-place upgrade method, there are a number of items to consider. Although there are several benefits to supporting this method, each of the following issues can affect the success of your implementation.

- **Compatibility**   You must review all hardware, drivers, and applications for Windows 10 compatibility. Older hardware, including peripherals, may not support the latest release of Windows 10 or have supported drivers, in which case they would need to be replaced or updated. Applications that are incompatible can cause the upgrade to fail and must be assessed as well. Later in this skill section, you will review Upgrade Readiness, a service provided by Microsoft to help identify compatibility issues.

- **Legacy BIOS to UEFI**   Windows 10 supports legacy BIOS and UEFI, both of which use different partition maps on the system drive. That said, there are security features, such as Secure Boot, that require UEFI. In this case, you can complete an in-place upgrade on a device running legacy BIOS and then use the MBR2GPT tool to convert the partition map from master boot record (MBR) to GUID partition table (GPT).

> ***NEED MORE REVIEW?* RUNNING MBR2GPT**
>
> For more information about the MBR2GPT tool, including prerequisites and instructions, visit *https://docs.microsoft.com/windows/deployment/mbr-to-gpt*.

- **Disk encryption**   The Windows 10 in-place upgrade supports BitLocker natively. If the system drive is encrypted with BitLocker, the upgrade will work without any additional administrative effort. If the drive is encrypted with a third-party solution, you must contact the vendor for instructions on how to address the encryption software during the upgrade.
- **Language packs**   The Windows 10 in-place upgrade will retain the system default user interface (UI) language. Any additional language packs that have been installed previously must be re-installed following the upgrade.
- **32-bit to 64-bit**   The Windows 10 in-place upgrade does not support upgrading devices from 32-bit versions of Windows to 64-bit versions. If this is a scenario you need to plan for, consider using the refresh or replace deployment method instead.
- **Windows to Go**   Windows to Go is a feature that enables customers to boot a Windows installation from a supported USB storage device. The Windows 10 in-place upgrade is not supported on Windows to Go devices running older versions of the operating system. Once a device is running Windows 10, however, future feature updates can be installed using this method.
- **Existing images**   If you have an existing operating system image for Windows 7 or Windows 8.1, installing that image, upgrading it to Windows 10, and recapturing it is not supported. A new operating system must be re-created for Windows 10 deployments. Alternatively, you can start using offline servicing to avoid traditional reference image designs.

> ***NEED MORE REVIEW?* WINDOWS 10 OFFLINE SERVICING**
>
> For more information about offline servicing for Windows 10, visit *https://docs.microsoft. com/windows-hardware/manufacture/desktop/understanding-servicing-strategies*.

- **Dual-boot**   The Windows 10 in-place upgrade supports devices running a single version of Windows. Devices configured in a dual-boot or multi-boot configuration are not supported.

Design an in-place upgrade for Windows 10

In this section, you take a closer look at the in-place upgrade deployment method. This is a common starting point for organizations that are planning their migration to Windows 10. In the following example, you will work with a task sequence in ConfigMgr, version 1810. In this version of ConfigMgr, a task sequence template is provided to support in-place upgrade scenarios.

To begin, you must download a copy of the Windows 10 installation media. You can retrieve this by downloading the latest Windows 10 ISO from the Microsoft volume license service center (VLSC). To access the VLSC, visit *https://www.microsoft.com/Licensing/servicecenter/default.aspx*. After you have downloaded Windows 10, you must extract the files from that ISO in preparation for creating the operating system upgrade package required by ConfigMgr. See Figure 1-27 for an example of the extracted files needed.

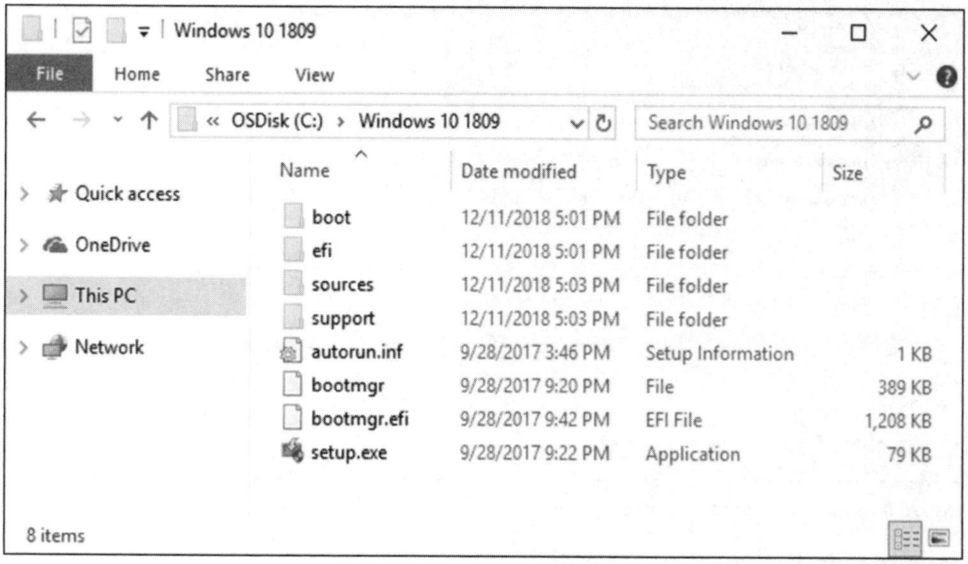

FIGURE 1-27 Windows 10 installation media

ConfigMgr requires the Windows 10 installation media in order to complete the in-place upgrade. The installation media is referenced in the task sequence as an operating system upgrade package. When this step runs, ConfigMgr executes setup.exe with a series of command-line options that instruct the setup operation on how to complete the upgrade. Setup.exe can be executed independently of ConfigMgr; it is worth reviewing the variety of supported options.

> **NEED MORE REVIEW? WINDOWS SETUP COMMAND-LINE OPTIONS**
>
> For more information about the supported Windows setup command-line options, including examples on how to use these options, visit *https://docs.microsoft.com/windows-hardware/manufacture/desktop/windows-setup-command-line-options*.

Figure 1-28 shows an example of the in-place upgrade task sequence template provided with ConfigMgr, version 1810. Each group in this task sequence template is provided to assist you with creating a working upgrade deployment. You can add, remove, or modify any of these steps to meet your requirements. Each group contains a basic description to provide additional guidance.

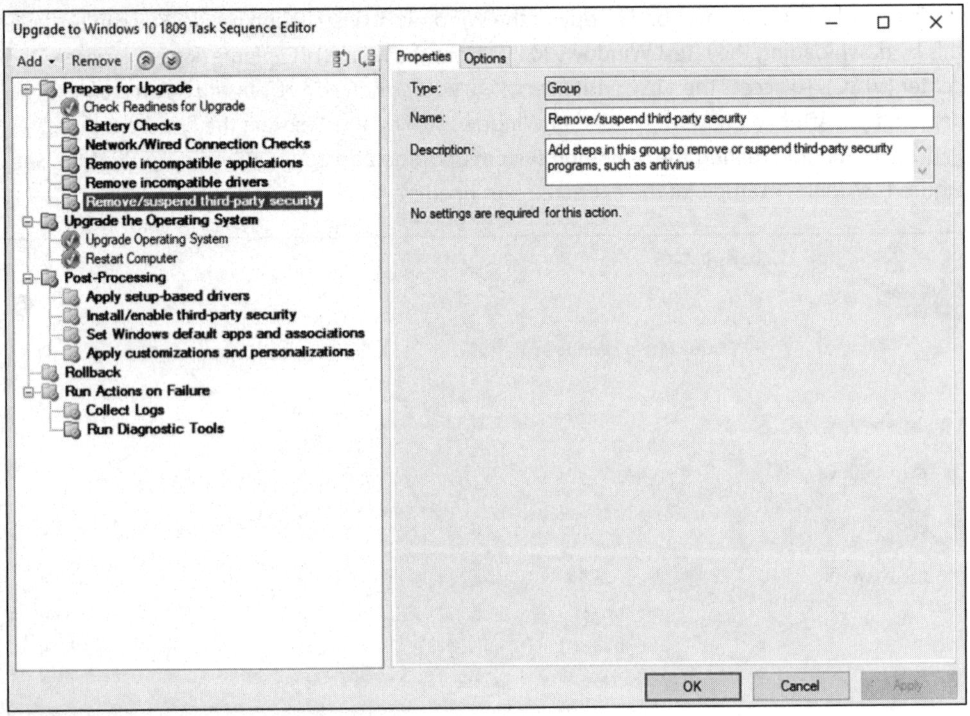

FIGURE 1-28   In-place upgrade task sequence

The groups are as follows:

- **Prepare for Upgrade**   This group is designed for steps that will run in the current operating system. These steps should be focused on pre-upgrade operations, such as checking for 20 GB of free disk space (a requirement for setup) or ensuring that the computer is connected to a wired connection (if you do not support upgrades over wireless).

- **Upgrade the Operating System**   This group is designed for steps that trigger the in-place upgrade. The Upgrade Operating System and Restart Computer steps are included as part of the template. The Upgrade Operating System step includes a number of options. (See Figure 1-29.) In this figure, the Perform Windows Setup Compatibility Scan Without Starting Upgrade check box is selected. This setting runs setup using the /Comapt option. The Windows setup will scan the device for possible incompatibilities. If any are found, a return code is generated with a series of logs that require further analysis.

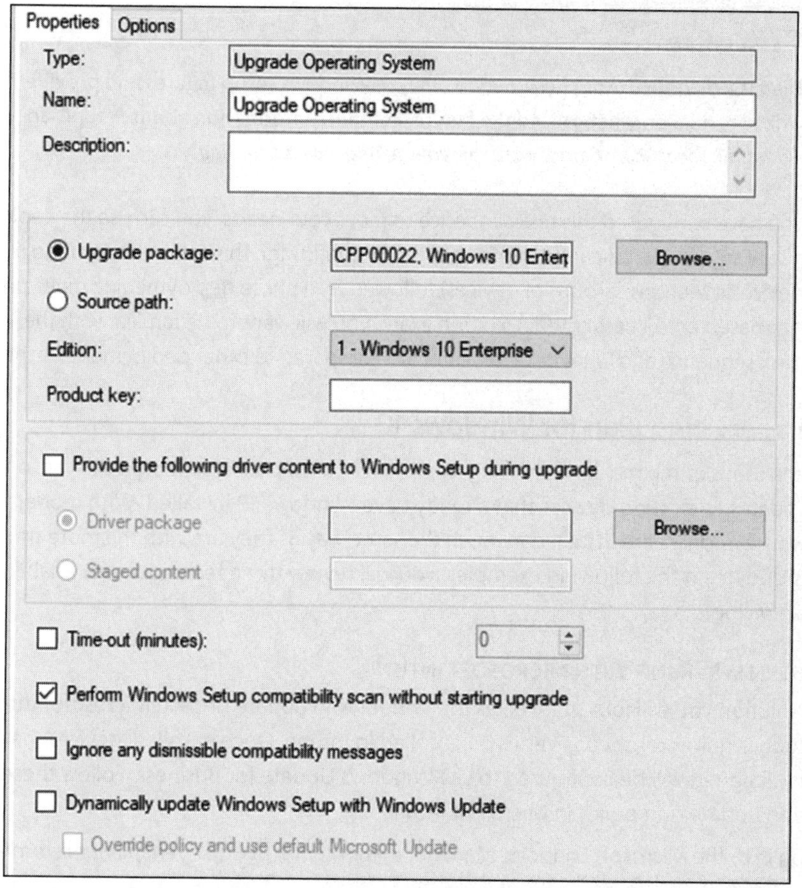

FIGURE 1-29 The Upgrade Operating System task sequence

- **Post-Processing**   This group is designed for steps that need to run after the upgrade has completed successfully. This group will run if the task sequence variable _SMSTSSetupRollback equals `false`. Possible steps might include installing applications, resuming disk encryption, and running custom configuration changes for your organization.

- **Rollback**   This group is designed for steps that need to run after an upgrade has failed and triggered a rollback. This group will run if the task sequence variable _SMSTSSetupRollback equals `true`. Possible steps might include sending an email notification to the device owner that the upgrade was unsuccessful and automatically creating an incident in your service desk system.

- **Run Actions on Failure**   Similar to the rollback group, this group is designed for steps that need to run after an upgrade has failed. This group will run if the task sequence variable _SMSTSOSUpgradeActionReturnCode does not equal 0. Possible steps might include running a log collector or diagnostic tool such as SetupDiag.

After you have configured this task sequence to meet your needs, you can use the deployment ring strategy discussed earlier in this chapter. In ConfigMgr, this can be done using a series of device collections (groups of devices) followed by a phase deployment (a multi-phase deployment based on success criteria). For the exam, you will want to be familiar with the in-place upgrade task sequence and what its capabilities are compared to other deployment methods.

Design a servicing plan for Windows 10

This section looks at the modern servicing deployment method. This method delivers new feature updates to existing devices that already have Windows 10 installed. With modern servicing, feature updates are installed in much the same way as they are with the more traditional Windows Update. In the following examples, you will review three techniques for enabling modern servicing.

USE MODERN SERVICING WITH MICROSOFT INTUNE

The first solution you will look at involves the Windows 10 update rings in Microsoft Intune. This solution requires target devices to be enrolled in Intune. Once enrolled, devices that have this policy assigned will be configured to use Windows Update for Business. Follow these steps to create an update ring policy in Microsoft Intune.

1. Log in to the Microsoft Endpoint Manager admin center at *https://endpoint.microsoft.com/*.

2. Click **Devices**.

3. Click **Windows 10 Update Rings**.

4. On the Windows 10 Update Rings page, click **Create Profile**.

Figure 1-30 shows the Update Ring Settings tab, which shows the update ring settings available through this policy.

The update ring settings are split into two sections: Update Settings and User Experience Settings. In the Update Settings section are two controls that are used to manage the deployment of feature updates. These include the following:

- **Servicing Channel**   This drop-down list includes each of the servicing channels you reviewed in Skill 4.1. Use this option to set up deployment rings for Windows Insider for Business or to configure deployments of public releases when they reach the semi-annual channel.

- **Feature Update Deferral Period (Days)**   This feature enables you to defer an update for as long as 365 days. It is designed to give you an additional grace period to accommodate your deployment workflow.

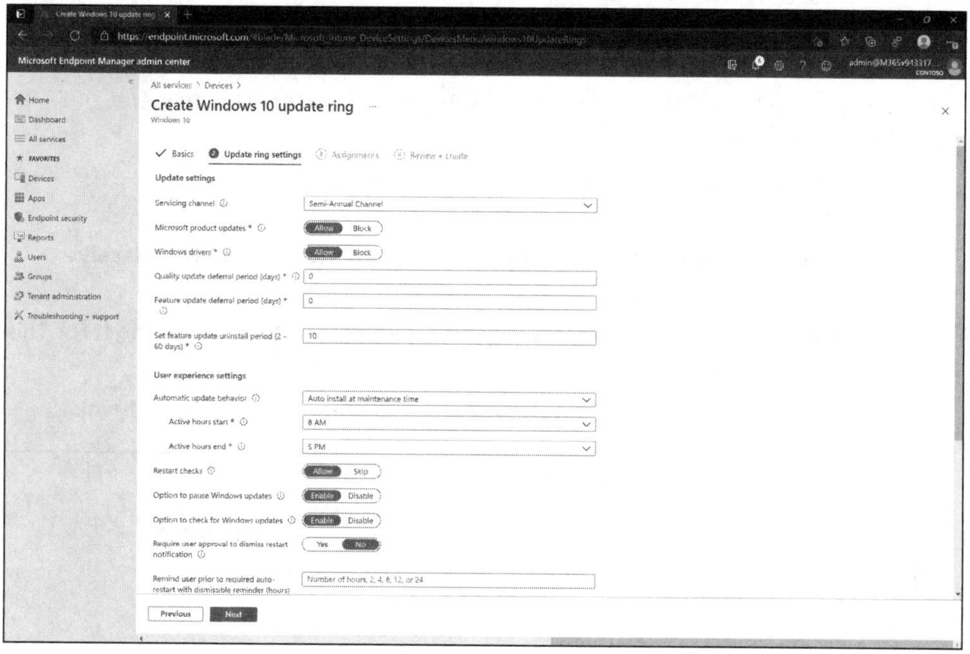

FIGURE 1-30   Windows 10 update rings

After configuring and assigning this policy, you have the option to pause the assignment for as many as 35 days in case you need to halt all upgrades to troubleshoot an issue. You can set this option in the **Software Updates – Windows 10 Update Rings** blade, which you access by selecting the policy and clicking **Pause** on its **Overview** page. When you are ready to resume the assignment, you can do so from the same blade; otherwise, the assignment will automatically resume after 35 days.

USE MODERN SERVICING WITH GROUP POLICY

The next solution you will review involves configuring WUfB using the group policy. These group policy settings are identical to the ones in Intune, so this will be a brief example. The major difference with group policy is how the various settings are split into individual policies. For instance, the settings for user experience are broken down between multiple policies. In the following example, you will configure a new GPO for WUfB using the latest ADMX templates provided with Windows 10, version 1809.

1. Open the **Group Policy Management Editor**.
2. Create a new GPO and name it **WUfB**.
3. Right-click the new **GPO** and click **Edit**.
4. Under **Computer Configuration**, expand **Policies**.
5. Expand **Administrative Templates**.
6. Expand **Windows Components**.

7. Expand **Windows Update**.

8. Expand **Windows Update for Business**.

9. Locate and edit the **Select When Preview Builds and Feature Updates Are Received** policy.

10. Select the **Enabled** option and configure the following options (see Figure 1-31). Then click **OK**.

   - **Select the Windows Readiness Level for the Updates You Want to Receive Semi-Annual Channel**

   - **After a Preview Build or Feature Update Is Released, Defer Receiving It for This Many Days   0**

   - **Pause Preview Builds or Feature Updates Starting**   Leave this value **blank**

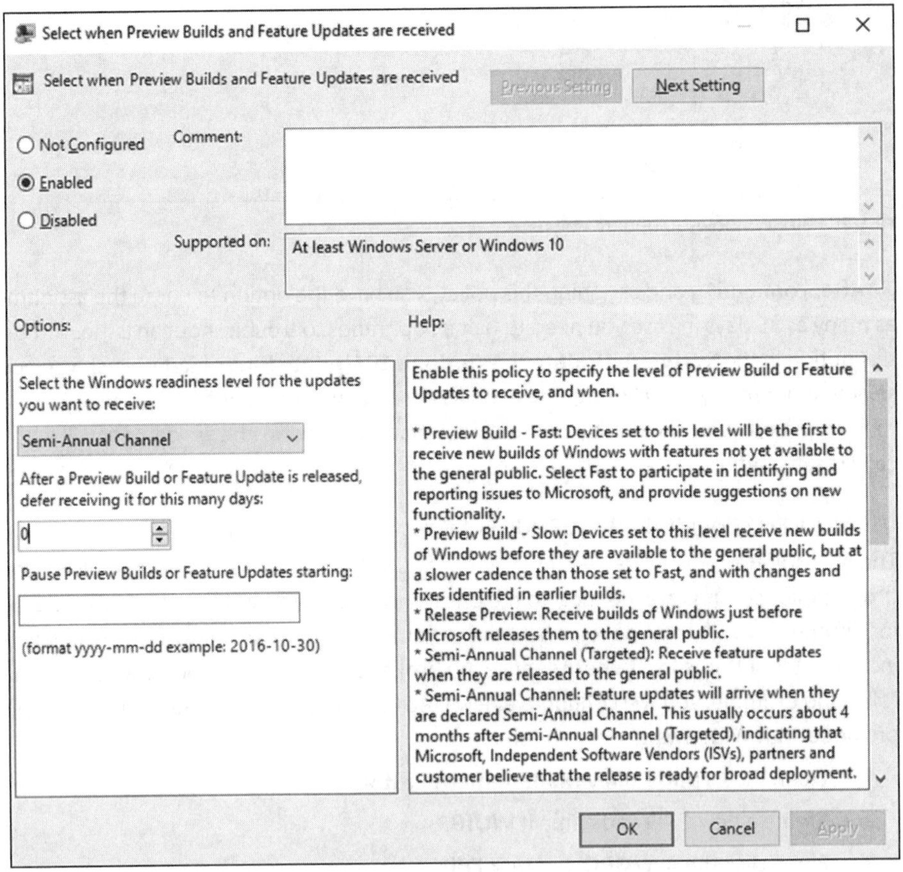

FIGURE 1-31   GPO for feature updates

MODERN SERVICING WITH CONFIGMGR

The last solution you will review is the Window 10 servicing feature in ConfigMgr. This deployment method is ideal for organizations that have chosen the ESD update format but still want to manage update deployments through ConfigMgr.

Windows 10 servicing uses ConfigMgr's Software Update feature. This feature employs WSUS to synchronize updates from the Microsoft Update catalog. Those updates can then be managed and deployed by ConfigMgr. The Windows 10 Servicing feature leverages these capabilities.

The creation wizard will walk you through creating a servicing plan, setting up deployment rings, and creating the deployment. In this example, you will create a servicing plan in ConfigMgr, version 1810.

1. Click **Start**, search for **Configuration Manager Console**, and select it.
2. In the **Configuration Manager Console**, click the **Software Library workspace**.
3. In the **Overview** page, expand **Windows 10 Servicing**, and select **Servicing Plans**.
4. In the ribbon, click **Create Servicing Plan**.

   Figure 1-32 shows an example of a Windows 10 servicing plan created in ConfigMgr. The summary page outlines the configuration options for each of the various controls available on each page in the creation wizard. The pages are as follows:

   - **General** Assign a name and description for the servicing plan.
   - **Servicing Plan** Select the device collection that will receive the deployment generated by this servicing plan.
   - **Deployment Ring** Select a servicing channel and delay deployment up to 120 days. Note that your only options for servicing channels are Semi-Annual Channel (Targeted) and Semi-Annual Channel. You do not have options for Windows Insider builds.
   - **Upgrades** Define the criteria for the updates you are deploying with this servicing plan. For example, if you are creating a servicing plan for just 64-bit devices, you can configure the architecture attribute to only retrieve 64-bit updates.
   - **Deployment Schedule** Define when the update will become available and when it will be enforced.
   - **User Experience** Configure what notifications are displayed to the user and how reboot behavior will be handled. If you are using maintenance windows in ConfigMgr, you can configure whether they are acknowledged for this deployment.
   - **Package** Assign a deployment package or configure the servicing plan to use the Microsoft cloud, reducing the need to download and replicate content internally.

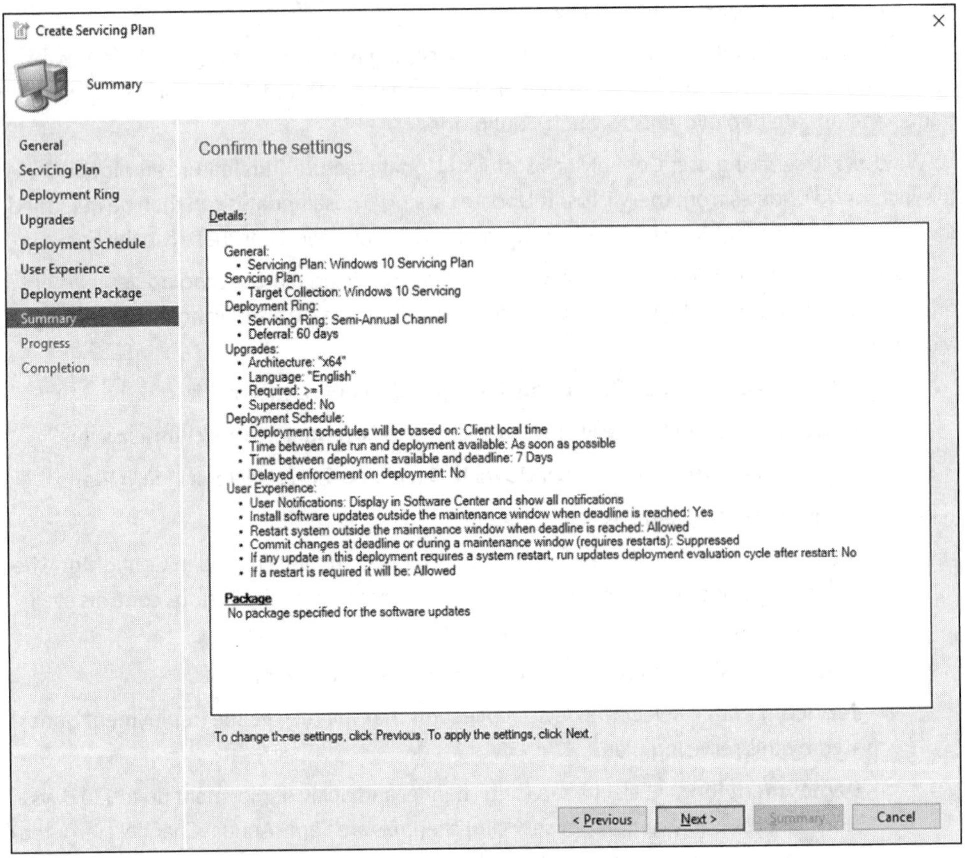

Create Servicing Plan

Summary

General
Servicing Plan
Deployment Ring
Upgrades
Deployment Schedule
User Experience
Deployment Package
Summary
Progress
Completion

Confirm the settings

Details:

General:
  • Servicing Plan: Windows 10 Servicing Plan
Servicing Plan:
  • Target Collection: Windows 10 Servicing
Deployment Ring:
  • Servicing Ring: Semi-Annual Channel
  • Deferral: 60 days
Upgrades:
  • Architecture: "x64"
  • Language: "English"
  • Required: >=1
  • Superseded: No
Deployment Schedule:
  • Deployment schedules will be based on: Client local time
  • Time between rule run and deployment available: As soon as possible
  • Time between deployment available and deadline: 7 Days
  • Delayed enforcement on deployment: No
User Experience:
  • User Notifications: Display in Software Center and show all notifications
  • Install software updates outside the maintenance window when deadline is reached: Yes
  • Restart system outside the maintenance window when deadline is reached: Allowed
  • Commit changes at deadline or during a maintenance window (requires restarts): Suppressed
  • If any update in this deployment requires a system restart, run updates deployment evaluation cycle after restart: No
  • If a restart is required it will be: Allowed

Package
No package specified for the software updates

To change these settings, click Previous. To apply the settings, click Next.

< Previous   Next >   Summary   Cancel

FIGURE 1-32 Windows 10 servicing plan summary

Analyze upgrade readiness for Windows 10

Earlier in this chapter, you explored some of the requirements that you must consider before deploying Windows 10. Most customers preparing to deploy a new operating system are going to perform extensive testing and validation of their hardware, drivers, and applications before they start large-scale deployments. This process can be time-consuming — even more so when that operating system is undergoing major changes every six months.

Upgrade readiness is a service provided by Microsoft to help customers identify compatibility concerns in support of WaaS. Customers that choose to enroll in this service can get metrics and visual indicators on which components need the most attention and which devices are ready to upgrade. This is made possible using Windows telemetry and the Microsoft cloud.

Plan for upgrade readiness

To prepare for upgrade readiness, you must be familiar with the requirements for Windows Analytics. To begin, let's cover the fundamentals of upgrade readiness and items that you should be familiar with:

- **Telemetry** The upgrade readiness service requires that you set the Windows telemetry level to basic (minimum) for any devices that you enroll in the service.

- **Operating system support** Upgrade readiness supports devices running Windows 7 SP1, Windows 8.1, or Windows 10. For Windows 7 SP1, you must install KB2952664. For Windows 8.1, you must install KB2976978.

- **Target operating system** Upgrade readiness can provide you with compatibility information for one operating system version at a time. For example, in Figure 1-33, you can see the **Target Version to be Evaluated** drop-down menu. This option is configured as part of the solution settings in Azure. The operating system version you select will be used for data analysis. When a new Windows 10 feature update is released, you must update this field to the new build number. A change to the target version can take up to 24 hours to apply.

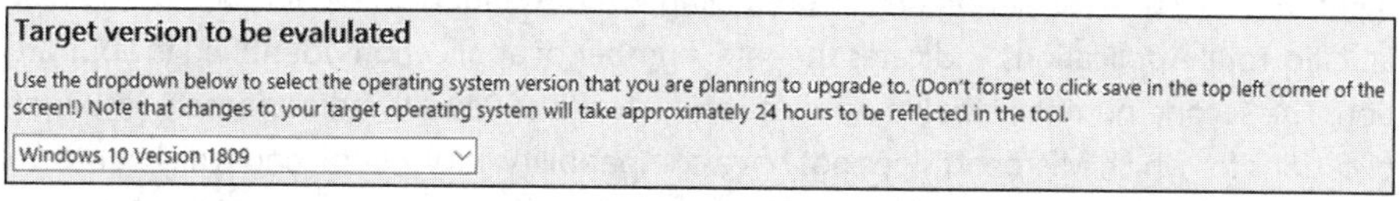

Target version to be evaluated

Use the dropdown below to select the operating system version that you are planning to upgrade to. (Don't forget to click save in the top left corner of the screen!) Note that changes to your target operating system will take approximately 24 hours to be reflected in the tool.

Windows 10 Version 1809

FIGURE 1-33 Upgrade readiness solution settings

- **Data availability** After a device is configured to upload telemetry and associate it with a commercial ID, it can take up to 72 hours for that data to become visible in upgrade readiness. After that, you can expect to see updates every 24 hours. For example, if a device has an incompatible application and you update that application, the change will be reflected within 24 hours.

- **Cost** The upgrade readiness service is offered free of cost. This free offering provides seven days of historical data and up to 500 MB of storage. If your organization decides it needs to retain 90 days of historical data, you must procure Azure storage to accommodate this requirement.

Navigate upgrade readiness

After you have set up your devices to upload telemetry to Microsoft with your organization's commercial ID, the results will be shown in the Log Analytics service in the Azure portal. From there, you can begin navigating through the different blades and assessing your organization's upgrade readiness.

The following steps will introduce you to the upgrade readiness solution in the Azure portal. For this demonstration, we have already created a Log Analytics workspace for Contoso Electronics, named -Analytics. The devices in this organization are also configured for upgrade readiness.

You will look at the Contoso Electronics environment to determine whether the organization is ready to adopt Windows 10. To access the upgrade readiness solution, follow these steps.

1. Log in to the Microsoft Azure portal at *https://portal.azure.com/*.
2. Click **All Services**.
3. Search for **Log Analytics** and select it.
4. On the **Log Analytics** blade, select the workspace containing your upgrade readiness solution — in this example, **-Analytics**.
5. On the **-Analytics** blade, under **General**, select **Solutions**.
6. On the **-Analytics – Solutions** blade, select the solution starting with **CompatibilityAssessment** — in this example, **CompatibilityAssessment(-Analytics)**.
7. On the **CompatibilityAssessment(-Analytics)** blade, click the **Upgrade Readiness** tile.

   The Upgrade Readiness Workflow page opens. It consists of multiple blades with data related to Windows 10 compatibility.

The next blade you are presented with relative to upgrade readiness is **STEP 1: Identify Important Apps**. (See Figure 1-34.) This blade is designed to highlight applications in your environment that may need attention before deploying Windows 10. The first number on this blade, labeled Total Applications, indicates the total number of applications identified in your organization. The second number, labeled Applications in Need of Review, indicates the number of applications for which Microsoft does not have compatibility information and which it recommends that you review. You can click either of these values to drill down into the various data categories.

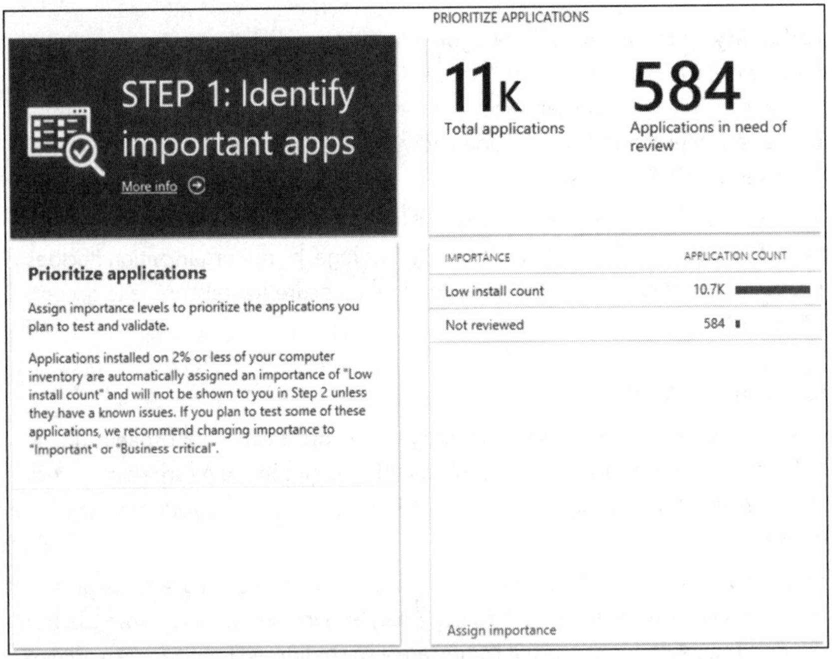

FIGURE 1-34 Upgrade Readiness - Identify Important Apps

Applications are automatically grouped based on importance. For example, applications that are installed on less than 2% of devices are grouped together. You also have the option to assign or modify the importance level with a selection of built-in options. You accomplish this by clicking the **Assign Importance** link at the bottom of the blade. Defining the importance level will assist in organizing your application portfolio and defining which applications are upgrade ready. Importance levels include the following:

- **Not reviewed**   This is the default importance level for applications that are installed on more than 2% of devices. To clearly understand which apps are important, you can modify this default value to something with additional meaning.

- **Mission critical**   This is an optional importance level, signifying a mission-critical dependency on the application.

- **Business critical**   This is an optional importance level, signifying a business-critical dependency on the application.

- **Important**   This is an optional importance level, signifying the application is important to the organization.

- **Best effort**   This is an optional importance level, signifying the application is not important and compatibility will be approached as a best effort.

- **Ignore**   This is an optional importance level, signifying the application is not important and can be safely ignored from future compatibility reports. Selecting this option will mark the application as upgrade ready, removing it as a blocker.

- **Review in progress**   This is an optional importance level, signifying the application is currently under review and the importance level has not yet been identified.

The next blade you are presented with is **STEP 2: Resolve Issues**. This step in the workflow includes a series of blades for addressing issues that are considered to be upgrade blockers. See the following list for more information about each of the blades in step 2.

- **Review Applications with Known Issues**   This blade highlights applications with known issues. Applications that Microsoft has a fix for will be marked accordingly, reducing the number of applications that you must review. As you review these apps, you have the option to adjust the upgrade readiness value, approving or blocking applications from the upgrade. These values include:

  - **Not Reviewed**   This is the default value for applications that are installed on more than 2% of devices and all drivers.

  - **Review in Progress**   Assigning this value to an application or driver will prevent it from being approved until it can be marked as ready to upgrade. This should be used for any applications or drivers that you still need to validate.

  - **Ready to Upgrade**   Assigning this value to an application or driver will mark it as upgrade ready.

  - **Won't Upgrade**   Assigning this value to an application or driver will mark all corresponding devices as not upgrade ready.

- **Review Known Driver Issues** This blade highlights drivers with known issues. Drivers that Microsoft has information on will be marked accordingly. For example, if newer versions of various drivers are available through Windows Update, those drivers will be grouped together. Similar to the previous application blades, you can define the same upgrade readiness values to approve or deny drivers.

- **Review Low-Risk Apps and Drivers** This blade highlights applications and drivers that need review but are determined to be low risk based on various conditions. For example, if Microsoft has identified an application as highly adopted (installed on more than 100,000 devices), that application will be marked as low risk.

- **Prioritize App and Driver Testing** This blade highlights applications and drivers that are currently blocking the upgrade for your target operating system on more than 80% of devices. Reviewing and prioritizing these items can yield a high return for upgrade readiness.

The next blade you are presented with is **STEP 3: Deploy** (see Figure 1-35). This step in the workflow consolidates all information that has been collected and categorizes devices based on upgrade readiness. There are three upgrade options on this blade:

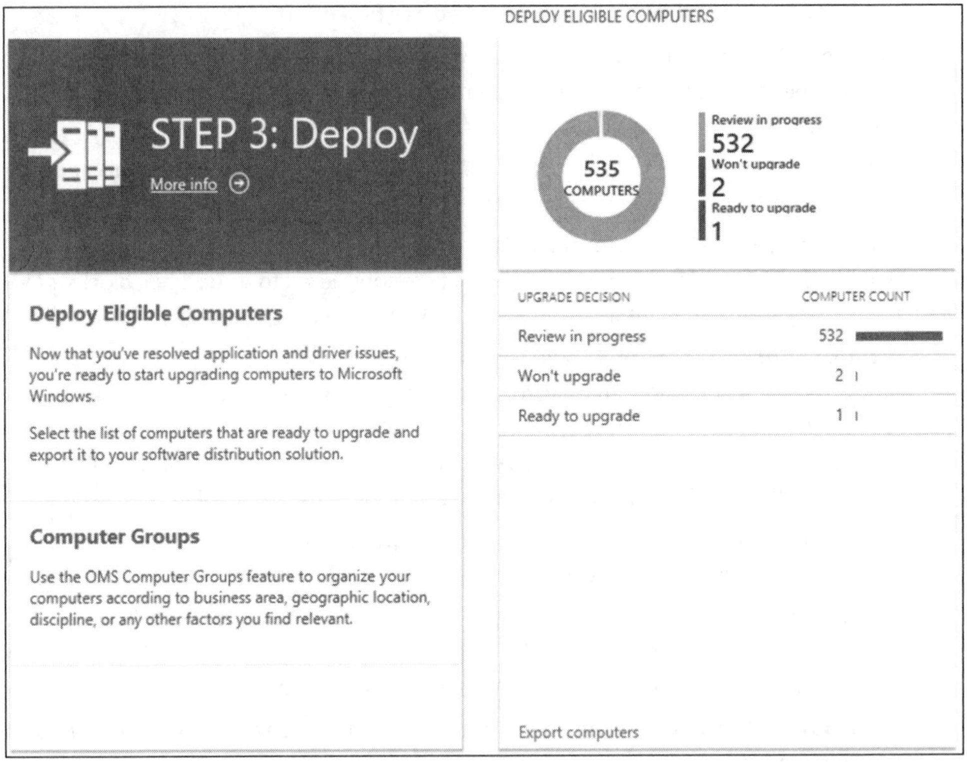

FIGURE 1-35 Upgrade Readiness - Deploy

- **Review in Progress**   Devices in this category have at least one application or driver installed that has been marked as review in progress. These markings are applied in step 1 and step 2 of the workflow.

- **Won't Upgrade**   Devices in this category have at least one application or driver installed that has been marked as won't upgrade. Alternatively, these devices do not meet a system requirement to complete the upgrade, such as free disk space.

- **Ready to Upgrade**   Devices in this category have all applications and drivers marked as ready to upgrade. When you are ready to deploy the upgrade to these devices, export the list of computers and target them with your preferred management solution.

The next blade you are presented with is **STEP 4: Monitor**. This step in the workflow includes a series of blades for monitoring the progress of your upgrade deployments. See the following list for more information about each of the blades in step 4.

- **Update Progress (Last 30 Days)**   This blade highlights the deployment status for all your devices. There are five deployment categories that group devices.

  - **Not Started**   Devices that have not started the upgrade. This includes devices that are upgrade ready and those that are not.

  - **Upgrade completed**   Devices that have successfully completed the upgrade to your target operating system.

  - **Failed**   Devices that attempted to upgrade to your target operating system but were unsuccessful.

  - **In Progress**   Devices that have started the upgrade to your target operating system and have not yet reported back their results.

  - **Progress stalled**   Devices that have started the upgrade and stalled.

- **Driver issues**   Drivers that are reporting issues following a successful upgrade. This information includes the problem code reported in device manager for the affected device(s).

- **User feedback**   User feedback submitted through the Feedback Hub app. Users that have submitted feedback using their Azure AD account will be consolidated and displayed here for review.

NEED MORE REVIEW?   **UPGRADE READINESS**

For more information about enabling upgrade readiness to support Windows 10, visit *https://docs.microsoft.com/windows/deployment/upgrade/use-upgrade-readiness-to-manage-windows-upgrades.*

Evaluate and deploy additional Windows 10 Enterprise security features

Windows 10 is a cloud-connected operating system, engineered to protect against modern-day security threats. Windows 10 introduces a new collection of security features and enhancements that earlier versions of the operating system do not offer. Some Windows 10 security features can be connected to Microsoft 365 for centralized management and reporting.

This section explores the core security features available with Windows 10, including those that integrate with Microsoft 365, as well as what options you have available to evaluate these features in your environment. For the exam, you must be familiar with these features and their capabilities.

> **NOTE** Moving to a semi-annual release cycle has enabled Microsoft to address major security vulnerabilities in a much shorter timeframe. This also means that these features are frequently evolving over time with new releases of Windows 10.

The security capabilities in Windows 10 are grouped into three categories:

- **Identity and access management** Security features in this category focus on enhancing security identities. This includes capabilities such as two-factor authentication and biometric credentials.

- **Information protection** Security features in this category focus on protecting the data in your organization. This includes capabilities such as drive encryption, data leakage protection, and information protection.

- **Threat protection** Security features in this category focus on protecting against vulnerabilities and threats. This includes capabilities such as antivirus, antimalware, and behavioral monitoring.

Table 1-8 includes a breakdown of each core Windows 10 security component, its protection category, the required Windows edition, and a description of its capabilities. In this table, you will see references to S Mode. Alongside the variety of security features built into Windows 10, S Mode adjusts the behavior of the operating system. When activated, new security requirements are enforced, such as only allowing apps from the Microsoft Store and limiting browser usage to Microsoft Edge.

> **NEED MORE REVIEW?** **WINDOWS 10 S IN MODE**
>
> For more information about Windows 10 in S mode, visit *https://support.microsoft.com/ help/4020089/windows-10-in-s-mode-faq.*

TABLE 1-8   Windows 10 security components

Technology	Protection Category	Windows Edition	Description
Windows Hello for Business	Identity and access management	S mode, Enterprise	Password replacement, enabling strong two-factor authentication for PCs and mobile devices. Leverages biometric credentials and supports Active Directory and Azure AD accounts.
Windows Defender Credential Guard	Identity and access management	S mode Enterprise, Enterprise	Virtualization-based security that protects secrets stored on the device, including NTLM password hashes, Kerberos credentials, and credential manager domain credentials.
BitLocker	Information protection	S mode, Pro, Enterprise	Drive encryption solution that is strongest when combined with a hardware-based Trusted Platform Module (TPM). Supports the escrowing of recovery keys in Azure AD.
Windows Information Protection	Information protection	S mode, Pro, Enterprise	Data leakage prevention (DLP) solution that can apply additional protection to company files, preventing data leakage.
Windows Defender Application Guard	Threat protection	S mode Enterprise, Enterprise	Enhanced security for Microsoft Edge that isolates untrusted sites to a Hyper-V enabled container, protecting the host operating system from potential threats.
Windows Defender Application Control	Threat protection	Enterprise	Policy-based protection that prevents access to non-approved applications.
Windows Defender Exploit Guard	Threat protection	S mode, Pro, Enterprise	Collection of host intrusion prevention tools focused at reducing fileless attacks. Features include exploit protection, attack surface reduction rules, network protection, and controlled folder access.
Windows Defender Antivirus	Threat protection	S mode, Pro, Enterprise	Antivirus and antimalware definition-based solution that is integrated with Windows 10.
Microsoft Defender for Endpoint	Threat protection	Enterprise	Cloud-connected integration with the built-in security features in Windows 10. Provides behavioral-based analysis using machine learning and cloud-based analytics. Includes monitoring and alerts based on threat intelligence data generated by Microsoft and collected by other partners.

From an evaluation perspective, the majority of these features are built into the operating system. As long as you have a compatible edition of Windows 10, you can enable these features for testing without any additional licensing. To keep current with the list of available features, including requirements and deployment documentation, visit *https://docs.microsoft.com/windows/security/*.

Skill 1.5: Enroll devices

Enrolling devices is the first step to enabling them to receive the compliance and configuration polices that you have created, and to gain access to the Microsoft Store for Business to access apps. Device enrollment also sets the baseline that you configured in skill section 1.2.

> **This skill covers how to:**
> - Plan for device join to Azure Active Directory (Azure AD) and plan for device enrollment
> - Enable device enrollment

Plan for device join to Azure Active Directory (Azure AD) and plan for device enrollment

When you enroll a device, you join that device to an Azure Active Directory tenant associated with Microsoft Intune. Before you can join or enroll a device, you must meet certain prerequisites that relate to the Azure AD tenant:

- The MDM authority must be set to Intune
- The devices you plan to manage must be supported. Supported device types include:
  - Android
  - iOS/iPadOS
  - macOS
  - Windows
- For iOS, iPadOS, and macOS, you must have an Apple ID and an MDM push certificate.
- Users and groups must have been configured with enrollment policies

If the device you plan to enroll was previously part of a different MDM policy or tenant, the device might need to be factory reset before Intune policies can be applied. The device platforms that require a reset include the following:

- Android Enterprise corporate-owned work profile
- Android Enterprise fully managed
- Android Enterprise dedicated devices
- iOS/iPad OS
- macOS

If you plan to enroll devices in bulk before distributing or assigning them to users, you should create a *device enrollment manager* (DEM) account in Microsoft Intune. The DEM account is a standard Azure Active Directory user that has been added to the list of DEM accounts in Intune. Follow these steps to add an existing user as a DEM account in Intune:

1. Sign in to the Microsoft Endpoint Manager admin center at *https://endpoint.microsoft.com*.

2. Click **Devices**, and then click **Enroll Devices**.

3. Click **Device Enrollment Managers**, and then click **Add**.

4. Specify the user principal name of an existing AD account that you want to serve as a DEM account and click **Add**. Figure 1-36 shows a DEM account in Intune.

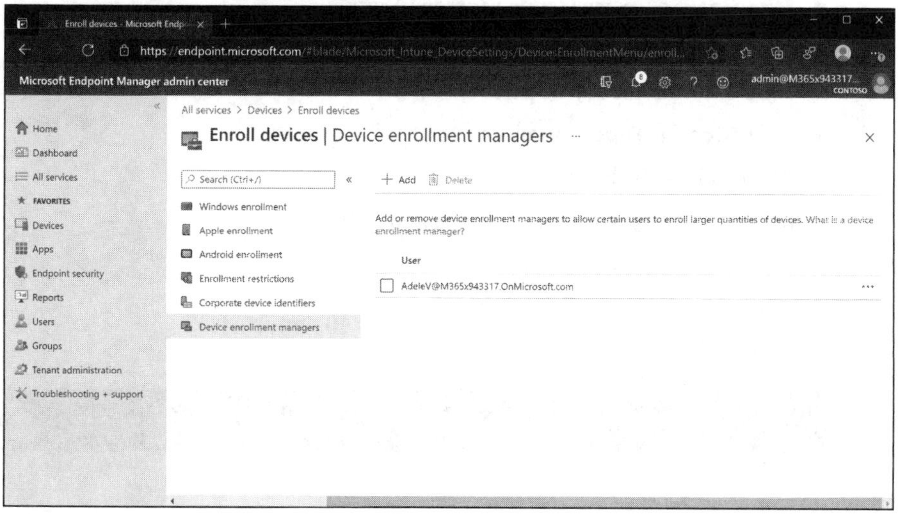

FIGURE 1-36   Device enrollment managers

> **NOTE**   User accounts that are DEMs can enroll up to 1,000 devices in Intune, compared to the default limit of 15 for a normal user account.

Enable device enrollment

You can manage device enrollment with Intune by creating deployment profiles, setting enrollment restrictions, and setting enrollment limits. You create deployment profiles for various platforms to control how devices are connected, depending on the device type.

Create deployment profiles

Deployment profiles customize the provisioning experience and preconfigured settings to simplify enrollment for end-users. To configure a deployment profile, follow these steps.

1. Sign in to the Microsoft Endpoint Manager admin center at *https://endpoint.microsoft.com*.

2. Click **Devices**, and then click **Enroll Devices**.

3. Click **Windows Enrollment**, and then click **Deployment Profiles**.

4. Click **Create Profile**, and then click **Windows PC**.

5. On the **Basics** tab, enter a name for the profile — for example, **AutopilotProfile1**.

6. On the **Out-of-Box Experience (OOBE)** tab, enter the following settings (see Figure 1-37), and then click **Next**.

- **Deployment Mode**   User-Driven
- **Join to Azure AD As**   Azure AD Joined
- **Microsoft Software License Terms**   Hide
- **Privacy Settings**   Hide
- **Hide Change Account Options**   Hide
- **User Account Type**   Administrator
- **Allow White Globe OOBE**   Yes
- **Language (Region)**   Operating System Default
- **Automatically Configure Keyboard**   Yes
- **Apply Device Name Template**   Yes
- **Name**   %SERIAL%

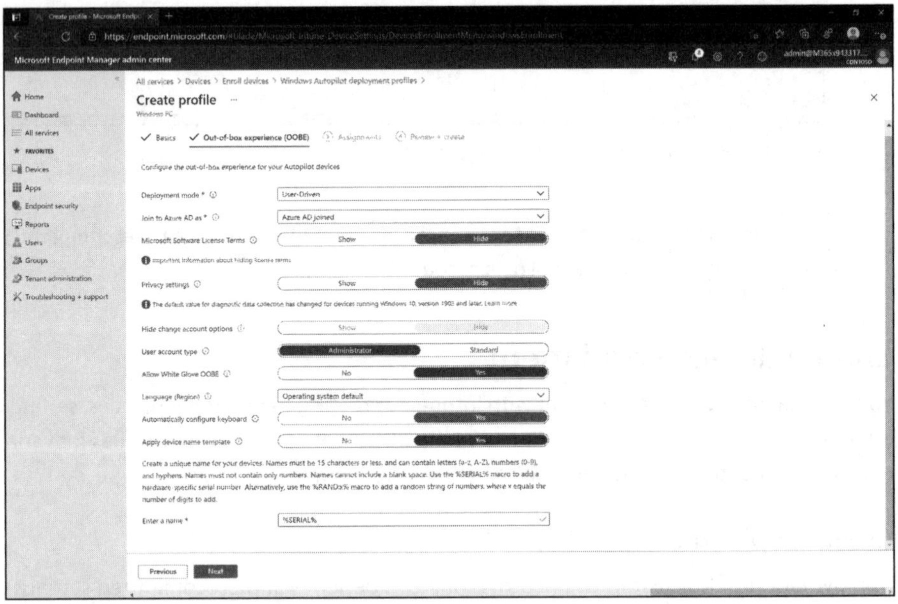

FIGURE 1-37   Out-of-box experience (OOBE) settings

7. On the **Assignments** tab, select the groups to add or exclude from being applied — for example, **All Devices.** Then click **Next**.

8. On the **Review + Create** tab, click **Create**.

Set device enrollment restrictions

This section covers the controls given to administrators to limit the number and type of devices a user can enroll. Limiting the number of devices assigned to a user can help with license constraints and organization. In addition, restricting devices that are running an older operating system is a requirement for many organizations due to security and compliance concerns. Finally, blocking personally owned devices may be a scenario you need to consider if your organization is not ready to support a bring your own device (BYOD) model. Table 1-9 explains the various enrollment restriction options.

TABLE 1-9   Device enrollment restrictions

Restrictions	Restriction Type	Description
Maximum number of enrolled devices	Limit restriction	Restrict the number of devices a user can enroll, ranging from 1 to 15.
Allow or block based on device platforms	Type restriction	Restrict device enrollment by device platform, including Android, Android work profile, iOS, macOS, and Windows (MDM).
Allow or block based on platform operating system	Type restriction	Restrict device enrollment by operating system, providing a minimum and maximum version number.
Allow or block personally owned devices	Type restriction	Restrict device enrollment to corporate-owned devices, requiring additional steps to define a device as corporate-owned.

> **NOTE**   **PERSONALLY OWNED DEVICES**
>
> The ability to allow and block personally owned devices depends on other factors in your MDM configuration. For Windows (MDM), if the device was previously enrolled through a bulk provisioning package, like ConfigMgr Co-Management or Windows Autopilot, it will be allowed to enroll.

DEVICE LIMIT RESTRICTION

In this section, you implement a restriction to limit the number of devices a user can enroll with:

1. Sign in to the Microsoft Endpoint Manager admin center at *https://endpoint.microsoft.com*.

2. Click **Devices**, and then click **Enroll Devices**.

3. Click **Enrollment Restrictions**.

4. On the **Enrollment Restrictions** blade, review the items under **Device Type Restrictions** and **Device Limit Restrictions**. (See Figure 1-38.)

   Note that there is a default enrollment restriction for each restriction. Both can be modified, but not deleted.

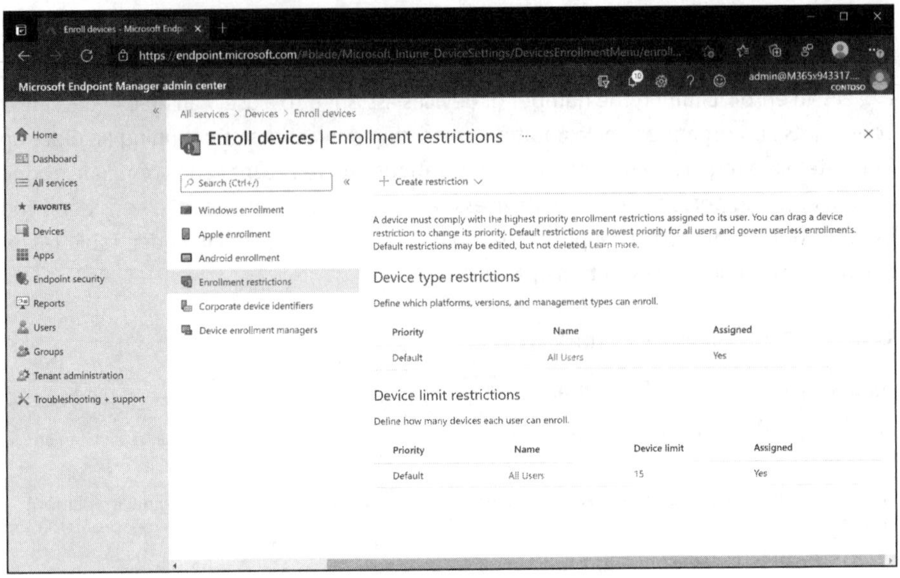

FIGURE 1-38 Device enrollment restrictions

5. Click **Create Restriction**, and then click **Device Limit Restriction**.

6. On the **Basics** tab, provide a name for the restriction — for example, **Custom Device Limit**.

7. On the **Device Limit** tab, open the **Device Limit** drop-down list and choose **5**.

8. On the **Scope Tags** tab, specify a scope if required for the deployment, and click **Next**.

9. On the **Assignments** tab, specify the groups that the enrollment restriction should apply to, and click **Next**.

10. On the **Review + Create** tab, click **Create**.

A new custom device restriction is created and is available on the Device Enrollment – Enrollment Restrictions blade.

Here you worked with limit restrictions. Assigning a limit prevents users from enrolling more than the defined value. The default restriction allows users to enroll up to five devices. Attempting to enroll more than five will result in a notification.

DEVICE TYPE RESTRICTIONS

The second enrollment restriction you will work with limits enrollment by the type of device:

1. Sign in to the Microsoft Endpoint Manager admin center at *https://endpoint.microsoft.com*.

2. Click **Devices**, and then click **Enroll Devices**.

3. Click **Enrollment Restrictions**

4. Click **Create Restriction**, and then click **Device Type Restriction**.

5. On the **Basics** tab, provide a name for the restriction — for example, **Custom Type Restriction**.

6. On the **Platform Settings** tab, select the desired combination of settings to allow or restrict devices by platform, version, whether they are personally owned, or device manufacturer. Figure 1-39 shows a configuration that blocks Android devices. Then click **Next**.

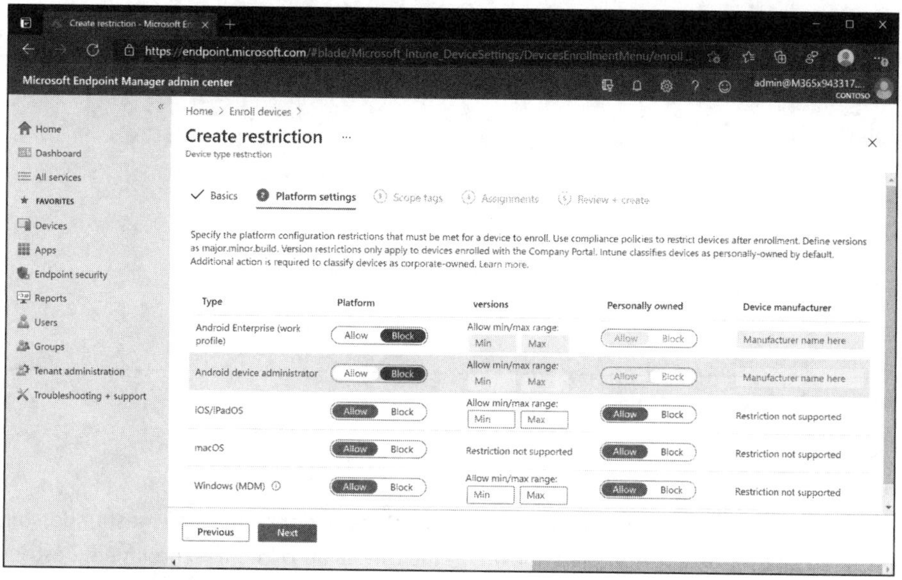

FIGURE 1-39 Device type restrictions

7. On the **Scope Tags** tab, specify a scope if required for the deployment, and click **Next**.

8. On the **Assignments** tab, specify the groups that the enrollment restriction should apply to, and click **Next**.

9. On the **Review + Create** tab, click **Create**.

With these steps complete, you should have a custom device type restriction available on the Enrollment Restrictions blade. In this example, you worked with platform restrictions. Platform restrictions provide a granular set of controls for approving specific device types and operating system versions. With an enrollment plan that supports BYOD, controlling the minimum and maximum operating system version can prevent known vulnerabilities or pre-release versions from entering your environment. Figure 1-40 shows the configured device type and limit restrictions.

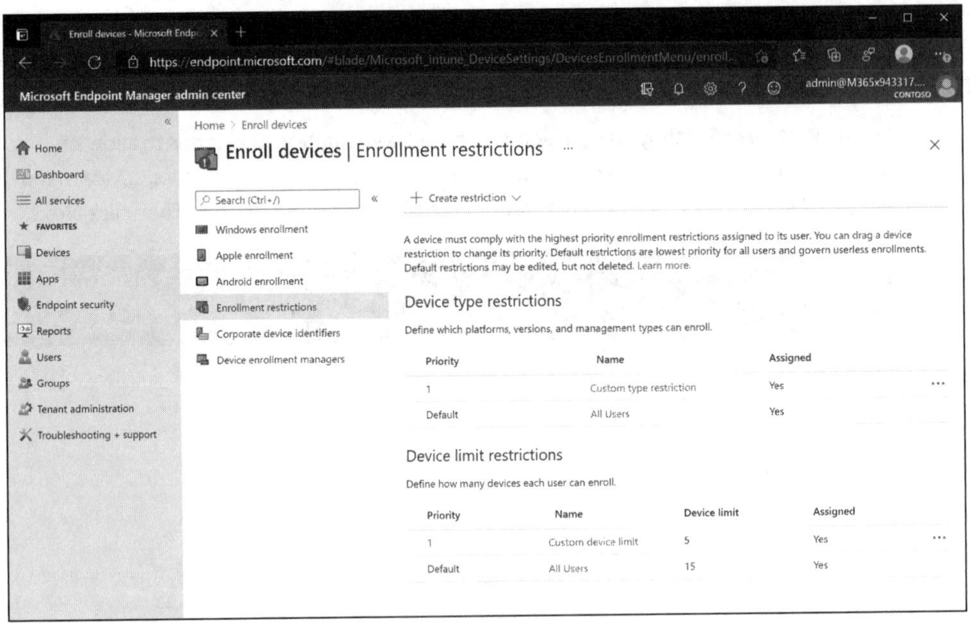

FIGURE 1-40 Custom restrictions

ASSIGN ENROLLMENT RESTRICTIONS

Let's examine the process for assigning enrollment restrictions. First, you must understand the priority system. The priority value, shown on the Device Enrollment – Enrollment Restrictions blade, is for users who are members of multiple groups, but may have different enrollment restrictions assigned. You can change the priority value in the portal by dragging a device restriction up or down the list.

> **REAL WORLD**   **DEVICE RESTRICTION PRIORITIES**
>
> Suppose Ethan is a member of two Azure AD groups: IT and All Employees. The IT group has device-enrollment restrictions that allow members to enroll all device types. This device restriction has a priority of 1. The All Employees group has device-enrollment restrictions that only allow members to enroll Windows (MDM) devices. This device restriction has a priority of 2. In this situation, Ethan would receive the IT device restrictions due to the higher priority.

Enrollment restrictions are assigned to Azure AD groups. The following steps assume you already have an Azure AD group created with the users you need to target.

1. Sign in to the Microsoft Endpoint Manager admin center at *https://endpoint.microsoft.com*.

2. Click **Devices**, and then click **Enroll Devices**.

3. Click **Enrollment Restrictions**

4. Click the ellipses (**...**) next to the custom device limit restriction that was previously created.

5. On the **Custom Device Limit** blade, click **Assign**.

The device restriction should become available in the portal and can be assigned to an Azure AD group of your choosing.

Thought experiment

In this thought experiment, demonstrate your skills and knowledge of the topics covered in this chapter. You can find the answer to this thought experiment in the next section.

Contoso Electronics is a global organization, spanning 200 locations and supporting 25,000 mobile devices. Some offices have slow WAN links, but all locations have fast internet connections.

The organization is using ConfigMgr for device management and deployment. All employees are registered in Azure AD and have an Office 365 license assigned. Last year they started introducing Windows 10 through a traditional bare metal deployment. The organization has 2,500 devices that run Windows 10, version 1803. The remaining devices run Windows 8.1.

Your manager has tasked you with creating a deployment plan for fully adopting Windows 10 over the next six months and keeping current with new releases. As the technical lead for enterprise device management, you have started testing the in-place upgrade using Config-Mgr, going from Windows 8.1 to Windows 10. Some devices upgraded successfully, but others failed. As part of your deployment design, you must address the following questions, while minimizing on-premises infrastructure:

1. The in-place upgrade from Windows 8.1 to Windows 10 has surfaced some compatibility issues. What solution should you implement to track compatibility for your fleet and what steps do you need to take to implement this solution?

2. Windows 10 Enterprise 64-bit is the target operating system for your fleet. Recently, you found that 5% of your Windows 8.1 devices are 32-bit. What solution will you use to upgrade these devices?

3. What servicing channels should you adopt to keep current with the latest releases of Windows 10 and what steps do you need to take to implement them?

4. The 2,500 devices running Windows 10 must be upgraded to version 1809. What solution should you implement to upgrade these devices?

5. Your CIO is asking you to begin migrating MDM workloads to Intune. What MDM solution addresses this requirement?

Thought experiment answers

This section contains the solution to the thought experiment. Each answer explains why the answer choice is correct.

1. To address compatibility issues with Windows 10, you should implement upgrade readiness. To accomplish this, you must create a Log Analytics workspace in Azure. After creating the workspace, you should create and deploy a GPO with Windows telemetry enabled and set to basic, along with your commercial ID. The Windows 8.1 computers will also need KB2976978 installed before they can upload data.

2. The Windows 8.1 computers must be upgraded using a refresh or replace deployment method. The user state can be captured with ConfigMgr and restored after the device has been re-imaged using a Windows 10 64-bit installation.

3. To support the latest release of Windows 10, you should adopt a semi-annual channel (targeted) and plan for the Windows Insider channel to prepare for new versions of the operating system. You should use a GPO to configure the servicing channel.

4. You should use Windows Update for Business to manage the upgrade from Windows 10, version 1803 to Windows 10, version 1809.

5. The best solution is to use Microsoft Intune with co-management enabled in ConfigMgr. This solution will deliver a cloud-based MDM with support for iOS, Android, and Windows 10. This will also enable the organization to transition workloads for Windows 10 from ConfigMgr to Microsoft Intune. The existing devices enrolled in MDM for Office 365 can also be assigned EMS licenses and can be converted to Intune.

Chapter summary

- There are two MDM solutions that you can deploy with Microsoft 365: standalone Intune and MDM with Microsoft 365.
- Cloud-based MDM solutions can reduce on-premises server infrastructure, but network bandwidth needs to be sized appropriately.
- Policy conflicts should be reviewed and addressed as part of your planning phase for implementing Intune.
- Setting an MDM authority is a requirement for managing devices with Intune, but is configured by default to Microsoft Intune for new tenants.
- The MDM authority can be changed when moving between MDM solutions.
- There are predefined device enrollment restrictions with Microsoft Intune.
- You should be familiar with the enrollment restrictions interface in Microsoft Intune, including where to create restrictions.
- You should be familiar with the priority system used by enrollment restrictions and how to assign them to devices.

- You should be familiar with the subscription requirements for Microsoft Intune and Azure AD, along with the supported platforms for compliance policies.

- You should be familiar with the fundamentals of a compliance policy, how they are assigned to devices, and how a device is marked for compliance.

- You should have some understanding on what rules a device-compliance policy can check for and use cases that align with those rules.

- You should be familiar with the conditional access conditions and how they correspond to the policies you create.

- You should be familiar with the conditional access controls available in the Azure portal, how these controls relate to each other, and how to design policies using these controls.

- You should be familiar with device-based and app-based policies, including how they are defined and what role they play in policy design.

- You should be familiar with navigating the New Conditional Access Policy blade, including items like named locations and terms of use.

- You should be familiar with how to create, assign, and enforce conditional access policies for users and groups.

- You should be familiar with navigating the Device Compliance blade, with a focus on the available compliance configurations settings and relative use cases for changing the default values.

- You should be familiar with how to create, assign, and evaluate device-compliance policies. Keep in mind that compliance policies are created on a per-platform basis and are used by conditional access policies when referencing compliance status.

- You must be familiar with the terminology used to describe WaaS. This includes terms such as feature updates, quality updates, and deployment rings.

- You must be familiar with servicing channels and how they operate. This includes the available channels and configuration options.

- You must be familiar with WUfB and its importance in supporting the WaaS model.

- You must be familiar with the different deployment methods and what their capabilities are. This includes traditional deployments, in-place upgrades, and modern servicing.

- You must be familiar with the Windows 10 in-place upgrade. This includes planning considerations, requirements, and solutions for deployment.

- You must be familiar with modern servicing. This includes understanding the differences between servicing and in-place upgrades, the limitations, and the various solutions that can enable modern servicing.

- You must be familiar with what upgrade readiness can provide and how it is implemented.

- You must be familiar with the upgrade readiness workflow. This includes the different blades and the information they provide.

- You must be familiar with each of the security features included with Windows 10. This includes an understanding of their capabilities and possible use cases.

- You should be familiar with MSfB, including how to navigate the management portal, add apps, and connect it with Intune for centralized management.

- You should be familiar with app deployment prerequisites. This includes conditional requirements depending on the needs of an organization.

- You should be familiar with creating and assigning apps in Intune. This includes navigating the client app blades in the Intune console.

- You should have a basic understanding of device health and upgrade readiness, including their requirements and capabilities.

- You should be familiar with the capabilities of device profiles and the use cases they address. This includes platform support and profile types.

- You should be familiar with using the portal to create and assign device profiles.

- You should be familiar with the requirements for app protection policies, with an emphasis on the required subscriptions and supported platforms.

- You should be familiar with navigating through the app protection policy blades, along with the extensive number of controls available for managing and securing app data.

- You should be familiar with the prerequisites and setup process required to activate the MSfB for an organization.

- You should be familiar with navigating the MSfB management portal, including searching for new apps in the Microsoft Store and adding them to an organization's app inventory.

- App collections and app visibility in the private store are managed through the MSfB portal, from the Private Store page.

CHAPTER 2

Implement Microsoft 365 security and threat management

In a traditional environment, applications and services are hosted and managed from an organization's on-premises data center. Intellectual property, employee data, and other sensitive information are contained within the confines of that organization. In the modern workplace, applications and services are hosted in cloud environments, such as Office 365, reducing overhead for IT and providing greater flexibility to the end user. This transition requires IT administrators to address new challenges around information protection and application security.

In this chapter we cover cloud-based security services for Microsoft 365. This includes a deep dive into Cloud App Security, Advanced Threat Analytics, and Windows Defender Advanced Threat Protection. With these services we walk through the various reports and alerts provided in each solution.

Skills covered in this chapter:

- 2.1: Manage security reports and alerts
- 2.2: Plan and implement thread protection with Microsoft Defender
- 2.3: Plan Microsoft Cloud App Security

Skill 2.1: Manage security reports and alerts

Microsoft 365 includes several cloud services under its umbrella, each one enabled with security controls. As an Azure cloud administrator, it is important that you know what these controls are, how to configure alerts, and how to generate reports so that you can keep informed when an event occurs. In this chapter we are going to be working with a few different technologies dealing with Microsoft 365 security. This will include an introduction to service assurance and the various security assessment reports that Microsoft is making available to customers. We will also be onboarding Azure AD Identity Protection and exploring its capabilities. Finally, we will be exploring the event-based alerts available in the Office 365 Security & Compliance center.

Evaluate and manage Microsoft Office 365 tenant security by using Secure Score

In this skill section we review the Microsoft Secure Score. The Microsoft Secure Score is a numerical value based on the current configuration of the Microsoft 365 tenant. Every tenant has a different possible number of points, and the Secure Score is represented as a percentage of the possible points. By configuring or deploying the recommended best practices, an organization can increase their Secure Score points and percentage. A higher percentage then indicates an increased security posture based on the settings and policies defined by the organization.

Secure Score overview

The Microsoft Secure Score is segmented into different groups:

- **Identity**   Actions to take with Azure Active Directory accounts and roles
- **Device**   Actions to take with Microsoft Defender for Endpoint
- **App**   Actions to take with email and cloud apps, including Office 365 and Microsoft Cloud App Security

To view the Secure Score for your organization, follow these steps.

1.   Sign in to the Microsoft 365 security center at *https://security.microsoft.com*.

2.   From the Navigation bar on the left, click **Secure score**.

The Secure Score for the organization is displayed on the Overview tab, as shown in Figure 2-1. By default, the Secure Score only includes the currently settings that have already been configured in the tenant. You can change the display to include theoretical possabilities, including:

- **Planned score**   A projected score based on improvement actions that have been marked as 'Planned'
- **Current license score**   The total possible score that can be achieved with the current licensed features
- **Achievable score**   The total score that can be achieved with both current licenses and risk acceptance

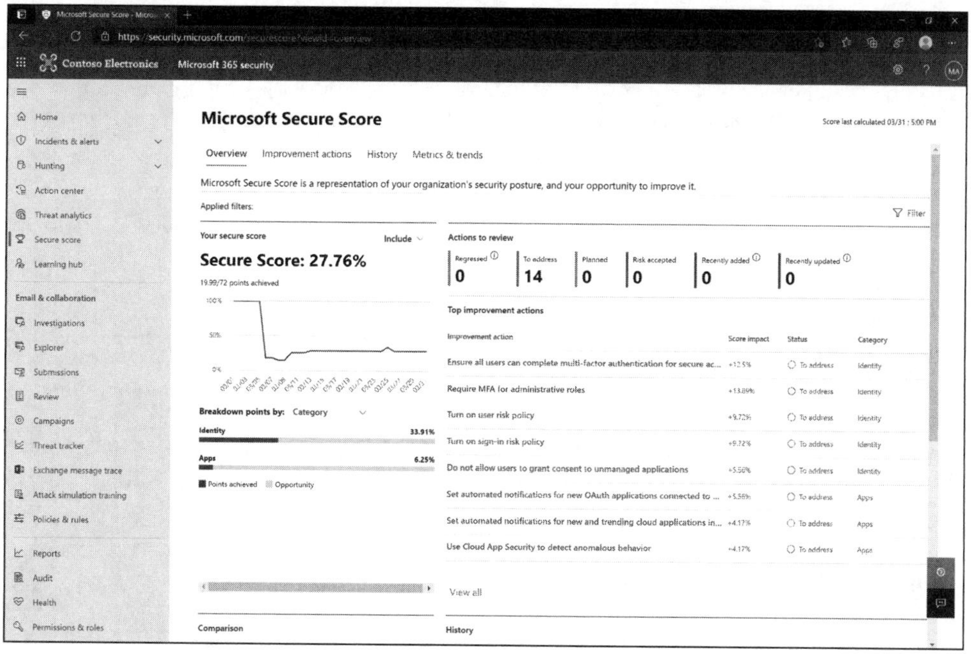

FIGURE 2-1 Microsoft Secure Score overview

Managing improvement actions

To increase the Secure Score in the tenant, you must take additional action for the various settings or features in identity, device, or apps. To see the list of improvement actions for your organization specifically, check the **Improvement actions** tab of Secure Score. Figure 2-2 shows the improvement actions that are available for the Contoso Electronics organization.

A variety of information is displayed for each improvement action that you can take in the organization. Some of the relevant columns for identifying how the improvement action changes the Secure Score are noted in these columns:

- **Score impact**   The percentage that the Secure Score will increase upon completing the action

- **Points achieved**   The numerical points that are added to your Secure Score by completing the action

- **Status**   The status of the action. Possible values are *Alternate mitigation, Completed, Planned, Risk accepted, Third party,* or *To address*

- **Regressed in last 90 days**   Whether the improvement action has been negatively impacted in the last 90 days by a configuration change

- **Have license?**   Displays if the organization already has the required license to make the recommended change

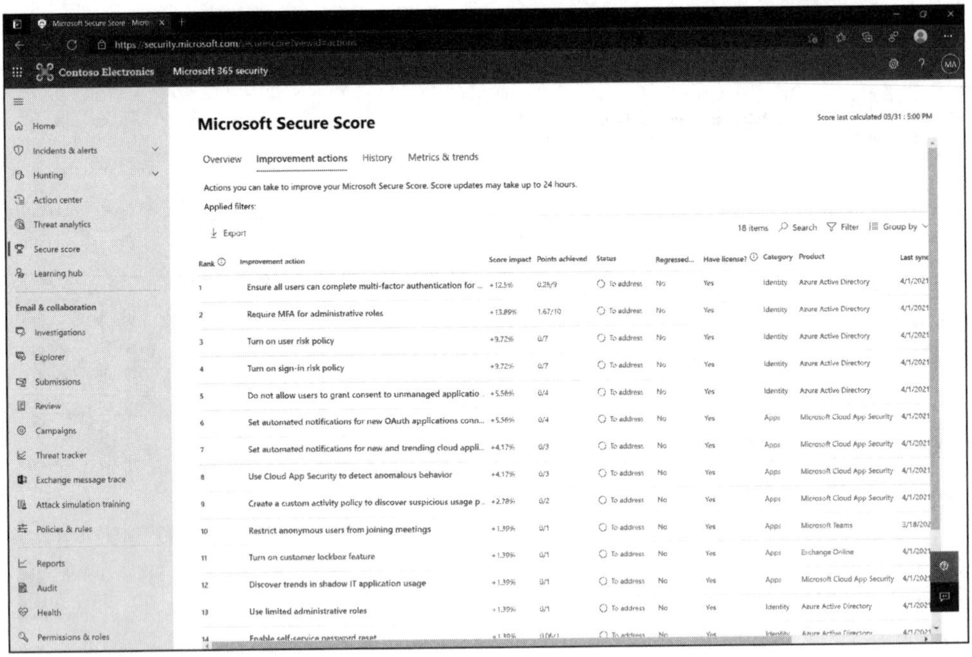

FIGURE 2-2 Microsoft Secure Score improvement actions

To manage an individual improvement action, click the action from the improvement actions tab. Each action has similar information that is displayed on the main tab. From the individual action, you can configure an **Action plan**, which changes the *Status* column on the previous page. The available settings for Action plan are *To address*, *Planned*, *Risk accepted*, *Resolved through third party*, and *Resolved through alternate mitigation*.

The Implementation section of the improvement action lists any prerequisites, such as licensing, as well as the general steps to customize and configure the desired state for that action. Figure 2-3 shows the management screen of an individual improvement action.

On the main Secure Score page, the History tab displays a line chart with the Secure Score history of the tenant. The History tab also shows a list of changes that have been made in the tenant with the resulting positive or negative point score change. You can also filter or search through the list of recent changes on the History tab. By default, the results show the past 90 days, but can be changed to 7 days, 30 days, or a custom date range. Other filter options include whether the change was an increase, regression, or no points change; the category of the change, the product the change was made in, the type of update that was made, and any tags that might have been associated with the change. Figure 2-4 shows the History tab with the default filtering options.

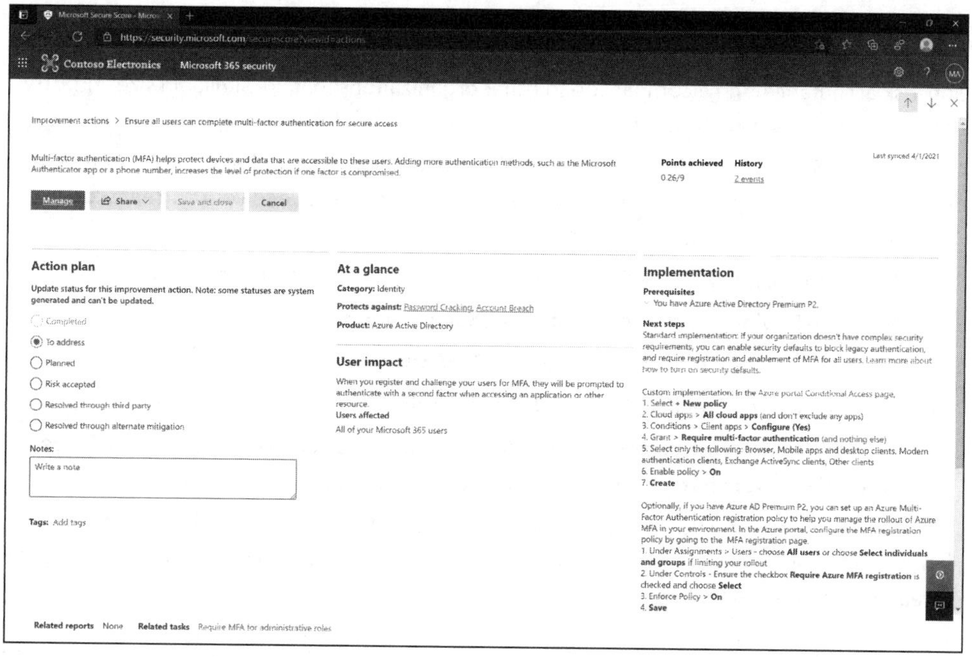

FIGURE 2-3 Microsoft Secure Score improvement action management

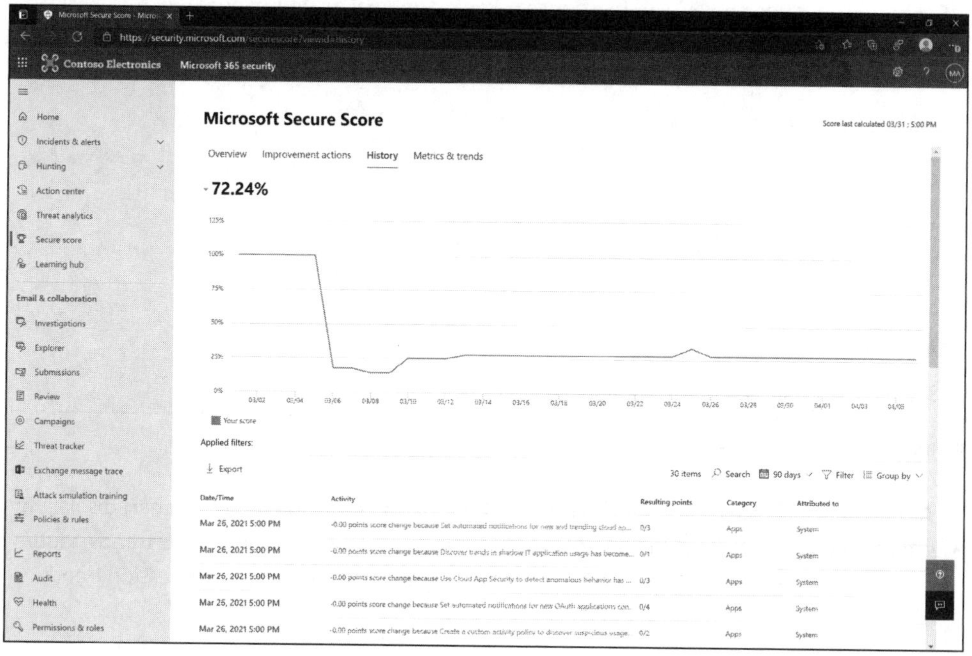

FIGURE 2-4 Microsoft Secure Score History

The final tab that is available with Secure Score is the Metrics & trends tab, which displays Secure Score changes, custom Secure Score zones, and trends in the environment for regression, risk acceptance, and a comparison to other organizations that are similar in size, industry, and the products that are licensed.

The Secure Score zones are a minimum and maximum percentage that you can set to display a chart that displays your score as bad, okay, or good relative to your current score. To create a custom zone, use the following steps.

1. Sign in to the Microsoft 365 security center at *https://security.microsoft.com*.

2. From the Navigation bar on the left, click **Secure score**.

3. On the Secure Score page, click **Metrics & trends**.

4. On the Metrics & trends tab, click **Add score zones**.

5. In the flyout window, customize the **Score is bad if less than or equal to and Score is good if greater than or equal to** fields, and then click **Save and close**.

Figure 2-5 shows the fields set to 40% and 70% respectively. This means that a bad score would be less than or equal to 40%, an okay score is in the 41% to 69% range, and a good score is greater than or equal to 70%.

Edit score zones ✕

Customize your good, okay, and bad zones based on internal goals. Changes you make will apply to zones seen by all users.

Score is bad if less than or equal to   40   %

Score is good if greater than or equal to   70   %

Score is okay if between 40-70%

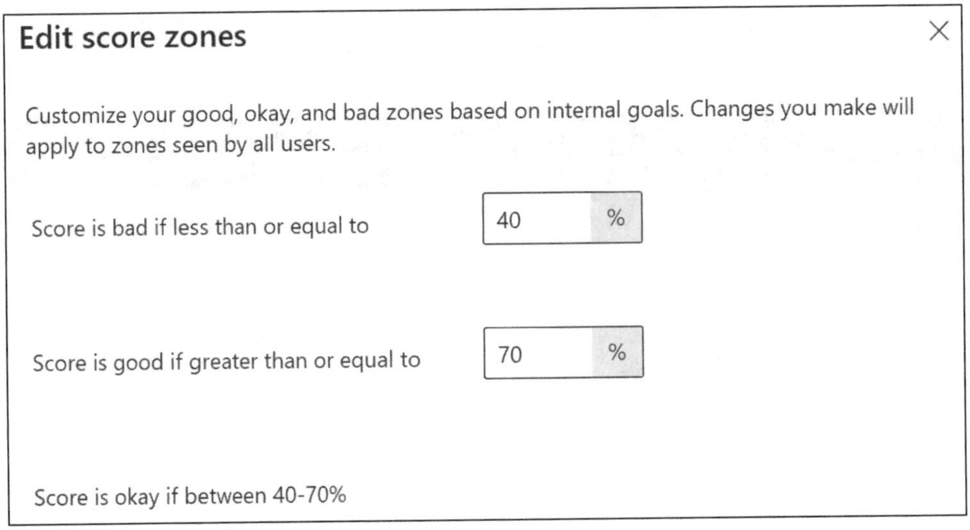

FIGURE 2-5 Custom Secure Score zones

After you save the custom zone, the Metrics & trends page will update with a chart displaying where your tenant is on the scale that you created. Figure 2-6 shows the Metrics & trends page with a custom zone created, Secure Score changes, and the comparison and regression trends.

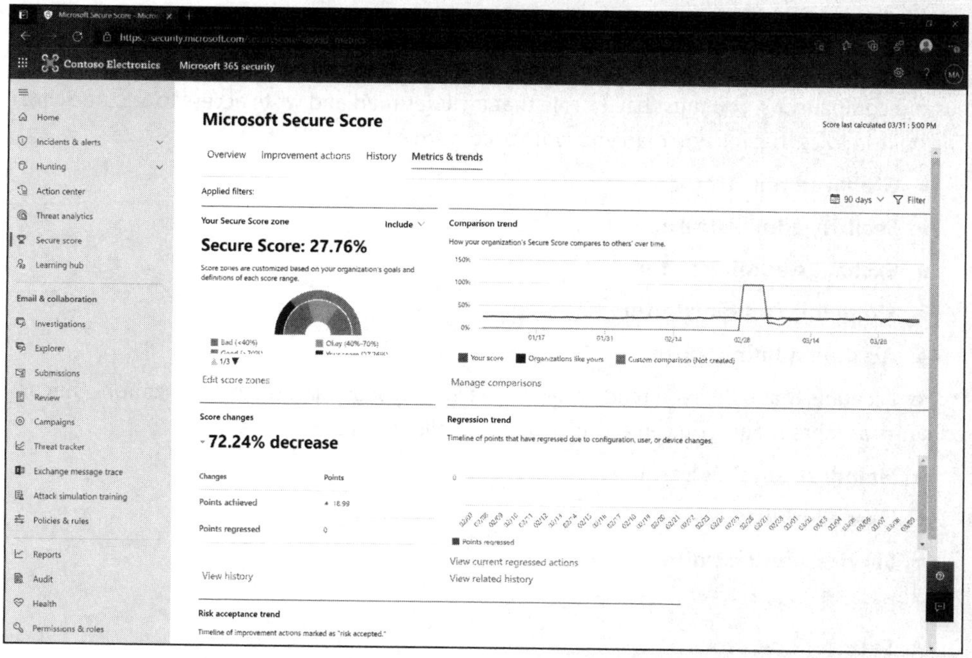

FIGURE 2-6 Secure Score Metrics & trends

To manage the comparison chart, click Manage comparisons on the Metrics & trends page. This will open another flyout window where you can set a custom comparison. The fields for a custom comparison are:

- **Industries**   The industries that you would like to compare with, for example, Manufacturing or Healthcare.

- **Organization size**   The size of the organization relative to the number of users being managed.

- **Licenses**   The licenses that are included in the organization.

- **Regions**   The geographic region of other organizations to compare with.

If you configure these options and click Save and close, the line chart on the Metrics & trends page will update with your custom settings. The line chart displays three lines, for Your score, organizations like yours, and your custom comparison.

The other charges that are displayed on the Metrics & trends for regression and risk acceptance are relative to the actions that have been taken in your specific environment. Actions that have resulted in a negative change to your Secure Score are displayed in the Regression trend chart. Improvement actions that have been marked as *Risk accepted* are displayed in the Risk Acceptance trend. You can also view the individual actions that were taken in either scenario if you need to review or report on when and why those actions were taken.

Required permissions

To have permissions to manage improvement actions, create custom score zones, or edit the custom comparisons, you must have a role that includes read and write access to Secure Score. The built-in roles that include read and write access are:

- **Global administrator**
- **Security administrator**
- **Exchange administrator**
- **SharePoint administrator**
- **Account administrator**

For accounts that only need read access to the Secure Score and the customizations that an administrator has made, you can assign any of the following roles:

- **Helpdesk administrator**
- **User administrator**
- **Service administrator**
- **Security reader**
- **Security operator**
- **Global reader**

It is also important to note that the Secure Score is simply a numerical value that represents the security posture of the current configuration in the organization. It is not guaranteed measure of how secure the organization might be. No online service is completely protected from security breaches, and a high or even 100% completion of Secure Score should not be interpreted as such.

Manage incident investigation

Incidents are triggered by alerts that correspond to a suspicious or malicious event that has occurred in the organization. We can look at incident response with two categories: manual investigation and automated investigation. In a large organization, there could be thousands of alerts at any given time that might require additional investigation. Some might be handled automatically, and others might require additional administrative input. In this section, we'll look at both investigation types.

Manual incident investigations

The Microsoft 365 security center includes an incidents queue, which displays any incidents that have occurred in the organization. The incidents queue can help you sort, filter, and prioritie the alerts and incidents that require additional actions to review and resolve the incident as either a *False alert* or a *True alert*. To open the incident queue, follow these steps.

1. Sign in to the Microsoft 365 security center at *https://security.microsoft.com*.
2. From the Navigation bar on the left, expand **Incidents & alerts**, and then click **Incidents**.

Figure 2-7 displays the incidents that have been identified in the Contoso Electronics organization.

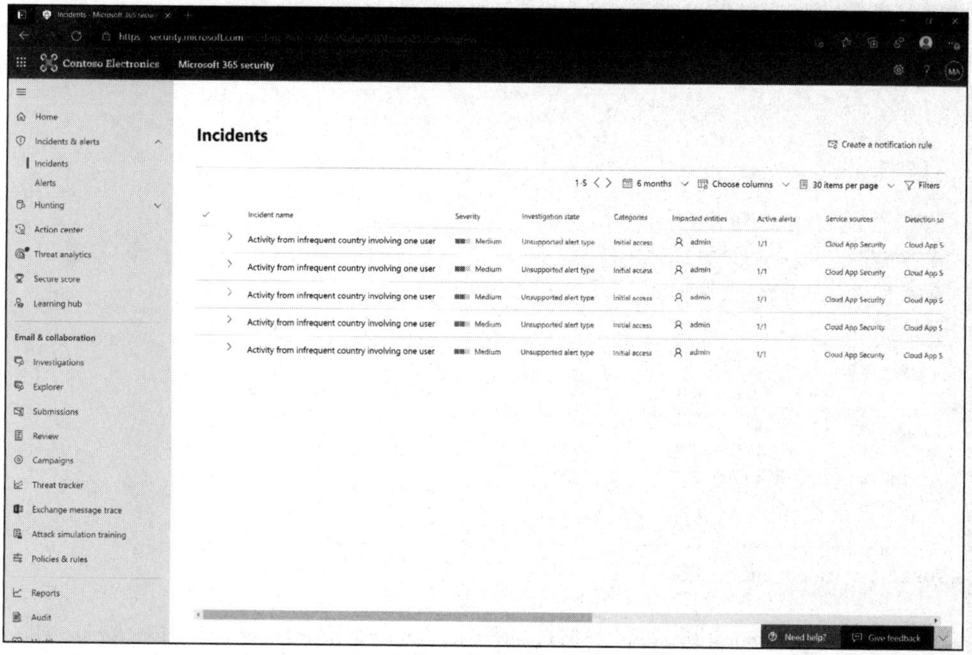

FIGURE 2-7   Microsoft 365 security center incident queue

The incident queue has a variety of columns that display relevant information for each incident that has outstanding actions. Some of these columns include:

- **Severity**   The severity of the incident, categorized as informational, low, medium, or high.
- **Investigation state**   Displays the alert type that the incident relates to.
- **Categories**   The category that the incident relates to.
- **Impacted entities**   The user accounts, devices, or other entity that the alert corresponds to.
- **Active alerts**   The number of alerts that are still active that correspond to the incident. One incident could have multiple alerts that correspond to the same event.
- **Service sources**   The Microsoft 365 service that the incident has potentially impacted.

To view more information about the incident, click the checkmark next to the name of the incident, without clicking the name itself. This will open a flyout window that displays more information about the incident, including the classification, activity times, and buttons to open the full incident page or assign the incident to your user account. Figure 2-8 displays a portion of the information from the flyout window.

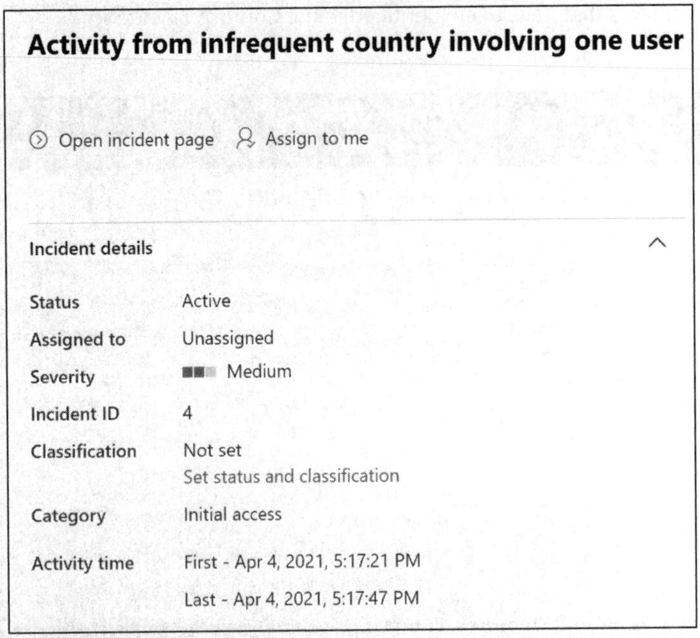

Activity from infrequent country involving one user

⊙ Open incident page   ℛ Assign to me

Incident details ⌃

Status	Active
Assigned to	Unassigned
Severity	▪▪▪ Medium
Incident ID	4
Classification	Not set
	Set status and classification
Category	Initial access
Activity time	First - Apr 4, 2021, 5:17:21 PM
	Last - Apr 4, 2021, 5:17:47 PM

FIGURE 2-8 Incident information

To view even more information, or to begin managing the properties of the incident, click the name of the incident or the **Open incident page** link. Every incident can be managed individually, and has a variety of tabs that display more information around the incident and alert. These tabs include

- **Summary** Displays the basic information about the incident and alert, including the MITRE ATT&CK tactics, impacted user accounts, and incident information.
- **Alerts** The alert(s) that was generated from the services as they relate to the overall incident.
- **Devices** Any impacted devices if the alert or incident occurred on a device that is being managed by the organization.
- **Users** The impacted user accounts that have been associated with the incident.
- **Mailboxes** Any Exchange Online mailboxes that might also be associated with the incident.
- **Investigations** Any automated investigation that occurred with the incident.
- **Evidence and response.** A summary of the evidence that relates to the alerts that were generated.

Depending on the incident and alert type, not all of these tabs might have information as it relates to the incident. Figure 2-9 shows the incident summary page for an alert related to user activity, but was not associated with a device or investigated automatically.

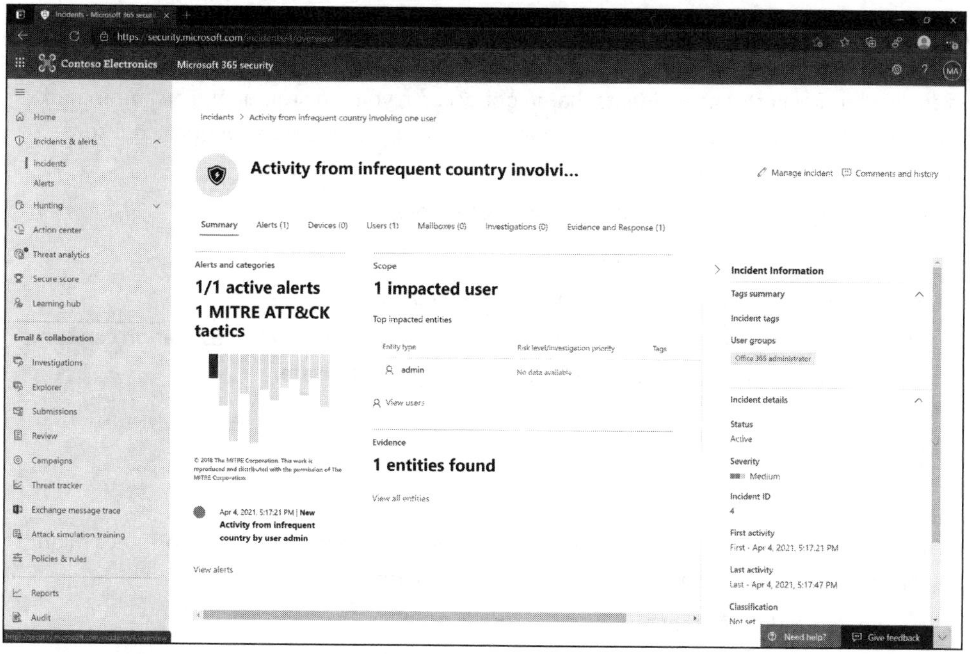

FIGURE 2-9 Incident summary

To manage the properties of the incident, click the **Manage incident** link from the summary tab. This will open a flyout window where you can change the properties of the incident, including:

- **Name** You can change the display name of the incident from the default provided.
- **Incident tags** Custom tags that can be assigned to the incident for reporting and tracking.
- **Assign to me** A toggle to assign the incident to your user account for further investigation or management.
- **Resolve incident** A toggle that marks whether the incident has been resolved and does not require further investigation.
- **Classification** The classification value for the incident, which could be *Not set, False alert,* or *True alert.*
- **Comment** A free text field that can be used to track investigation comments for later reporting or other administrators.

EXAM TIP

When you set the classification at the incident level, it will also be applied on the individual alerts that have been linked to the incident.

Automated incident investigations

If your organization is using Microsoft 365 Defender, you can take advantage of having a built-in analyst for the alerts and incidents that might occur in your environment. The automated investigation and remediation that is included with Microsoft 365 Defender provides some automated capabilities around for each alert, including:

- Determining if an alert requires additional actions
- Recommending or taking remediation actions
- Determining if additional investigation should occur

When an alert is generated and creates an incident, the automated investigation can come to a vedict about the alert. The three verdicts of an investigation are:

- Malicious
- Suspicious
- No threats found

If an alert is found to be malicious or suspicious, some automatic remediation steps might be performed. Some of the more common actions include:

- Sending a file to quarantine
- Stopping a process on a managed device
- Isolating a device from the network
- Blocking a URL from being accessed

> **NEED MORE REVIEW?** **REMEDIATION ACTIONS**
>
> For more information on the possible remediation actions with Microsoft 365 Defender, visit *https://docs.microsoft.com/en-us/microsoft-365/security/defender/m365d-remediation-actions?view=o365-worldwide.*

To configure automated investigation and response, there are a few prerequisites that the organization must meet to enable this configuration. Table 2-1 explains the various requirements for the tenant.

After you have verified that your organization meets the requirements, you can set the automation level for device groups. To configure the automation level, follow these steps.

1. Sign in to the Microsoft 365 Defender security center at *https://securitycenter.windows.com.*
2. Go to **Settings**.

TABLE 2-1 Automated investigation and response requirements

Requirement	Details
Subscription and license type	One of the following subscription and license types: ■ Microsoft 365 A5 ■ Microsoft 365 E5 ■ Microsoft 365 A5 Security ■ Microsoft 365 E5 Security ■ Office 365 E5 with Enterprise Mobility + Security E5, and Windows E5
Network requirements	■ Microsoft Defender for Identity enabled ■ Microsoft Cloud App Security configured ■ Microsoft Defender for Identity integration configured
Windows device requirements	■ Windows 10, version 1709 or later ■ Microsoft Defender for Endpoint ■ Micosoft Defender Antivirus
Protection for email content and Office files	■ Microsoft Defender for Office 365 configured
Permissions	■ Global Administrator ■ Security Administrator

3. Under **Permissions**, click **Device groups**.

4. For each device group, set the desired *Remediation level*. For example, the recommended setting is *Full – remediate threads automatically*. Figure 2-10 shows the setting configured for the Mobile Devices device group.

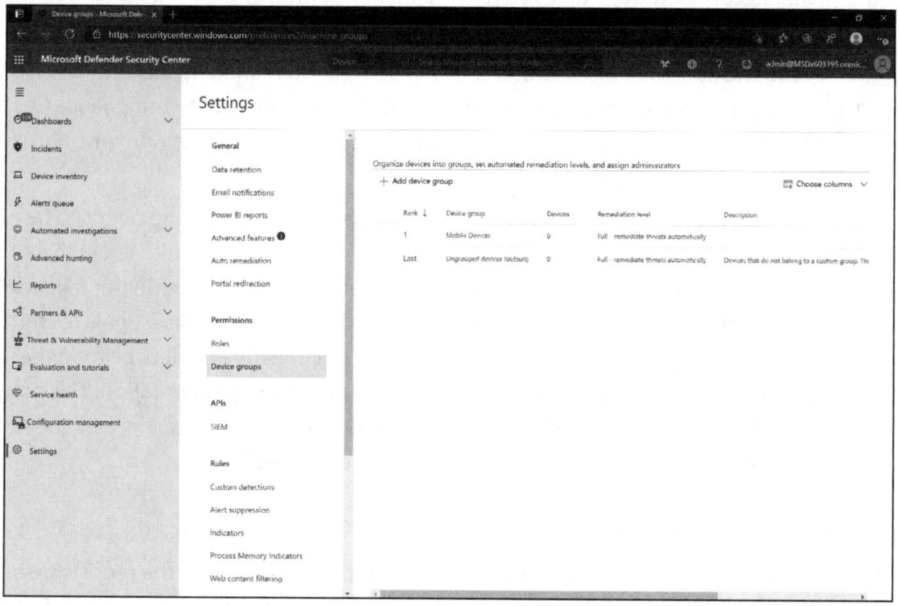

FIGURE 2-10 Microsoft Defender Security Center remediation level

Automated investigations appear in the Investigations tab of the incident. From this tab, you can view the conclusions and actions that the investigation resulted in.

> **NEED MORE REVIEW?** **AUTOMATED INVESTIGATION**
>
> For more information and a video on automated investigation and self-healing, visit *https://docs.microsoft.com/en-us/microsoft-365/security/defender/m365d-autoir?view= o365-worldwide.*

Manage and review security alerts

In this section we work with alerts in the Office 365 Security & Compliance Center. The alerts available in this portal deal with user, administrator, and general Office 365 activity. These alerts are based on information contained in the Office 365 audit log. While you can review the audit logs to retrieve this information, creating an alert policy can ensure that you are notified about critical events. There are a handful of pre-defined alert policies that cover major events, such as a user account being elevated to Exchange administrator. New alert policies can also be created by an administrator to provide additional visibility around the Office 365 platform.

Plan for Office 365 alerts

Before you begin working with alerts in the Office 365 Security & Compliance Center, there are a few planning considerations that you need to be familiar with. These are the prerequisites for accessing managing Office 365 alerts.

- **Permissions** The administrator that will be creating managing alerts must be granted the Organization Configuration role in the Office 365 Security & Compliance Center. This role is automatically granted to members of the Compliance Administrator and Organization Management role groups.
- **Audit logging** Before you can start creating alerts, audit logging needs to be enabled for Office 365. Office 365 alerts are based on the information contained in the audit logs. To do this, navigate to the Office 365 Security & Compliance Center, select **Alerts**, then **Alert policies**. Select any one of the built-in alerts. On the alert policies settings you will be prompted to turn on auditing if it is not already enabled. Beyond these hard requirements, you should also create an action plan for implementation. This might include items such as who will be administering Office 365 alerts, who should be receiving notifications, and what items you need to create policies for.

Navigate Office 365 alerts

The alerts for Office 365 are visible in a few different formats, similar to the reports we saw with Azure AD Identity Protection. The first page we will look at is the Alerts dashboard. This can be accessed by signing in to the Office 365 Security & Compliance Center, clicking Alerts, and selecting Dashboard. Refer to Figure 2-11 for an example of what to expect when you access the dashboard. There are a few different resources available in this view.

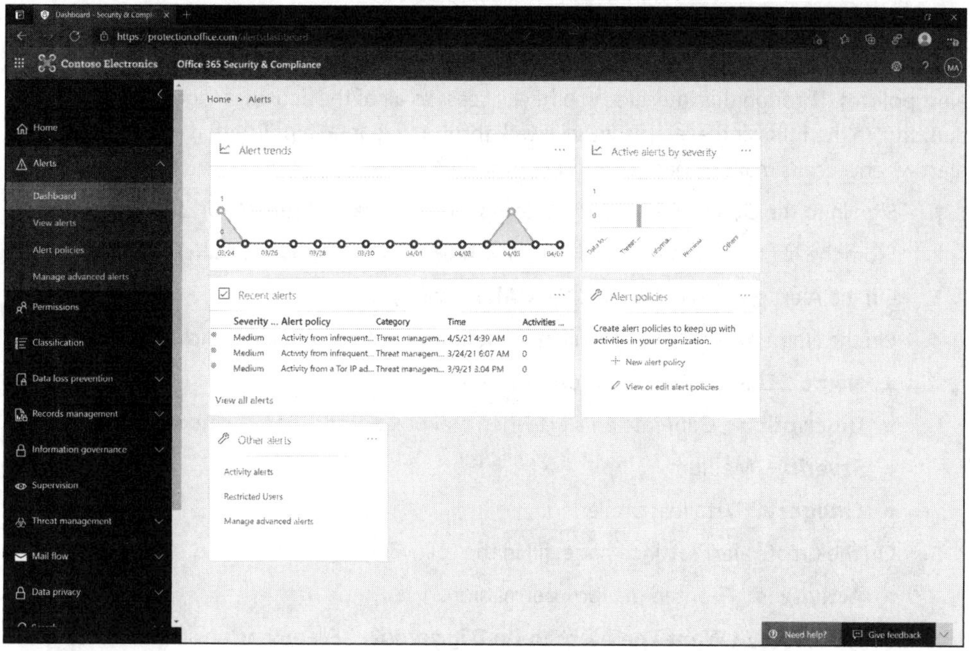

FIGURE 2-11 Office 365 Alerts Dashboard

- **Alert Trends**   The Alert Trends tile shows recent activity by count for each of the different alert categories. Hovering your mouse cursor over the report tile will summarize event accounts for each category. This tile does not have a drilldown view.

- **Active Alerts By Severity**   The Active Alerts By Severity tile provides summarizes active alerts by category and severity (low, medium, high). Hovering your mouse cursor over the report tile will summarize the event counts by severity. This tile does not have a drilldown view.

- **Recent Alerts**   The Recent Alerts tile provides a list of recent alerts, including Severity, Alert Policy, Category, Time, and Number Of Activities. Clicking any of the events on this tile will bring up a blade with additional details about the event. From there you can see additional information about that specific event. You also have controls to resolve, suppress, or notify users about the alert.

- **Alert Policies**   The Alert Policies tile provides helpful links to quickly create a new alert policy or manage the existing policies.

- **Other Alerts**   The Other Alerts tile provides helpful links to quickly create activity-based alerts, view restricted user accounts, and access advanced alert management.

It is worth noting that each of these tiles can also be pinned to the Office 365 Security & Compliance Center home page for quick reference. For situations where you need to browse all alerts, navigate to **Alerts**, then **View Alerts**. This page provides you with functionality to quickly filter all alerts, including those that have been resolved. Once you have isolated the alerts you need, you can also export them to CSV format from this page.

Configure Office 365 alert policies

The policy editor for Office 365 alerts enables you to create and manage additional custom alert policies. Through this interface you have access to all of the activities logged through auditing. In the following example we will walk through creating a policy that generates an alert when a user's mailbox permissions are modified.

1. Sign in to the Office 365 Security & Compliance Center at *https://protection.office.com*.

2. From the Navigation bar on the left, click **Alerts** and select **Alert Policies**.

3. On the Alert policies page, click **New Alert Policy**.

4. On the Name Your Alert page, fill in the following information and click **Next**.

   - **Name**   Change to mailbox permissions.
   - **Description**   Generate an alert when mailbox permissions are modified.
   - **Severity**   Medium.
   - **Category**   Data loss prevention.

5. On the Create alert settings page, fill in the following information and click **Next**.

   - **Activity Is**   Granted mailbox permission.
   - **How Do You Want The Alert To Be Triggered?**   Every time an activity matches the rule.

6. On the Set your recipients page, fill in the following information and click **Next**.

   - **Email Recipients**   Your email address.
   - **Daily Notification Limit**   No limit.

7. On the Review your settings page, review the proposed policy as shown in Figure 2-12. Select the option **Yes, Turn It On Right Away** and click **Finish**.

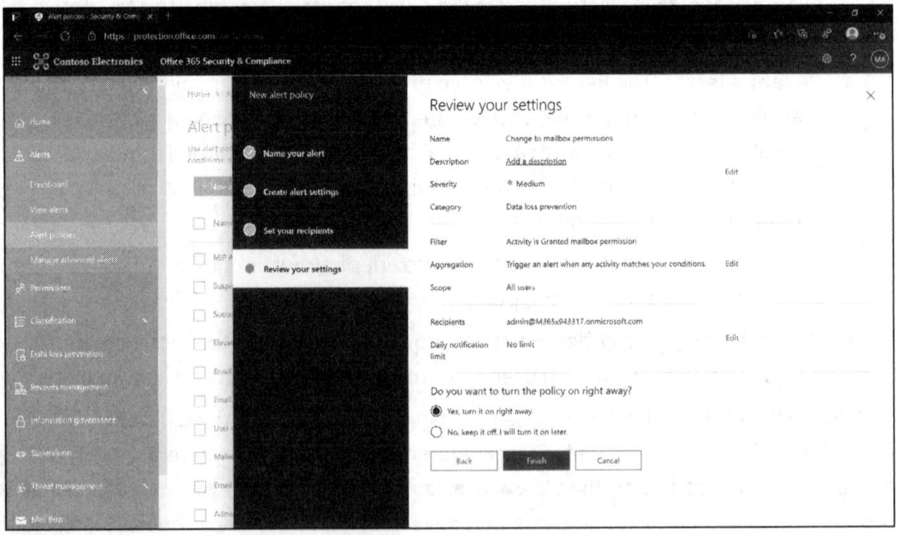

FIGURE 2-12   Office 365 Alerts - Alert Policy

Once the new alert policy has been applied you will start seeing associated events recorded in the Dashboard And Alerts page. The recipients that you configured in the policy will also begin receiving email notifications. These notifications will summarize each event and include a link that takes you back to the portal for further investigation.

NEED MORE REVIEW? **MANAGING ACTIVITY ALERTS**

For more information about activity alerts in Office 365, visit *https://docs.microsoft.com/ en-us/microsoft-365/compliance/alert-policies?view=o365-worldwide.*

Skill 2.2: Plan and implement threat protection with Microsoft Defender

A threat is any activity that could cause problems for your information technology environment, whether on-premises or in the cloud. When you hear the term "threat," you might immediately think of a malicious person trying to gain unauthorized access to your device or your environment. That is a threat. But threats are also accidental, such as an accidental administrative action that brings down a critical service. And threats can also be environmental, such as a heavy rain or hurricane near you or your primary data center. Managing these threats is called threat protection. In skill section, we'll look at implementing threat protection solutions that are integrated with Microsoft Defender for Endpoint, Microsoft Defender for Office 365, and Microsoft Defender for Identity.

This skill covers how to:

- Plan Microsoft Defender for Endpoint
- Design Microsoft Defender for Office 365 policies
- Implement Microsoft Defender for Identity

Plan Microsoft Defender for Endpoint

Microsoft Defender for Endpoint is one of the components of Microsoft 365 Defender and uses features that are available in Windows 10 along with cloud native services to protect these endpoints. Some features of Microsoft Defender for Endpoint include:

- **Endpoint behavioral sensors** Sensors that are built-in to Windows 10 that collect and process signals from the operating system and send the data to Microsoft Defender for Endpoint.
- **Cloud security analytics** Cloud-native analytics solution to translate the signals, insights, and detections into actionable responses.
- **Threat intelligence** Identify attacks and techniques that might occur in the organization with alerts and procedures to follow up and investigate when necessary.

Requirements for Microsoft Defender for Endpoint

Before you can onboard devices to Microsoft Defender for Endpoint, the tenant and configuration must meed some minimum requirements. From a licensing perspective, one of the following licenses must be available in the tenant:

- Windows 10 Enterprise E5
- Windows 10 Education A5
- Microsoft 365 E5 which includes Windows 10 Enterprise E5
- Microsoft 365 A5
- Microsoft 365 E5 Security
- Microsoft 365 A5 Security
- Microsoft Defender for Endpoint

To actively manage devices that run Windows, the supported versions include:

- Windows 7 Pro or Enterprise, SP1 and later (with a support agreement)
- Windows 8.1 Pro or Enterprise
- Windows 10 Pro, Enterprise, or Education
- Windows Server 2008 R2 SP1 and later
- Windows Virtual Desktop

Additionally, other devices can be managed even if they do not run Windows. Other supported operating systems include:

- Android
- iOS
- macOS
- Linux

Select a deployment method

The deployment method that you select depends on the type of architecture that you might use in your organization. The types of architecture are:

- Cloud-native
- Co-management
- On-premises

The objective domain and available materials for the MS-101 exam do not specifically call out if on-premises are in scope for the exam. The objectives that are listed refer to the cloud-native products, and that is what we will focus on in this skill section.

NEED MORE REVIEW? **PLANNING DEPLOYMENT**

For more information about planning a Microsoft Defender deployment and the various architectures, visit *https://docs.microsoft.com/en-us/microsoft-365/security/defender-endpoint/deployment-strategy?view=o365-worldwide.*

After you have verified that your devices run a supported operating system, you then need to determine how to on-board the devices to the service. Table 2-2 shows the variety of supported deployment options that exist for onboarding these devices.

TABLE 2-2 Supported deployment methods

Endpoint type	Deployment tool
Windows	Local script (up to 10 devices) ■ Group Policy ■ Microsoft Endpoint Manager ■ Microsoft Endpoint Configuration Manager ■ VDI scripts
macOS	■ Local script ■ Microsoft Endpoint Manager ■ JAMF Pro ■ Mobile Device Management
Linux	■ Local script ■ Puppet ■ Ansible
iOS	■ App-based
Android	■ Microsoft Endpoint Manager

The deployment guide for Microsoft Defender for Endpoint is broken up into three phases:

1. Prepare
2. Set up
3. Onboard

Phase 1 - Preparing for deployment

The preparation phase is mainly documentation and verification of what you intend to do in the orgization. These steps include:

- **Stakeholders and approval** Identifying the appropriate stakeholders and mapping sign-off and RACI assignments.
- **Environment** Collecting the data about the existing environment and ensuring everything is supported by the desired configuration. This could include endpoints, servers, and security information and event management (SIEM)

- **RBAC** Identifying the appropriate personas that are applicable to the organization, and if the built-in roles meet the desired security requirements.
- **Adoption order** Prioritizing the services or features that will be consumed by the organization; then deploying and configuring the services in that order.

NEED MORE REVIEW? **PLANNING DEPLOYMENT**

For more information about planning a Microsoft Defender deployment and the various architectures, visit *https://docs.microsoft.com/en-us/microsoft-365/security/defender-endpoint/prepare-deployment?view=o365-worldwide*.

Phase 2 – Setting up Microsoft Defender for Endpoint

The setup phase is where you validate existing licenses and begin setting up the tenant. The primary steps include:

- Validating licenses
- Configuring the tenant
- Configuring the network

You can validate that you have one of the required licenses from the Azure portal. To check your currently licensed products, follow these steps.

1. Sign in to the Office 365 Security & Compliance Center at *https://portal.azure.com*.
2. From the Navigation bar on the left, **Azure Active Directory**.
3. From Azure Active Directory, click **Licenses**.
4. From Licenses, click **All Products**. Verify that the licenses assigned to users include Microsoft Defender for Endpoint.

Figure 2-13 displays the licensed products for Contoso Electronics, including 20 Microsoft 365 E5 licenses.

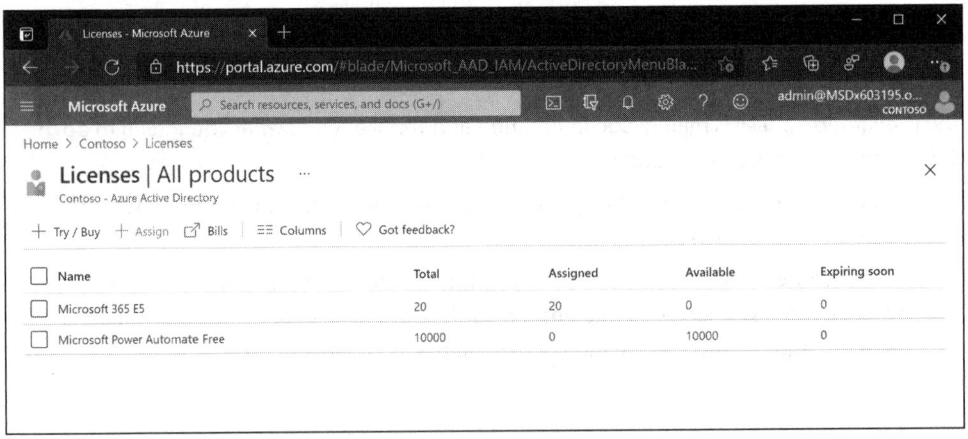

FIGURE 2-13 Microsoft 365 E5 licenses

After confirming that you have licenses available or already assigned to users, the next step is to begin the tenant configuration. The first time that you access the Microsoft Defneder Security Center, a short wizard will guide you through the first steps to configure the tenant. The primary configuration options are on the preferences step, which include:

- **Data storage location**   The physical location that data will be stored in, and cannot be changed after deployment. These options are the US, UK, or Europe.

- **Data retention policy**   The amount of time that Microsoft retains data for your tenant instance. The default policy is 180 days.

- **Organization size**   An approximation of the number of devices that you plan to onboard in the tenant.

Figure 2-14 displays these preferences being configured during the setup wizard.

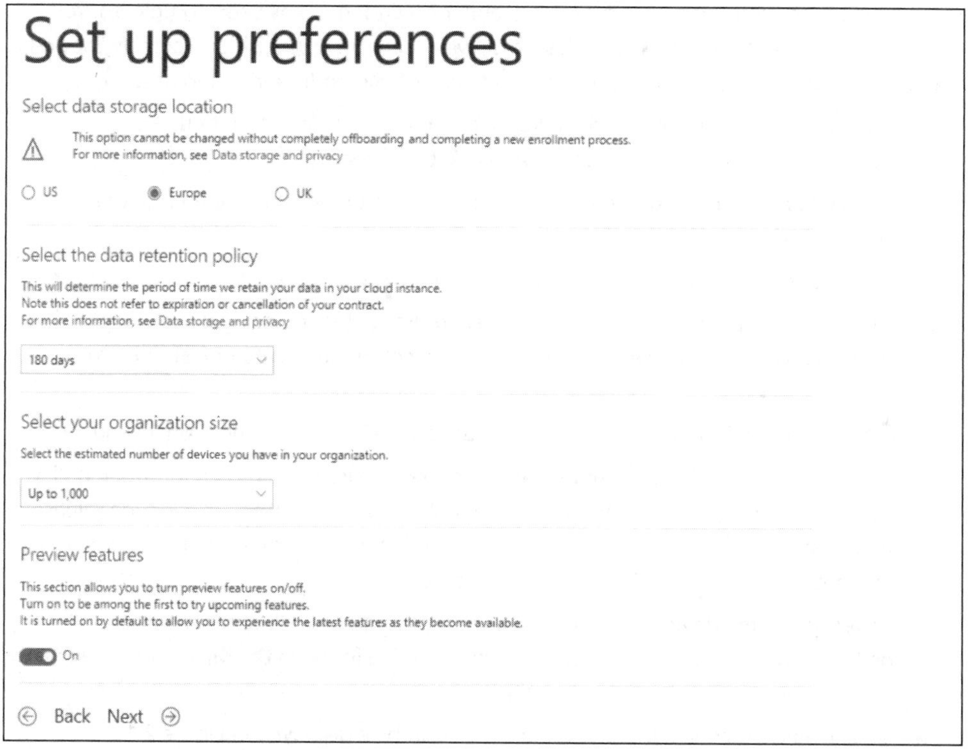

Set up preferences

Select data storage location

⚠ This option cannot be changed without completely offboarding and completing a new enrollment process.
For more information, see Data storage and privacy

○ US   ● Europe   ○ UK

Select the data retention policy

This will determine the period of time we retain your data in your cloud instance.
Note this does not refer to expiration or cancellation of your contract.
For more information, see Data storage and privacy

| 180 days | ⌄ |

Select your organization size

Select the estimated number of devices you have in your organization.

| Up to 1,000 | ⌄ |

Preview features

This section allows you to turn preview features on/off.
Turn on to be among the first to try upcoming features.
It is turned on by default to allow you to experience the latest features as they become available.

（◯）On

← Back   Next →

FIGURE 2-14   Microsoft Defender preferences

The network configuration portion of the setup is only required if you organization requires an outgoing proxy. By default, the Microsoft Defender for Endpoint service uses Microsoft Windows HTTP protocols to send sensor and signal data from the device to the cloud service. If the device can communicate directly with the internet, then the autodiscovery methods will allow communication by default. However, if your organization requires the use of a proxy, these services might be blocked until the proxy has been configured.

The recommended method of configuring these proxys is to use DNS-based URLs that can be accessed by the Defender for Endpoint service. Microsoft publishes a spreadsheet of specific DNS records for the various geographic regions and operating systems. If your network configuration settings do not allow DNS-based rules, you can also use IP ranges.

> **NEED MORE REVIEW?** **PROXY CONFIGURATION**
>
> For more information about configuring a proxy with Microsoft Defender for Endpoint, including the spreadsheet of DNS records, visit *https://docs.microsoft.com/en-us/ microsoft-365/security/defender-endpoint/production-deployment?view=o365-worldwide.*

Phase 3 – Onboarding Microsoft Defender for Endpoint

After the initial configuration of Microsoft Defender for Endpoint has been completed, you can onboard devices to the service. In this phase we'll focus on using using Microsoft Endpoint Manager and Intune to onboard devices to the Microsoft Defender for Endpoint service.

1. Sign in to the Azure Portal and configure automatic enrollment for Intune by configuring the MDM User Scope in Azure Active Directory.

2. Assign Intune licenses to users in Azure Active Directory and ensure their devices are enrolled.

3. Sign in to the Microsoft Defender Security Center and complete the initial setup wizard.

4. Sign in to the Microsoft Endpoint Manager admin center and navigate to Open the Microsoft Defender Security Center to connect to the Microsoft Defender for Endpoint service.

5. In the Microsoft Defender Security Center, turn on the Microsoft Intune connection setting.

6. In the Microsoft Endpoint Manager admin center, create a device configuration policy using the Microsoft Defender for Endpoint (Windows 10 Desktop) profile type (please note that non-Windows devices require an installation package that must be downloaded from the Microsoft Defender Security Center).

7. To verify that the devices are properly onboarded and reporting, run a detection test on the newly onboarded devices (commands can be found in the Microsoft Defender Security Center settings under Onboarding).

The end-to-end process that is identified in these steps is displayed in Figure 2-15.

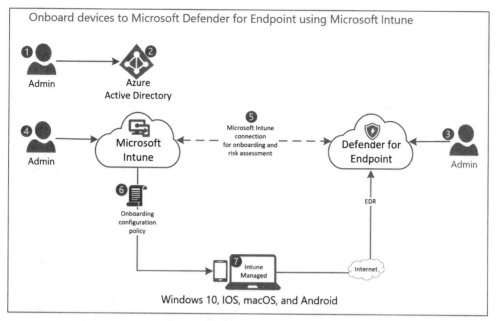

Onboard devices to Microsoft Defender for Endpoint using Microsoft Intune

FIGURE 2-15 Onboarding devices to Microsoft Defender for Endpoint

Design Microsoft Defender for Office 365 policies

Threat protection policies assist in the overall security posture of the organization. There are a number of of built-in policies with the Office 365 Security & Compliance center that you can customize for your organization. The built-in policies include:

- Anti-phishing
- Anti-spam
- Anti-malware
- Safe attachmetns
- Safe Links
- DomainKeys Identified Mail
- Enhanced filtering
- Tentant allow/block lists

Design anti-phishing policies

Anti-phishing policies are used to minimize or eliminate phishing attempts at your organization. Remember, phishing is the act of trying to fool recipients into clicking a malicious link, open a malicious attachment, or provide sensitive information (spear phishing is the same thing but targeted at a specific person). While phishing can happen over email, telephone, or in person, we will focus on phishing over email since that is the focus of the exam.

Office 365 includes built-in anti-phishing technology. However, you can expand on that by adding additional anti-phishing policies. The following list describes the capabilities of custom policies, presuming that you have Office 365 E3:

- You can deploy policies to domains, specific recipients, or groups. Thus, you can deploy one policy for a department and a separate policy for another department.
- Instead of moving spoofed messages to the Junk Email folder, you can quarantine the messages.
- You can turn off anti-spoofing protection.

With the Office 365 Security & Compliance center, you have greater control over your anti-phishing policies and more features. The following list describe the key capabilities you get with E5.

- **Greater control of who and what to protect**   You can add up to 60 users to protect from being impersonated.
- **Automatic domain protection**   You can configure a policy to automatically protect all of the domains you own.
- **You can control the actions during impersonation**   You can delete the message, deliver it and BCC somebody, or redirect the email to a different email address.
- **Mailbox intelligence.**   This feature analyzes user email to help identify phishing attempts.
- **Add trusted senders and domains**   You can add specific senders or trusted domains to a safe list so that message from the senders or domains won't be classified as impersonation.
- **You can adjust the aggressiveness of the anti-phishing engine**   Setting it to 1 is the default and represents a standard level of aggression. You can set it to 2, 3, or 4 where 4 is the most aggressive setting. As you increase the aggressiveness of the engine, the chance of having false positives increases (whereby a legitimate email is marked as a phishing attempt).

Outside of the anti-phishing policies, you can control anti-phishing in anti-spam policies too. In anti-spam policies, you have additional options for acting on email identified as phishing email. For example, you can redirect the phishing email to a shared mailbox that is monitored by your information security team.

Configure anti-phishing policies

By default, you will not have an anti-phishing policy. Instead, you have built-in anti-phishing protection, which is built into the other policies such as the anti-spam default policy. If you want additional protection, you should create a new anti-phishing policy.

To create a new policy, you need to be in the Azure AD global administrator, Azure AD security administrator, or the Exchange Online Organization Management role. When you create a new anti-phishing policy, you give it a name, an optional description, and then specify who the policy applies to (domain, group, or user). Thereafter, you can increase the priority of the policy, if desired. So where are the settings? After creation, you can edit the policy. That's where you'll find the settings. There aren't many configuration options. The following settings can be adjusted in the anti-phishing custom policy:

- **Description** A description helps you identify the purpose of a policy.
- **Who the policy applies to** You can apply a policy to a domain, a group, or directly to a user. You can have multiple conditions and can also include exceptions. For example, you can configure a policy to apply to all users except the executive team. Then you configure a separate policy to only apply to the executive team.
- **Whether anti-spoofing protection is enabled** This can be enabled or disabled but should be enabled for anti-spoofing protection.
- **The action to apply when somebody spoofs your domain**. You can choose to move messages to the Junk Email folder (default option) or to quarantine the message.

While there aren't many settings with the default anti-phishing solution, anti-phishing gives you access to impersonation settings and advanced settings, such as:

- **Define protected users** You can define up to 60 protected users. For example, you might define the CEO of your organization. If an email comes from outside the company and attempts to impersonate the CEO, all users who have the anti-phishing policy will be protected. Don't confuse protected users as the only users protected from the phishing attempt.
- **Show tip for impersonated users** This is a safety tip that notifies users of impersonated users.
- **Show tip for impersonated domains** This is a safety tip that notifies users of impersonated domains.
- **Show tip for unusual characters** This is a safety tip that notifies users if a message contains unusual characters (such as symbols).
- **Mailbox intelligence** This optional feature enhances impersonation results. This option is only available for mailboxes hosted in Office 365 (not for mailboxes hosted on-premises).

You receive an attack simulator toolset separately from anti-phishing, as part of Office 365 Threat Intelligence. At least one of these tools is helpful to find out if your organization is susceptible to phishing attacks. Office 365 Threat Intelligence offers three tools to simulate attacks. These tools are meant to help you test your environment for susceptibility to attacks. Office 365 Threat Intelligence is available as part of Office 365 Enterprise E5. Beyond the three tools we cover here, there is also a threat tracker (which helps you track publicly known campaigns or specific malware and phishing policies you've earmarked), a threat explorer that enables you to browse malware and phishing activity for your organization, and a threat management review tool that is a high-level view of incidents, quarantine, and blocked users.

- **Credential Harvest** This attack is a social engineering type of attach that sends users an email with a URL in the message. The URL takes the user to an authentication page, with the purpose of phishing their credentials.

- **Malware attachment**   An email is sent to the specified users that includes an attachment. When the user opens the attachment, a macro or code is run automatically on the user's device.

- **Link in attachment**   This attack simulation is a combination of the Credential Harvest and Malware attachment simulations. The user is sent an email that contains an attachment. The attachment contains a URL to a website that phishes for their credentials.

- **Link to malware**   This attack simulation uses an attachment within an email, and the attachment contains a link directly to malware.

- **Drive-by URL**   This attack simulation sends an email to the specified users and includes a URL in the email. The URL is a website that trys to run code in the background to obtain control of the device.

From an implement perspective for the exam, be aware of the following information:

- **Anti-phishing policies are configured in the Security and Compliance portal at https://protection.office.com**   There are wizards that walk you through tasks, step-by-step. We've opted not to show step-by-step walkthroughs if they are very simple (Next, Next, Next) and don't add value to the book.

- **Be familiar with permissions**   You can be in the Organization Management role, Security Administrator role, or Security Reader role to view reports. Organization Management enables you to control permissions for others and configure everything. Security Administrator has less permissions than Organization Management, but more than Security Reader. Security Reader is a read-only view of the Office 365 Security & Compliance Center.

To configure an anti-phishing policy in the Office 365 Security & Compliance center, follow these steps.

1. Sign in as an administrator to the Office 365 Security & Compliance portal at *https://protection.office.com*.

2. In the left pane, expand **Threat management**, and then click **Policy**.

3. From Threat policies, click **Anti-phishing**.

4. On the anti-phishing page, click **Create**.

5. Provide a name for the policy, for example *Default Policy*, and then click **Next**.

6. Click the **Add a condition** button, and select a desired condition. For example, **The recipient is a member of**, and then enter the name of an Azure Active Directory group. Repeat this step as many times as necessary to include or exclude specific users in the organization, and then click **Next**.

7. Click **Create**.

8. On the anti-phishing page, click the name of the policy that you created.

9. Click the **Edit** button for any policy setting, impersonation setting, or spoofing setting that you need to customize for your organization. Figure 2-16 shows the default policy settings.

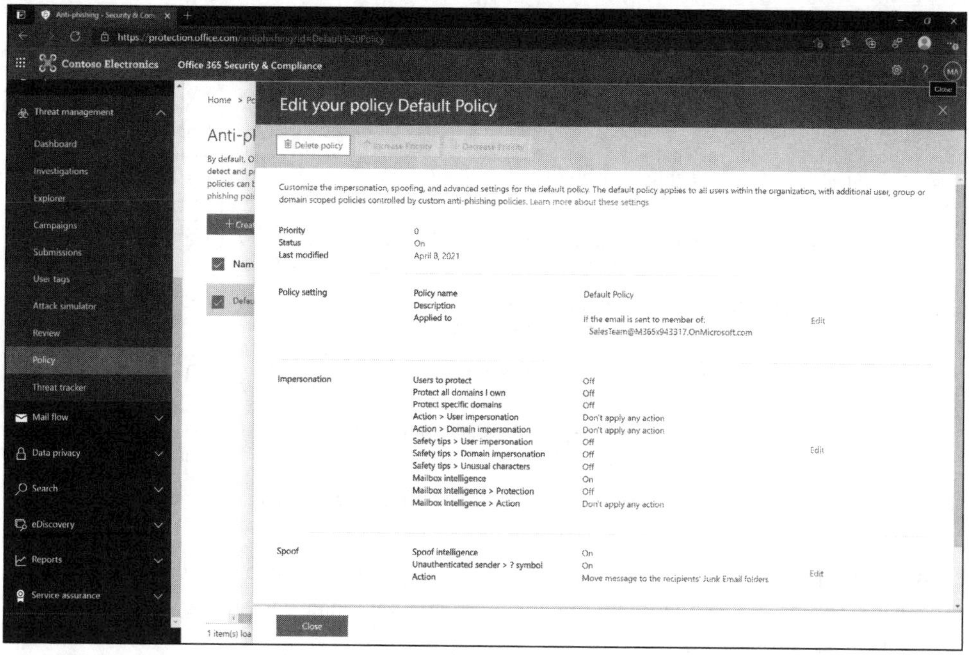

FIGURE 2-16 Default anti-phishing policy settings

Design anti-spam policies

When you think about spam, you think about unwanted email. Whether it is marketing-related email or unsolicited advertisements, spam is generally benign. With anti-spam policies, however, you can also control how potential malicious email is handled. For example, with control over some phishing email settings, you can block email from specific regions or countries, and you can block specific senders or domains.

When studying the anti-spam policies for the exam, you should keep something in mind: there are tons of settings and a myriad of ways to configure things. You won't possibly be able to memorize every setting or combination of settings. And you won't need to for the exam. For this section of the exam, focus on the design components. You need to know, at a high level, what your design options are, the pros and cons of various choices, and some of the most common settings.

Standard settings

By default, the standard anti-spam settings are turned on. This provides a basic level of protection and includes many of the most commonly used options. Table 2-3 shows the standard settings and default values.

TABLE 2-3 Standard settings for anti-spam

Setting name	Description	Default Value
Spam action	What to do with messages classified as spam.	Move message to Junk Email folder
Mark bulk email as spam	Whether to mark bulk email as spam.	On
Bulk threshold	A numerical value is assigned to each message. The threshold determines when a message is classified as bulk.	7
Mark NDR backscatter as spam	Backscatter messages are email bounce messages sent to you when your email address is spoofed or forged.	Off
Safety Tips	Color-coded message that warns you about potentially malicious messages.	On
Bulk email	What to do with messages classified as bulk (for example, marketing or newsletters).	Move message to Junk Email folder
Phishing email	What to do with messages classified as phishing attempts.	Quarantine message

Want to adjust the standard settings? Then you must switch to custom settings. When you use custom settings, you can modify the default spam filter policy and create your own policies. Custom settings are discussed next.

Custom settings

You have complete control of anti-spam when using custom settings. You can also have multiple policies (each having a specified priority). Using custom settings, however, also requires more administrative overhead (design time, setup time, testing time). Be sure to understand the different policies and what they are used for. Table 2-4 outlines these policies.

TABLE 2-4 Custom settings and multiple policies for anti-spam

Setting name	Description
Default spam filter policy	This is the default policy, which you can adjust. The default spam filter policy, however, applies to all users and you cannot change that.
Connection filter policy	You can use the connection filter policy to add safe IP address to the IP Allow List, which will ensure messages are always accepted. You can also add IP addresses to the IP Block List to always block messages from those IP addresses. You can turn on the safe list that ensures that messages from senders on the safe list are not checked for spam.
Outbound spam filter policy	This is a built-in policy to scan outbound messages for spam. This policy is always on. You can't turn it off. The only updates you can make to the outbound spam filter are to send a copy of suspicious outbound emails to somebody (such as your information security team) and notify specific people if a sender is blocked due to sending outbound spam.
Spoof intelligence policy	This policy is always on. You can review senders that have spoofed your domain and decide if you want to block them or not.

When you use custom settings, you gain access to a wider array of anti-spam settings. The following custom setting sections are available:

- **Spam and bulk actions**   This is the section where you decide which action to take. For example, with spam, you can move messages to the Junk Email folder, add an X-header, prepend a subject line with text (such as "<Possible spam>"), redirect messages to a specified email address, delete messages, or quarantine messages. You get the same options for high confidence spam, phishing emails, and bulk email. You set the spam threshold. The default is 7, and 1 represents the most aggressive while 9 is the least aggressive threshold. Finally, you can turn off safety tips.

- **Allow lists**   Here, you can add specific senders or domains to ensure that email is always delivered from them.

- **Block lists**   Here, you can mark all email from specific senders or domains as spam.

- **International spam**   You can filter email messages based on the language used, or based on country or region.

- **Spam properties**   Here, you can adjust the spam score based on email message attributes such as whether an email address has links to remote sites or uses an IP address in a URL. You can also flag email messages as spam if they meet certain criteria, such as having object tags in HTML. And you can also configure SPF, Sender ID filtering, and NDR backscatter.

- **Applied to**   You can apply a policy to a user, a group, or a domain. You can also use exceptions for granular control.

There are some key points to keep in mind for the exam:

- You cannot configure the default spam policy to apply to specific groups, users, or domains. Instead, create a new policy that can be targeted at groups, users, or domains.

- You cannot target the connection filter policy to specific groups, users, or domains.

- The outbound spam filter cannot be turned off.

- You cannot disable the spoof intelligence policy.

Configure anti-spam policies

The most important aspect of configuring anti-spam policies is knowing what the settings do. The configuration part is simple; mostly you configure a setting in a dropdown menu, click to enable features, and gives names and descriptions to policies.

Below are the steps to use custom settings in Office 365 anti-spam and create a basic anti-spam policy.

1. Sign in as an administrator to the Office 365 Security & Compliance portal at *https://protection.office.com*.

2. In the left pane, expand **Threat management**.

3. Under Threat management, click **Policy**.

4. On the threat policy page, click **Anti-spam**.

5. Click the **+ Create a policy** button.

6. In the New spam filter policy, type a name for the policy, and then type a description for the policy.

7. Expand the six configuration areas and configure your desired settings.

8. Click **Save** to finish creating the new policy.

9. After creating a policy, you can adjust the priority of the policy (if you have more than one policy). Figure 2-17 shows the settings of the default anti-spam policy.

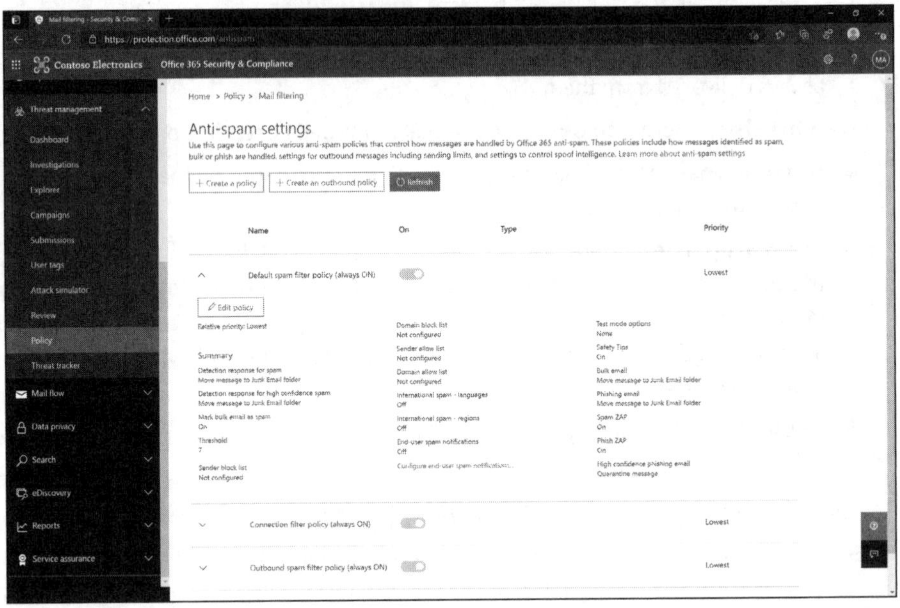

FIGURE 2-17 Default anti-spam policy settings

Here are additional key exam points about configuring anti-spam in Office 365:

- **Anti-spam protection is enabled by default**   By default, all users are protected. Many organizations will need to customize the anti-spam settings to reduce spam and improve the user experience.

- **Changes can take up to 1 hour to propagate**   Office 365 is spread across multiple data regions. Changes that you make in the services can take up to one hour to propagate throughout the centers.

- **Anti-spam isn't enhanced in Office 365**   Instead, anti-spam settings are the same. Only anti-phishing is enhanced. Additionally, you get safe attachments and safe links functionality with Office 365.

- **Use the Message Trace tool to find email messages**   If you want to find out if an email was dropped due to being flagged as spam, you can use the Message Trace tool to figure that out.

Design anti-malware policies

With anti-malware, you start with one default policy. It can be modified, but it cannot be disabled, and it has some limitations. For example, you cannot target the policy at specific groups or users. If you want more control, you must create a new anti-malware policy. Like anti-spam, Office 365 does not enhance anti-malware (in other words, there isn't an anti-malware like there is an anti-phishing solution).

Table 2-5 describes the available anti-malware policies.

TABLE 2-5 Description of anti-malware settings

Setting name	Description	Default value
Malware detection response	Whether to notify recipients if their messages are quarantined	Notify with default notification text
Common attachment types filter	Whether to block attachment types that might be harmful to a computer	On
Malware Zero-hour Auto Purge	Automatically takes the action to quarantine message if malware is detected	On
Notifications	Whether to notify a sender of the quarantined message	Off
Administrator notifications	Whether to notify an administrator about quarantined messages	Off
Custom notifications	Whether to customize the name, email address, subject, and message when notifications are used	Off

If you create a new anti-malware policy, you will be able to adjust the same settings. In other words, it has feature parity with the default policy. A custom policy can be targeted at specific domains, groups, or users. For the exam, this is important to remember.

In Figure 2-18 the scoping of a policy is targeted at members of the Sales Team group, with an exception for the MOD Administrator user.

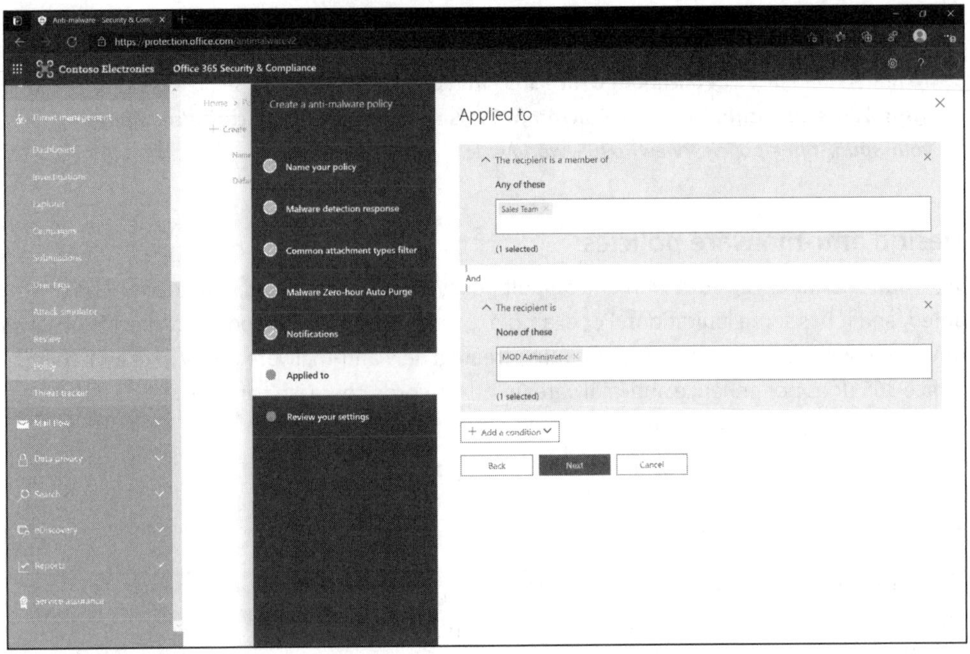

FIGURE 2-18 Scoping an anti-malware policy

There are some key things to remember about anti-malware for the exam:

- Messages are scanned when sent or received; however, messages are not scanned when viewed.
- Custom policies take precedence over the default policy. The default policy always has the lowest precedence.
- You can have multiple custom policies and specify a policy that takes precedence over other custom policies.
- You can test anti-malware policies by creating a text file named EICAR.TXT. In the file, type the following string: **X5O!P%@AP[4\PZX54(P^)7CC)7}$EICAR-STANDARD-ANTIVIRUS-TEST-FILE!$H+H***. Then, attach the file to an email message and try to send it to another mailbox. Note that your desktop anti-virus program might intercept the file. To avoid that, you can put it in a folder excluded from anti-virus scanning to test anti-malware.
- You can run a message trace to find out if a message was detected as malware.

Configure anti-malware policies

Office 365 anti-malware has a default policy. You can customize that. Or, optionally, you can create your own anti-malware policies. Many organizations use multiple policies based on departmental or organization needs. For example, you might create a custom policy for executives and ensure that the executives are not notified about malware detection. Instead, you could route notifications to the IT executive support team to handle.

Let's talk through the process of creating a new anti-malware policy and discuss these options.

1. Sign in as an administrator to the Office 365 Security & Compliance portal at *https://protection.office.com*.

2. In the left pane, expand **Threat Management**.

3. Under Threat Management, click **Policy**.

4. On the threat policies page, click **Anti-Malware**.

5. Click the **+Create** icon to create a new anti-malware policy.

6. Type a name for the new policy. For example, type "Executive anti-malware policy."

7. Type a description for the policy. For example, type "Disables notifications for executives and routes notifications to executive IT support team."

8. Choose a malware detection response setting. By default, it is set to not notify recipients if malware is quarantined. You can opt to notify recipients with the default text or notify with custom text.

9. Choose a common attachment types filter. By default, the feature is on and blocking dangerous file types (such as .exe and .vbs). You can turn it off, add more file types, or remove some file types.

10. Choose whether to automatically quarantine messages with Malware Zero-hour Auto Purge, which is on by default.

11. Configure the sender notifications. By default, senders are not notified if an email is not delivered due to malware. You can opt to notify senders if they are internal, notify senders if they are external, or notify all senders.

12. Configure administrator notifications. By default, administrators are not notified. You can opt to notify an administrator (based on email address) when undelivered messages originate from an internal sender or an external sender.

13. Configure customized notifications. By default, customized notifications are not enabled. You can enable custom notification text including the from name, from address, subject, and message. The subject and message can be unique based on whether the sender is internal or external.

14. Configure who the policy applies to. You can specify users, groups, or domains. You can also add conditions and exceptions. For example, you can configure the policy to apply to contosoelectronics.com if the recipient is a member of Group1 but isn't named Brian.

15. Click **Save** to complete the creation of the anti-malware policy. Figure 2-19 displays the review screen of a custom anti-malware policy.

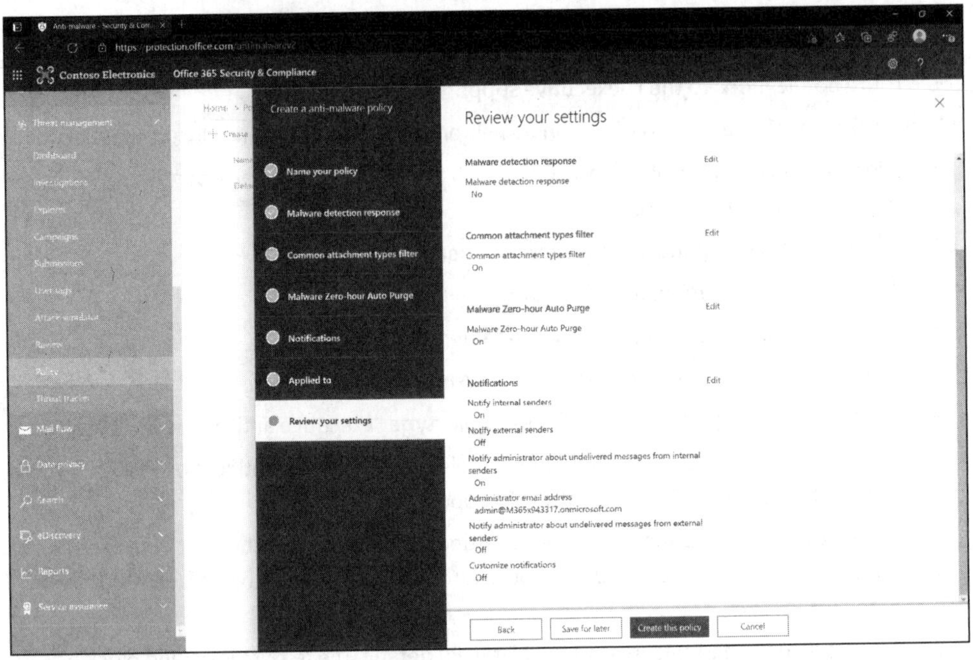

FIGURE 2-19 Customizing an anti-malware policy

For the exam, also know the following information about Office 365 anti-malware.

- **Standalone customers - most email messages are scanned** Whether sent or received, most messages are scanned. Messages sent from an internal recipient to another internal recipient are not scanned. Also, scanning does not occur upon email access.

- **Exchange Online customers (such as Office 365 Enterprise plans) - all email messages are scanned**. This includes messages sent from one internal recipient to another internal recipient.

- **The Message Trace tool can help you find out what happened to an email message** If you want to watch an email go through the Office 365 email service, use the Message Trace tool. It will also tell you if a message contains malware.

- **You can use PowerShell to manage anti-malware** Be familiar with the Get-MalwareFilterPolicy cmdlet, the Set-MalwareFilterPolicy cmdlet, the New-MalwareFilterPolicy cmdlet, and the Remove-MalwareFilterPolicy cmdlet.

- **You can use the EICAR.TXT file to test anti-malware functionality** As we discussed earlier, you can use EICAR.TXT to test the functionality of your anti-malware settings.

Design DomainKeys Identified Mail

DomainKeys Identified Mail (DKIM) provides a method for validating a domain name associated with an email message. With DKIM, you can greatly reduce the chances of your domain name being used maliciously, especially outside of your network (such as during spoofing). DKIM can help cut down on spam and malicious email, although this requires more widespread adoption. The high-level process involves the following steps:

1. Add required CNAME records for DKIM.

2. Add DKIM signature to your domain.

3. Send email.

4. The receiving organization receives an email message and the email server recognizes that it is signed by DKIM. A DNS query obtains the public key from the domain, which allows for the DKIM verification.

Table 2-6 shows the two CNAME record formats for the DNS records.

TABLE 2-6 DNS configuration items for DKIM

DNS item	Value
Hostname	selector1-<domainGUID>._domainkey.<initialDomain>
Points to address or value	selector1-<domainGUID>._domainkey.<initialDomain>
TTL	3600
Hostname	selector2._domainkey.<domain>
Points to address or value	selector2-<domainGUID>._domainkey.<initialDomain>
TTL	3600

You might be wondering how to obtain the domainGUID. You can check the MX record for the domain. Use the nslookup command, as follows:

```
nslookup
set type = MX
contosoelectronics.com
```

The output will contain the mail exchanger:

```
contosoelectronics.com   MX preference = 0, mail exchanger =
contosoelectronics-com.mail.protection.outlook.com
```

The part of the mail exchanger before mail.protection.outlook.com is the domainGUID (in this example, contosoelectronics-com). Full disclosure: contosoelectronics.com (on the internet), doesn't have this MX record. If you want to try this on the internet, use microsoft.com.

There are a few key points to note about DKIM for the exam:

- Your initial domain in Office 365, such as contosoelectronics.onmicrosoft.com, will have DKIM enabled by default.
- It is a good practice to use DKIM, Sender Policy Framework (SPF), and Domain-based Message Authentication, Reporting, and Conformance (DMARC) together to prevent spoofing of your domain. SPF and DMARC use DNS TXT records to help prevent spoofing. While the exam blueprint doesn't specifically call out SPF and DMARC, you should familiarize yourself with them.
- Office 365 supports inbound validation of DKIM messages. You can use a transport rule to process messages based on the results of the DKIM validation.
- There is a default Office 365 DKIM policy that applies to all domains. If you enable DKIM for your customer domain, then it takes precedence over the default DKIM policy.

> **NEED MORE REVIEW?** **HOW OFFICE 365 USES SPF TO PREVENT SPOOFING**
>
> To understand more detail about how SPF works in Office 365, see *https://docs.microsoft.com/office365/securitycompliance/how-office-365-uses-spf-to-prevent-spoofing*.

Implement Microsoft Defender for Identity

Microsoft Defender for Identity, formerly named Azure Advanced Threat Protection, is a cloud-native security solution that integrates with on-premises Active Directory Domain Services. This integrates enables detection, investigation, and reporting for threats against the identities used in your organization. There are two primary components of Microsoft Defender for Identity:

- **Defender for Identity Portal** The cloud-native portal where the collected data is displayed for monitoring and reporting.
- **Defender for Identity sensor** The Defender for Identity sensors are installed on domain controllers and federation servers to capture signals and events.

Defender for Identity prerequisites

As with the other Defender services that we have introduced, Defender for Identiy requires specific licensing to use the service. You can use either a bundled license with Enterprise Mobility + Security E5, or a standalone Defender for Identity license.

The sensor that is installed on the domain controllers in the environment also has specific requirements. The domain controller must be able to communicate with the cloud service through the internet, either directly or by using a proxy. The sensor also requires a user account or group managed service account that has read access to all objects in the domain.

Defender for Identity uses the Network Name Resolution protocol and requires the use of several ports:

- NTLM over RPC (TCP 135)
- NetBIOS (UDP 137)

- RDP (TCP 3389)
- DNS (UDP 53)
- Netlogon and SMB (TCP 445)

In addition to the port numbers, the sensor needs to communicate with *https://*.atp.azure.com.*

Setting up Defender for Identity

After you have verified that both the licensing and networking prerequisites are satisfied, you can continue with setting up Defender for Identity. Overall, there are three critical steps for getting Defender for Identity configured:

1. Connect to Active Directory
2. Download the sensor packages
3. Install the sensors

First, to connect to Active Directory, you need a user account or group managed service account (gMSA) that has read access to all objects in the domain. The recommended action is to use a gMSA, but this is only available on servers running Windows Server 2012 or later. If any domain controller instances run Windows Server 2008 or Windows Server 2008 R2, then those servers must use a standard account. Figure 2-20 shows using a gMSA to connect Defender for Identity to the contoso.com domain.

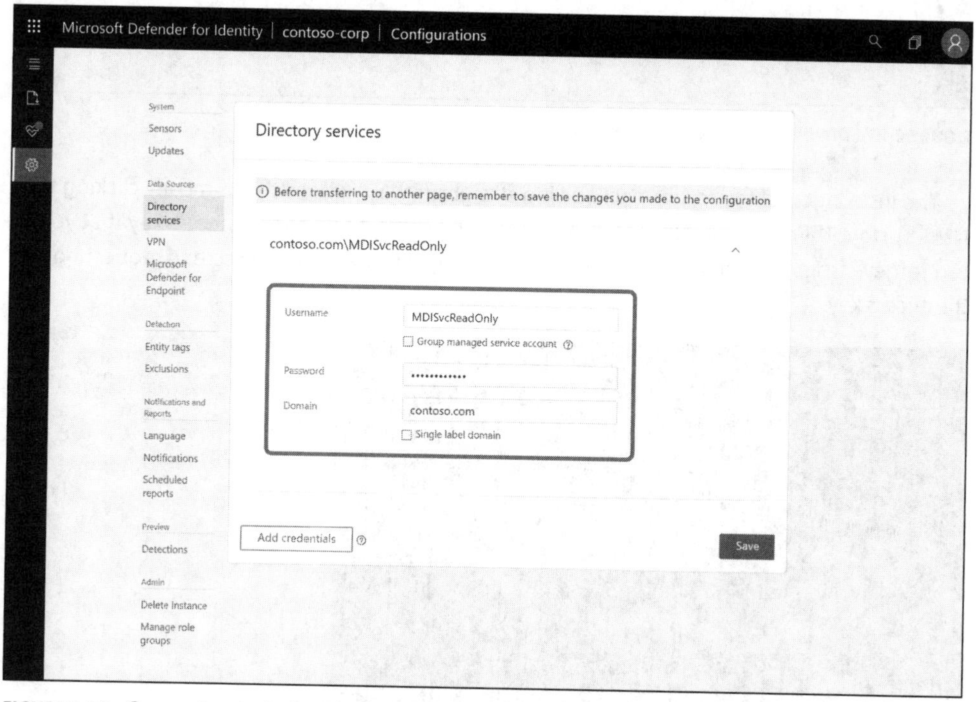

FIGURE 2-20 Connecting to Active Directory

After connecting to Active Directory, you will be prompted to download the sensor packages and provided an access key. When you download the sensor package, it is a compressed ZIP file that contains the installation file for the sensor, and a configuration file with the information to connect to Defender for Identity. Figure 2-21 shows the Sensors screen of Defender for Identity where you can download the sensor and access key.

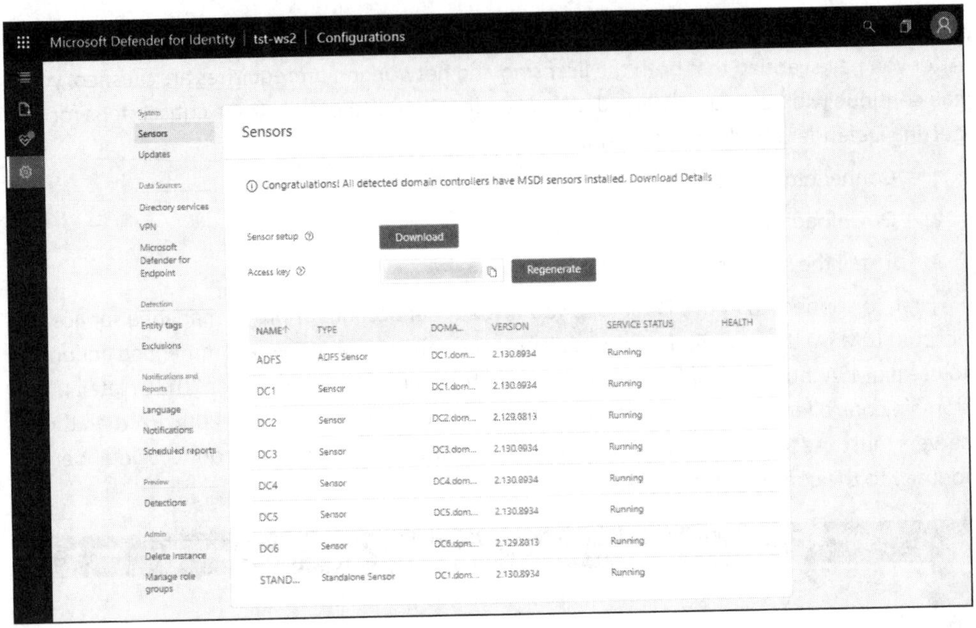

FIGURE 2-21 Download sensor and access key

The installation of the sensor package is a straightforward wizard that is mostly clicking the Next button. There is a Configure the Sensor screen, where it asks for the access key that you can retrieve from the Defender for Identity portal. Figure 2-22 shows the screen requesting the access key.

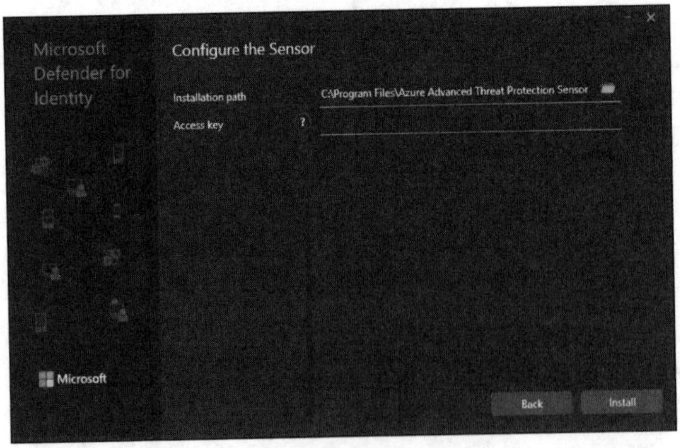

FIGURE 2-22 Defender for Identity sensor access key

Skill 2.3: Plan Microsoft Cloud App Security

Cloud App Security is a Microsoft cloud solution that helps organizations address the challenges associated with information protection and application security. This solution interfaces with your cloud applications, providing enhanced visibility and control such as monitoring activity, enforcing policies, identifying possible risks, and addressing threats. There are two flavors of Cloud App Security: Microsoft Cloud App Security and Office 365 Cloud App Security. For the exam we are covering Microsoft Cloud App Security, which covers cross-SaaS support, as opposed to just the Office 365 stack.

In this skill section we work with Cloud App Security and administration. We begin by reviewing the prerequisites for enabling Cloud Discovery and the configuration settings that are necessary for the exam. Next, we walk through creating policies and connecting cloud apps to your subscription for monitoring and alerts. Finally, we cover configuring alerts in the portal and how to upload traffic logs for snapshot reporting.

This skill covers how to:

- Plan information protection by using Cloud App Security
- Plan for application connectors
- Configure Cloud App Security policies
- Review and respond to Cloud App Security alerts

Plan information protection by using Cloud App Security

Let's begin by focusing on identifying the prerequisites for the Cloud App Security solution. After addressing the prerequisites, we will have access to the portal and can begin reviewing the various configuration settings. The list of hard prerequisites is minimal. You will need to address the following requirements before accessing the Cloud App Security portal.

- **Licensing**   A Cloud App Security license is required to use the product. Azure Active Directory Cloud App Security is included with Azure AD Premium P1, but has a limited set of features. The full Microsoft Cloud App Security solution is included with an EMS E5 subscription.

- **Security role**   To administer Cloud App Security, you need to be a Global Administrator, Compliance Administrator, or Security Reader in Azure AD.

- **Web portal**   Accessing the Cloud App Security portal is supported on the latest version of Internet Explorer 11, Microsoft Edge, Google Chrome, Mozilla Firefox, and Apple Safari.

- **Networking**   Accessing the Cloud App Security portal may require an update to your firewall's whitelist. For an updated list of IP addresses and DNS names, refer to the following link: *https://docs.microsoft.com/cloud-app-security/network-requirements*.

Beyond the list of prerequisites that Microsoft highlights, you should also plan to map out your organization's goals and objectives for this implementation. Consider setting up a trial account to evaluate the solution's capabilities and compatibility with your environment. This can help identify issues and areas where you can request support or provide feedback to Microsoft.

Configure Cloud App Security

Like many of the portals we cover throughout this book, the Cloud App Security portal has a series of configuration settings to meet different needs. For the best learning experience, consider setting up a trial account and navigating through the portal. The more you work with this solution, the more comfortable you will get with navigating these options.

Many of these settings are pre-configured with a standard default option. In Table 2-7 we cover each of the available settings, their functionality, and the default values.

TABLE 2-7 Cloud App Security settings

Setting	Category	Description	Default Values
Organization details	System	Contains settings for configuring your organization's details, including name, environment, and managed domains.	The default values are pulled from your tenant details.
Mail settings	System	Contains settings for configuring the email settings for alerts, including custom email properties, and templates.	Mail settings is configured to use the Default settings.
Export settings	System	Contains the option to export your portal's configuration, including policy rules, user groups, and IP ranges.	N/A
Score metrics	Cloud Discovery	Contains settings for configuring the weight of each app property, customizing the score assigned to discovered apps.	All metrics are set to Medium (x2) with Exclude N/As enabled.
Snapshot reports	Cloud Discovery	Contains the option to upload traffic logs from your environment for analysis of app activity.	N/A
Continuous reports	Cloud Discovery	Contains the option to create custom continuous reports, filterable by user group, IP address tags, and IP address ranges.	N/A
Automatic log upload	Cloud Discovery	Contains options for creating and managing data sources and log collectors for automatic upload.	N/A
App tags	Cloud Discovery	Contains the option to create and manage tags for discovered apps, used for filtering apps in the portal.	The default tags include Sanctioned and Unsanctioned.
Exclude entities	Cloud Discovery	Contains options for creating and managing user and IP range exclusions. Entries on this page are excluded from all future Cloud Discovery.	N/A

Setting	Category	Description	Default Values
User enrichment	Cloud Discovery	Contains the option to enable user enrichment. This feature replaces usernames found in traffic logs with the corresponding Azure AD username.	User enrichment is disabled by default.
Anonymization	Cloud Discovery	Contains options for enabling data anonymization for Cloud Discovery. This feature replaces username and device name information with encrypted values.	Anonymization is disabled by default.
Delete Data	Cloud Discovery	Contains the option to delete all Cloud Discovery data for the active tenant.	N/A
Admin quarantine	Information Protection	Contains the option to configure an admin quarantine location for files that violate your information protection policies.	The admin quarantine folder is not selected by default.
Azure Information Protection	Information Protection	Contains options for enabling Azure Information Protection to scan new files.	Azure Information Protection is not enabled by default.
Azure security	Information Protection	Contains the option to enable or disable monitoring of activities generated by the connected subscription.	Azure security is enabled by default.
Files	Information Protection	Contains the option to enable or disable monitoring of files in your software as a service (SaaS) apps.	File monitoring is enabled by default.
Default behavior	Conditional Access App Control	Contains the option to allow or block access to cloud apps when Cloud App Security is unavailable.	Allow access is enabled by default.
User monitoring	Conditional Access App Control	Contains the option to notify users that their activity is being monitored when accessing apps that have a policy assigned.	Notify users is enabled by default.
Device identification	Conditional Access App Control	Contains options for configuring device identification that can be leveraged for assigning access and session policies.	N/A
Provide feedback	Conditional Access App Control	Contains the option for enabling feedback collection for a list of defined users.	No usernames are provided by default.

There are a few important configuration settings you need to be familiar with as you begin working with Cloud App Security. The first area is covered on the Organization details page. Follow these steps to configure your organization details:

1. Sign in to the Cloud App Security portal at *https://portal.cloudappsecurity.com*.

2. From the menu bar, click the settings cog and select **Settings**.

3. On the Organization details page, fill in the following information:

   ■ **Organization Display Name**   The name you provide in this field will be included in emails and web pages sent to employees.

   ■ **Environment Name**   The name you provide in this field is used to differentiate between different environments owned by the same organization.

- **Organization Logo**   The image you provide in this field will be included in emails and web pages sent to employees. The image must be in PNG format with a maximum size of 150x150 pixels.

- **Managed Domains**   The domains you provide in this field determine which users are internal and external. This information is used for reports, alerts, and file sharing access levels.

4. Click **Save**. Figure 2-23 shows these settings for the Contoso organization.

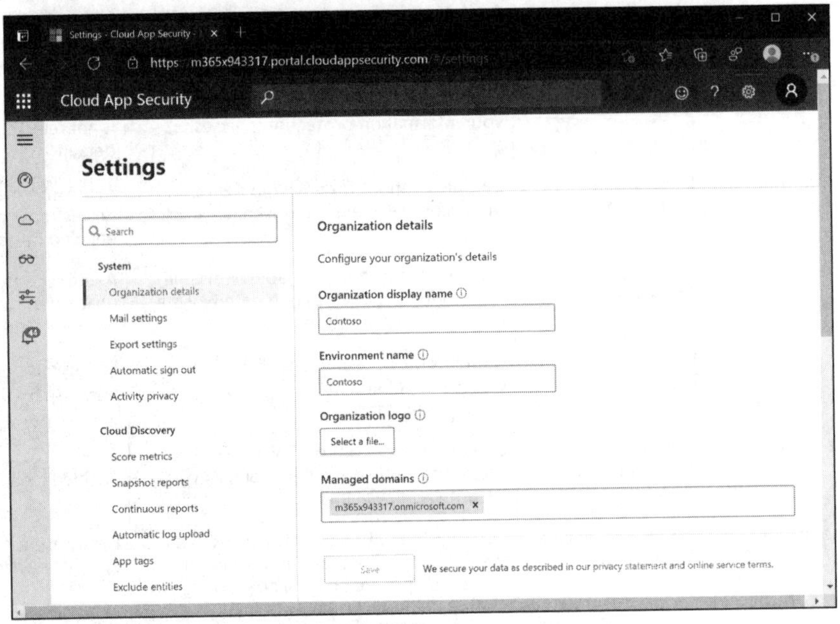

FIGURE 2-23   Cloud App Security settings

After configuring your organization details, navigate to the Mail settings page and confirm that the applied values work for your environment. These settings include the following:

- **Default Settings**   This is the default option and will apply the following configuration to emails:
  - **Display Name**   Microsoft Cloud App Security
  - **Email Address**   no-reply@cloudappsecurity.com
  - **Reply-To-Address**   no-reply@cloudappsecurity.com
- **Custom Settings**   Select this option if you want to customize the mail sender identity.
  - **From Display Name**   Enter a custom display name.
  - **From Email Address**   Enter your preferred sender email address.
  - **Reply-To Email Address**   Enter your preferred reply-to email address.

- **Custom Settings Approval** You must agree to the terms of service when using custom mail settings.
- **Email Design** Upload a custom email template, formatted in HTML.
- **Send A Test Email** Initiate a test email.

The remaining configuration settings serve different purposes depending on your needs. Activities such as uploading logs, tagging apps, and customizing score metrics play an important role as you begin importing data and connecting apps. We will cover additional settings throughout the chapter.

Design Cloud App Security solutions

Organizations that are moving their infrastructure, applications, services, and data to the cloud need a comprehensive security solution to protect against modern day security threats. Microsoft has positioned Cloud App Security as the solution for these needs. As you prepare to deploy Cloud App Security in your organization, you need to understand the requirements, capabilities, and connected technologies in order to design the best possible solution. In this skill we will review design consideration for Cloud App.

There are several technologies that Cloud App Security uses or integrates with to deliver a full-featured security solution. Table 2-8 outlines these technologies, along with their requirements and the design considerations that you can use to build a solution appropriate to your organization's needs.

TABLE 2-8 Cloud App Security designs

Technology	Requirements	Design Considerations
Connected apps	There are seven supported cloud apps available. Customers can request support for additional apps through the portal.	Review the list of supported connected apps and plan your solution accordingly. Connected apps give greater visibility and control to Cloud App Security, increasing your ability to manage threats.
Conditional Access App Control	Azure AD Premium P1 subscription.	Access and session policies require Conditional Access App Control. These policies enable you to restrict and monitor access to cloud apps based on defined criteria. Incorporating these in your design will enable you to automate actions that could prevent unwanted behavior.
Windows Defender for Endpoint integration	Windows Defender for Endpoint subscription Windows 10, version 1809 or later.	Integrating Cloud App Security with Windows Defender for Endpoint enables extended visibility beyond your network and provides machine-based investigation. Consider designing a solution that leverages Windows Defender for Endpoint and automatic log uploads for maximum coverage.
Microsoft Flow	Microsoft Flow subscription.	Integrating Cloud App Security with Microsoft Flow enables administrators to create custom automation and orchestration playbooks based on alerts. This integration can further automate remediation tasks for known threats.

As you design your Cloud App Security solution, identify the cloud apps that you need to prioritize monitoring for and establish a policy structure that meets your needs. For example, if you are using Dropbox Business for file sharing and backups, consider first establishing an app connector for greater visibility into app usage. Next, consider creating the following policies.

- **Activity policy**   Create this policy to monitor for mass file downloads from a single user in a short period of time.
- **File policy**   Create this policy to monitor file sharing behavior in Dropbox with unauthorized domains.
- **Cloud Discovery Anomaly Detection policy**   Create this policy to monitor unusual behavior for all cloud apps.

This policy structure can be used as a starting point, with additional policies being created as you begin receiving alerts. For the exam, expect to see multi-question scenarios that deliver an organization's design and outlines specific requirements. For these scenarios you will need to understand how the various technologies and policies interact.

Plan for application connectors

Cloud App Security supports multiple methods for consuming your data for analysis so that you can monitor and act on it. In this section we cover connected apps as one of these data sources. Cloud applications that offer an Application Programming Interface (API) can be connected to your Cloud App Security instance. This enables greater visibility into user activity and offers additional capabilities for governance.

Plan for Connected Apps

Before you get started with creating Connected Apps in the Cloud App Security portal, there are a few planning considerations that you should be familiar with.

- **Management Account**   As a best practice, plan to create a dedicated Cloud App Security management account for each cloud app that you connect using the API integration.
- **Networking**   Depending on the application, you may need to update your firewall's whitelist to allow connectivity. For an updated list of IP addresses and DNS names, refer to the following link: *https://docs.microsoft.com/cloud-app-security/network-requirements*.
- **Supported Apps**   At the time of this writing, the Cloud App Security portal supports nine Connected apps. These include the following:
    - **Amazon Web Services (AWS)**   There are no additional licensing requirements. For connectivity, create a new user account that has programmatic access in the AWS console.
    - **Box**   This app requires an enterprise license. The connecting account can be either a co-admin or full admin. However, the co-admin role will have limited visibility.

- **Cisco Webex**   This app does not require a license for recent data. To view more data, you must have a Cisco Webex pro license. The connecting account must be an admin.
- **Dropbox**   This app requires a business/enterprise license. The connecting account must be an admin.
- **G Suite**   This app requires an enterprise or unlimited license. The connecting account must be a super admin.
- **Github**   This app uses OAuth authentication to Github Enterprise Cloud.
- **Exchange**   There are no additional licensing requirements. The connecting account must be a global admin.
- **Office 365**   There are no additional licensing requirements. The connecting account must be a global admin.
- **Okta**   This app requires an enterprise license. The connecting account must be an admin.
- **Salesforce**   This app requires a Eureka license or higher. The connecting account must be an admin with the +RestAPI role.
- **ServiceNow**   There are no additional licensing requirements. The connecting account must be an admin.
- **Workday**   This app requires a business/enterprise license. The connecting account must be an admin.

Configure Connected Apps

The process of creating a Connected App will depend largely on the app that you are working with. If you do not have an account available for the supported apps, trial accounts are an option in some cases. This can be useful for testing Connected Apps in a lab environment.

In this section we are going to walk through the process of creating a Connected App. For this example, we will be working with a Dropbox business account for Contoso Electronics. We have an active business license and have created a dedicated admin user account for establishing the connection with Cloud App Security. To create the Connected App, follow these steps:

1. Sign in to the Cloud App Security portal at *https://portal.cloudappsecurity.com*.
2. From the menu bar, click the settings cog and select **App Connectors**.
3. On the Connected Apps page, take a moment to familiarize yourself with the interface. Refer to Figure 2-24 for an example of the Connected Apps page. Note that there are two tabs available. The App connectors tab shows all API connected apps. The Conditional Access App Control apps tab shows all apps connected through Azure AD Conditional Access. Refer back to this page when you need to manage app connectors or troubleshoot connectivity.

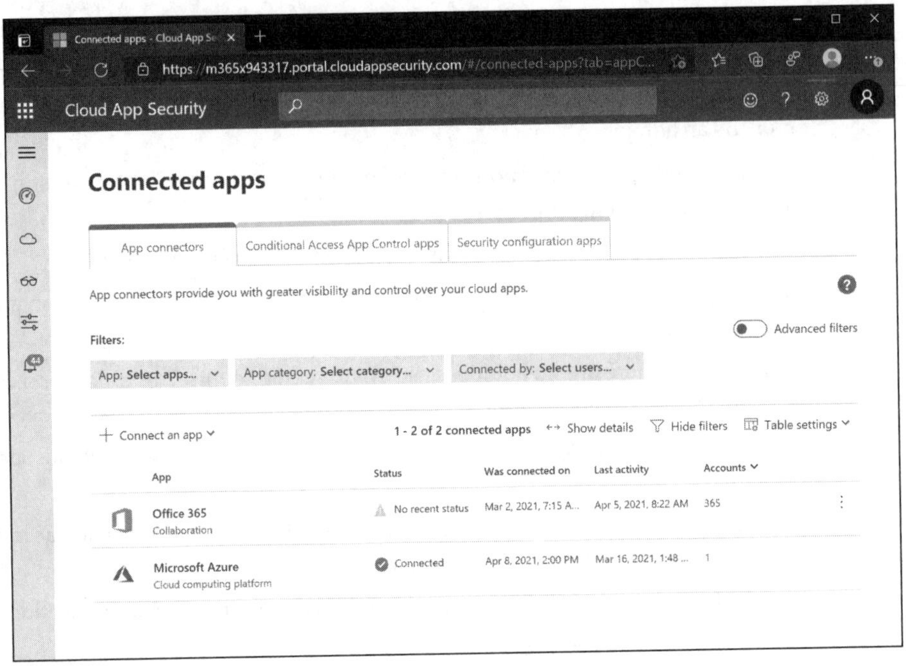

FIGURE 2-24 Connected Apps

4. On the Connected Apps page, click the plus button and select **Dropbox**.

5. On the Dropbox connection page, enter a name for the connected app instance and click **Connect Dropbox**. This name can be changed later from the Connected apps page.

6. On the Dropbox connection page, under Enter Details, enter the email address for the admin Dropbox account.

7. Under Save settings, click **Save Settings** and confirm the operation completes successfully.

8. Under Follow the link, click **Follow This Link**.

9. On the Dropbox sign-in page, enter the credentials for the Dropbox admin account and click **Allow**.

10. After completing the connection, navigate back to the Connected Apps page and locate the new app. Click the app and select **Test Now** to verify the app is connected successfully.

After creating a new Connected App, you will see the app listed on supported policies with additional governance capabilities. If you come across a situation where you need to rename the Connected App instance or update the admin account information, navigate back to the Connected Apps page and click the more options button for the app in question.

> **NOTE** **REMOVING CONNECTED APPS**
>
> At the time of this writing there is no option to remove Connected Apps from the Cloud App Security portal. If you identify an app that you need to remove, you will need to contact support and have them assist you with removing the app.

Configure Cloud App Security policies

Let's examine the available policy types and cover some example scenarios. There are seven types of policies available in the Client App Security portal. These policies enable administrators to define what behavior is acceptable and what is not. Policies can be created to accomplish multiple automated tasks, such as generating email alerts, blocking access to apps, or quarantining suspicious files. Policies are a core component of Cloud App Security and are an important feature that you need to be familiar with for the exam.

Configure access policies

Access policies are the first policy type we are going to work with. An access policy delivers real-time monitoring and control when users log in to your cloud apps. For example, you can create an access policy that generates an alert when a user accesses Office 365 from a non-US location.

Before you begin creating access policies there are some additional prerequisites that you need to consider. These include the following:

- **Licensing**   Access policies have a dependency on Azure AD Conditional Access. You will need an Azure AD Premium P1 subscription to use access policies in Cloud App Security.

- **Conditional Access**   Applications that you want to control with an access policy will need to be referenced in a Conditional Access policy with the option **Use Conditional Access App Control** enabled. The Conditional Access policy also needs to be assigned to a test user so you can complete an initial sign-in for the app to be discovered.

After addressing these prerequisites, you can start creating access policies in the portal. In the following walkthrough we are going to create an access policy that generates an alert when non-domain joined devices access Microsoft Exchange Online.

1.   Sign in to the Cloud App Security portal at: *https://portal.cloudappsecurity.com*.
2.   In the navigation menu, expand **Control** and select **Policies**.
3.   On the Policies page, click **Create Policy** and select **Access Policy**.
4.   On the Create access policy page, fill in the following information:
     - **Policy Name**   Enter a name that clearly identifies the policy. In this example we named our policy Access Monitoring For Non-Domain Joined Devices.
     - **Policy Severity**   Select a severity level for your policy. The policy severity is shown in the portal and can be used to determine if an alert should be generated. In this example we set the severity level to **Medium**.
     - **Category**   Select a category that best describes the policy. This field is for administrative use and can be used as search criteria to isolate policy types. In this example we kept the category set to access control (default).
     - **Activities Matching All Of The Following**   Define your activity filter(s) by selecting the desired conditions that you want the policy to monitor. Refer to Figure 2-25 for an example of the settings we are using.

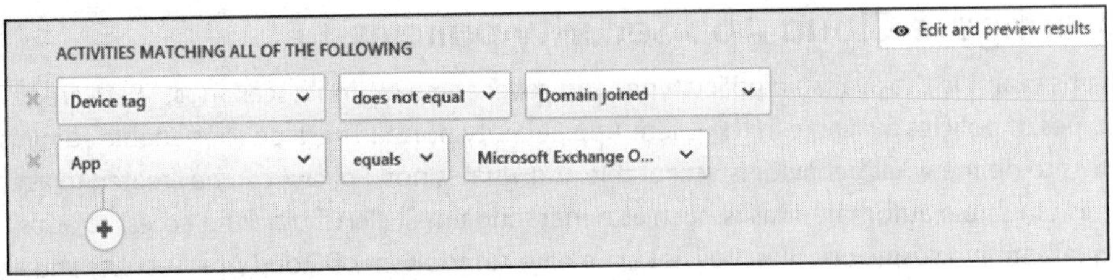

ACTIVITIES MATCHING ALL OF THE FOLLOWING			Edit and preview results
Device tag	does not equal	Domain joined	
App	equals	Microsoft Exchange O...	

FIGURE 2-25 Access Policy - Matching Activities

- **Actions** Select an action you want to take when this policy is triggered. In this example we are selecting **Test**, which will monitor activity but will not block the user from accessing the application.

- **Alerts** Select which alerts you want to occur when this policy is triggered. In this example we are selecting **Create An Alert For Each Matching Event With The Policy's Severity** and **Send Alert As Email**.

5. Click **Create**.

Confirm your new access policy has been created successfully by reviewing the list of policies on the Policy page of the Cloud App Security portal.

Configure activity policies

The next scenario covers working with activity policies. An activity policy leverages the APIs in your cloud applications to collect metadata and generate alerts and actions. For example, you can create an activity policy that monitors user login events. If a user fails to log in successfully multiple times in a row, the policy will generate an alert and notify the user.

In the following walkthrough we will create an activity policy that accomplishes this behavior.

1. Sign in to the Cloud App Security portal at: *https://portal.cloudappsecurity.com*.

2. From the navigation bar on the left, expand **Control** and select **Policies**.

3. On the Policies page, click **Create Policy** and select **Activity Policy**.

4. On the Create Activity Policy page, review the available policy templates by clicking the dropdown under Policy template. Microsoft provides you with a few pre-built templates to help you get started. Select the template **Multiple Failed User Log On Attempts To An App**.

5. Click **Apply Template** when prompted.

6. Review the options defined under Create Filters for the policy. Refer to Figure 2-26 for an example of the selections defined in the template. In this section you can control whether the policy triggers on single events or repeated activity, along with the minimum number of repeats and the timeframe.

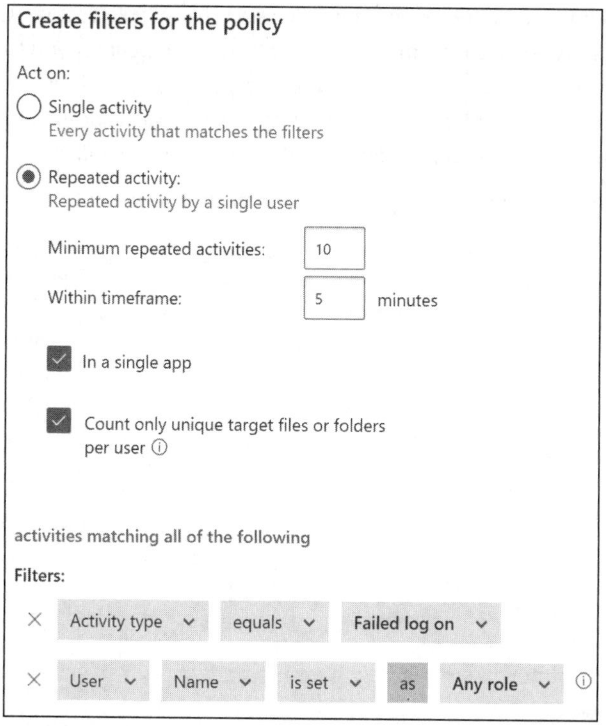

Create filters for the policy

Act on:

○ Single activity
Every activity that matches the filters

● Repeated activity:
Repeated activity by a single user

Minimum repeated activities: `10`

Within timeframe: `5` minutes

☑ In a single app

☑ Count only unique target files or folders per user ⓘ

activities matching all of the following

Filters:

✕ [Activity type ∨] [equals ∨] [Failed log on ∨]

✕ [User ∨] [Name ∨] [is set ∨] [as] [Any role ∨] ⓘ

FIGURE 2-26 Activity Policy - Filters

7. Review the options defined under Alerts. Refer to Figure 2-27 for an example of the selections defined in the template. In this section you can control if an alert is generated, the maximum number of alerts for this policy per day, and what platform to deliver the alert to. Note that Microsoft Flow is available as a preview feature at the time of this writing. Flow enables you to create additional automation when alerts occur.

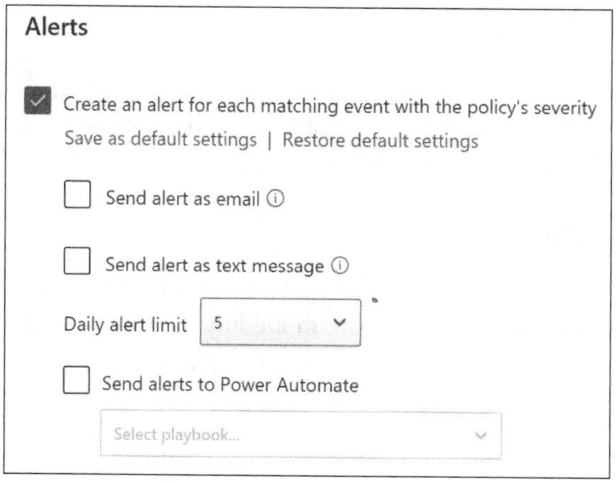

Alerts

☑ Create an alert for each matching event with the policy's severity
Save as default settings | Restore default settings

☐ Send alert as email ⓘ

☐ Send alert as text message ⓘ

Daily alert limit [5 ∨]

☐ Send alerts to Power Automate

[Select playbook... ∨]

FIGURE 2-27 Activity Policy - Alerts

8. Expand the **All Apps** container under Governance. Review the available options. Check the box for **Notify User**. After checking this box, a new field will appear for you to enter a custom notification for this policy. Refer to Figure 2-28 for an example of the selected options. In this section you can control additional actions when an alert occurs, such as notifying the user, suspending the user, or requiring the user to sign in again.

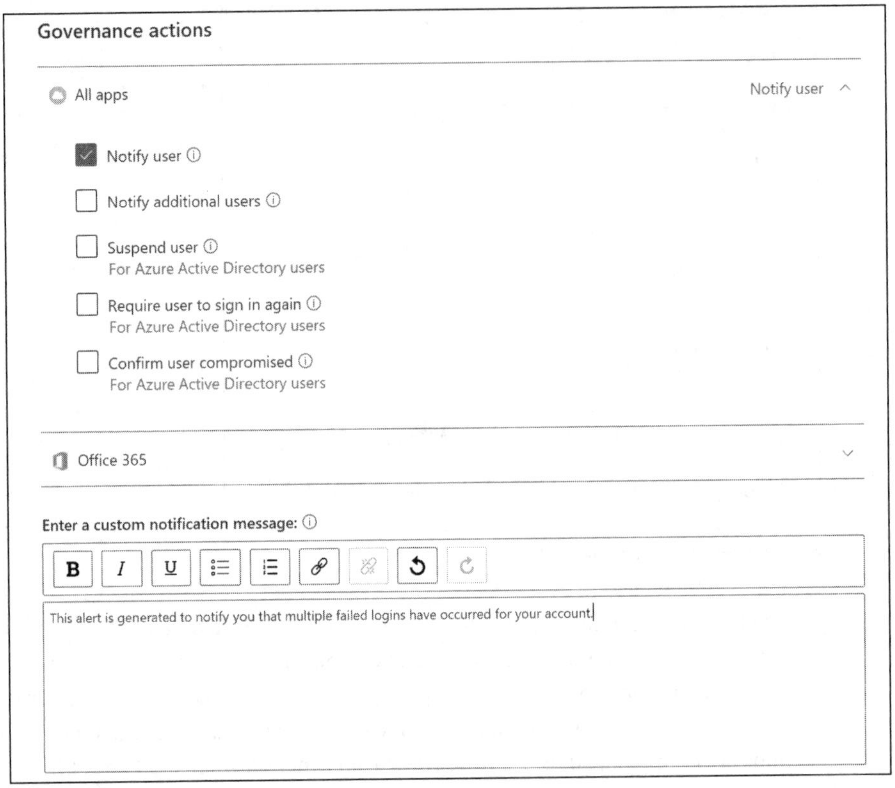

FIGURE 2-28 Activity Policy - Governance

9. Click **Create**.

Confirm your new access policy has been created successfully by reviewing the list of policies on the Policy page of the Cloud App Security portal.

Configure app discovery policies

Next, we are going to work with app discovery policies. An app discovery policy enables you to receive alerts for events such as detecting new applications or identifying risky app behavior. For example, you can create an app discovery policy that generates an alert when a new app is detected across multiple users and has cloud storage capabilities.

In the following walkthrough we will create an app discovery policy that accomplishes this behavior.

1. Sign in to the Cloud App Security portal at: *https://portal.cloudappsecurity.com*.

2. From the navigation bar on the left, expand **Control** and select **Policies**.

3. On the Policies page, click **Create Policy** and select **App Discovery Policy**.

4. On the Create App Discovery policy page, review the available policy templates by clicking the dropdown under Policy template. Microsoft provides you with a few pre-built templates to help you get started. Select the template **New Cloud Storage App**.

5. Click **Apply Template** when prompted.

6. Review the following configuration options.

   - **Apps Matching All Of The Following** Define your app discovery filter(s) by selecting the desired conditions that you want the policy to monitor. Refer to Figure 2-29 for an example of the settings we are using.

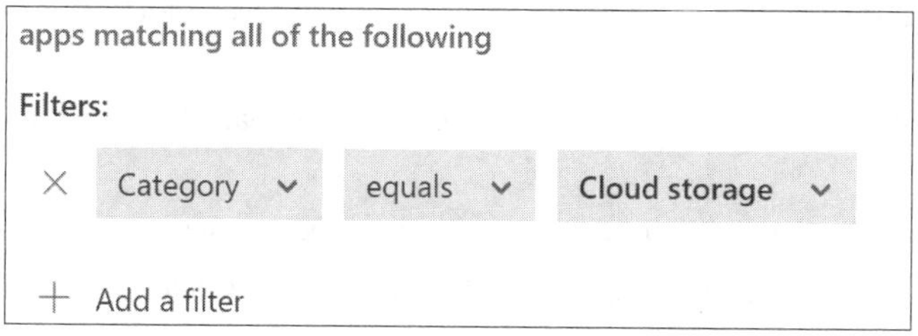

FIGURE 2-29 App Discovery Policy - Matching Activities

   - **Apply To** Select which reports you want the policy to apply to. In this example it will apply to **All Continuous Reports**.

   - **Trigger A Policy Match If All The Following Occur On The Same Day** This setting differs slightly from the previous filter. These conditions must occur on the same day for the policy to trigger. Define your same day criteria by selecting the desired conditions that you want the policy to match on. Refer to Figure 2-30 for an example of the settings we are using.

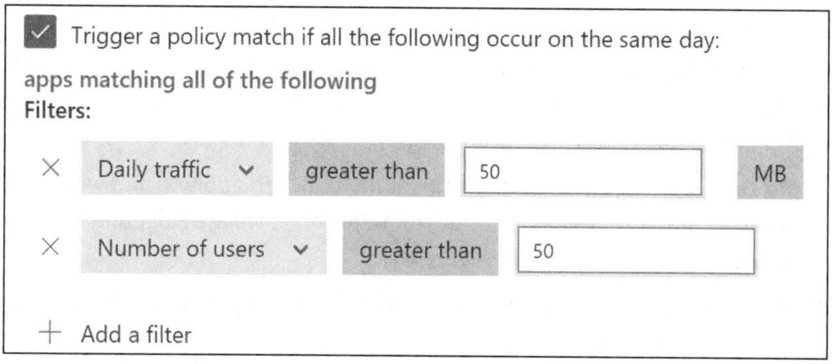

FIGURE 2-30 App Discovery Policy - Matching Activities

- **Alerts** Select which alerts you want to occur when this policy is triggered. In this example we are selecting **Create An Alert For Each Matching Event With The Policy's Severity**.

- **Governance** Select an app tag to apply to the app when this policy triggers. In this example we will leave all options unchecked (default template). If you would like to apply a custom tag you can create new ones by navigating to **Settings**, and **App Tags**.

7. Click **Create**.

Confirm your new app discovery policy has been created successfully by reviewing the list of policies on the Policy page of the Cloud App Security portal.

Configure Cloud Discovery anomaly detection policies

Next, we'll work Cloud Discovery anomaly detection policies. These policies are responsible for detecting unusual activity in application usage as part of the Cloud Discovery process. Cloud Discovery refers to the process of analyzing your network traffic logs. For this example, consider a policy that will generate an alert when suspicious activity is detected for cloud storage apps. Suspicious activity is determined using Microsoft's behavior analysis information. As an administrator, you can adjust the sensitivity of this feature.

In the following walkthrough we will create a Cloud Discovery anomaly detection policy that relates to this scenario.

1. Sign in to the Cloud App Security portal at: *https://portal.cloudappsecurity.com*.

2. From the navigation bar on the left, expand **Control** and select **Policies**.

3. On the Policies page, click **Create Policy** and select **Cloud Discovery Anomaly Detection Policy**.

4. On the Create Cloud Discovery anomaly detection policy page, fill in the following information.

- **Policy Template** Review the list of available templates. In this example we will not be using a template.

- **Policy Name** Enter a name that clearly identifies the policy. In this example we named our policy Monitoring Unusual Activity For Cloud Storage Apps.

- **Description** Enter a description for your policy.

- **Category** The category value cannot be changed from Cloud Discovery.

- **Apps Matching All Of The Following** Define your activity filter(s) by selecting the desired conditions that you want the policy to monitor. Refer to Figure 2-31 for an example of the settings we are using.

- **Apply To** Select which reports you want the policy to apply to and whether you are targeting users, IP addresses, or both. In this example we are Selecting **All Continuous Reports** and **Users And IP Addresses**.

- **Raise Alerts Only For Suspicious Activities Occurring After Date** Enter the current date (default value).

- **Alerts** Adjust the **Select Anomaly Detection Sensitivity** to **4**.

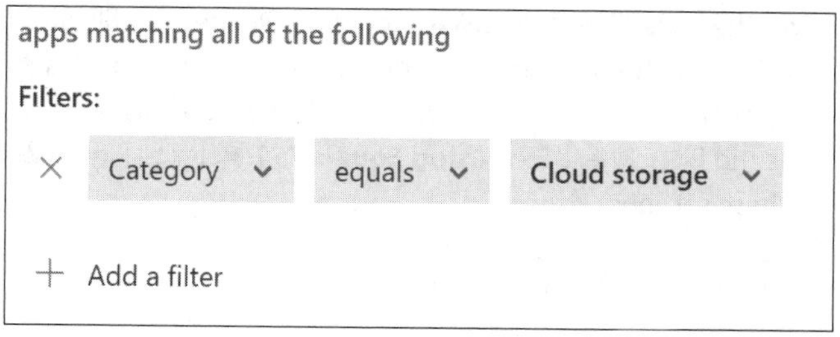

apps matching all of the following

Filters:

✕   Category ∨   equals ∨   Cloud storage ∨

+ Add a filter

FIGURE 2-31   Cloud Discovery Anomaly Detection Policy - Matching Activities

5. Click **Create**.

Confirm your new Cloud Discovery anomaly detection policy has been created successfully by reviewing the list of policies on the Policy page of the Cloud App Security portal.

Configure file policies

Next, we are going to work with file policies. File policies can be configured to scan for specific files or file types in your cloud apps. If detected, you can generate an alert or apply a governance action, such as quarantining the file. For example, you can create a file policy that monitors for Outlook data files (PST) with Microsoft OneDrive. If the policy detects a PST file being shared externally it will generate an alert and quarantine the file. To accomplish this behavior, you must enable two settings in the Cloud App Security portal.

- **File monitoring**   Navigate to **Settings**, then **Files** and confirm that **Enable File Monitoring** is enabled.

- **Quarantine**   Navigate to **Settings** then **Admin Quarantine** and select a folder location.

In the following walkthrough we will create a file policy that monitors PST file types and quarantines them if shared externally.

1. Sign in to the Cloud App Security portal at: *https://portal.cloudappsecurity.com*.
2. From the navigation bar on the left, expand **Control** and select **Policies**.
3. On the Policies page, click **Create Policy** and select **File Policy**.
4. On the Create file policy page, fill in the following information.

   - **Policy Template**   Review the list of available templates. In this example we will not be using a template.
   - **Policy Name**   Enter a name that clearly identifies the policy. In this example we named our policy Monitoring Unauthorized Sharing Of PST Files.
   - **Description**   Enter a description for your policy.
   - **Policy Severity**   Set the severity level to **Medium**.
   - **Category**   Set the category to **DLP**.

- **Create A Filter For The Files This Policy Will Act On**   Define your file filter(s) by selecting the desired conditions that you want the policy to monitor. For this example, create a filter where **Access Level Equals Public (Internet), External, Public**. Create a second filter where **Extension Equals PST**. Refer to Figure 2-32 for an example of these settings.

Create a filter for the files this policy will act on

files matching all of the following

Filters:

| ✕ | Access level ⌄ | equals ⌄ | Public (Internet), External, Public ⌄ |
| ✕ | Extension ⌄ | equals ⌄ | pst | + |

FIGURE 2-32   File Policy - File Type Filter

- **Apply To**   Set apply to **All Files** and **All File Owners**.
- **Inspection Method**   Set to **None**.
- **Alerts**   Check the box to **Create An Alert For Each Matching File** with a daily limit of **5**.
- **Governance**   Expand the application **Microsoft OneDrive for Business** and check the box to **Put In Admin Quarantine**.

5. Click **Create**.

Confirm your new Cloud Discovery anomaly detection policy has been created successfully by reviewing the list of policies on the Policy page of the Cloud App Security portal.

Configure OAuth app policies

Let's take a look at OAuth app policies. Third-party cloud apps that utilize Open Authorization (OAuth) can introduce security risks on a per-user basis. If users accept the terms of the app, they may be granting access to their information without knowing the impact. OAuth app policies can trigger an alert if an unapproved cloud app requires a high level of permissions.

In the following walkthrough we will create an OAuth policy that accomplishes this behavior.

1. Sign in to the Cloud App Security portal at: *https://portal.cloudappsecurity.com*.
2. From the navigation bar on the left, expand **Control** and select **Policies**.
3. On the Policies page, click **Create Policy** and select **OAuth App Policy**.
4. On the Create OAuth app policy page, fill in the following information:
    - **Policy Name**   Enter a name that clearly identifies the policy. In this example we named our policy Monitoring For Unapproved High Permission Apps.
    - **Description**   Enter a description.

- **Policy Severity**   Set the severity to **Medium**.
- **Category**   Set the category to **Threat Detection**.
- **Create Filters For The Policy**   Define your OAuth filter(s) by selecting the desired conditions that you want the policy to monitor. For this example, create a filter where **Permission Level Equals High Severity**. Create a second filter where **App State Does Not Equal Approved**. Refer to Figure 2-33 for an example of these settings.

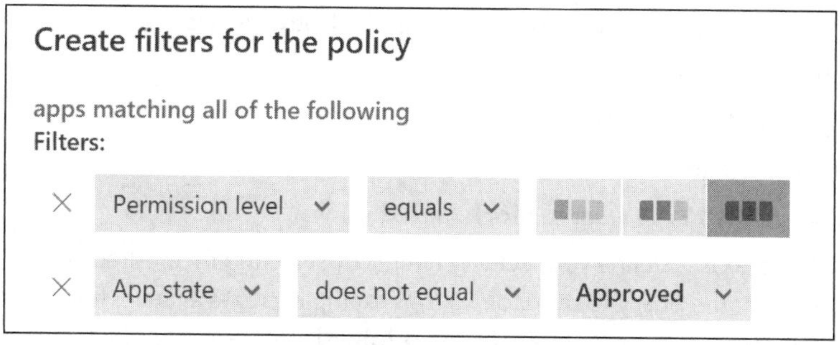

Create filters for the policy

apps matching all of the following
Filters:

✕   Permission level ⌄   equals ⌄   ▮▯▯   ▮▮▯   ▮▮▮

✕   App state ⌄   does not equal ⌄   Approved ⌄

FIGURE 2-33   OAuth Policy - App Filter

- **Alerts**   Check the box to **Create Alert** with a daily limit of **5**.
- **Governance**   Review the list of available apps and options. Leave these with their default options.

5.   Click **Create**.

Confirm your new OAuth policy has been created successfully by reviewing the list of policies on the Policy page of the Cloud App Security portal.

Configure session policies

For our final scenario we will be working with session policies. Session policies have the same prerequisites as access policies. To review, these include the following:

- **Licensing**   Access policies have a dependency on Azure AD Conditional Access. You will need an Azure AD Premium P1 subscription to use access policies in Cloud App Security.

- **Conditional Access**   Applications that you want to control with an access policy will need to be referenced in a Conditional Access policy with the option **Use Conditional Access App Control** enabled. The Conditional Access policy also needs to be assigned to a test user so you can complete an initial sign-in for the app to be discovered.

With these prerequisites in place, a session policy will deliver session-level visibility to your cloud apps, enabling you to monitor the session or block specific activities within the session. For example, you can monitor for sessions accessing Exchange Online from untrusted devices. If a session is found, you can block the user from printing.

In the following walkthrough we will create a session policy that accomplishes this behavior.

1. Sign in to the Cloud App Security portal at: *https://portal.cloudappsecurity.com*.

2. From the navigation bar on the left, mouseover **Control** and select **Policies**.

3. On the Policies page, click **Create Policy** and select **Session Policy**.

4. On the **Create Session** policy page, fill in the following information:

   - **Policy name**   Enter a name that clearly identifies the policy. In this example we named our policy Block Print From Exchange On Untrusted Devices.

   - **Description**   Enter a description.

   - **Policy Severity**   Set to **Medium**.

   - **Category**   Set to **DLP**.

   - **Session Control Type**   Set to **Block Activities**.

   - **Activity Source**   Define your activity filter(s) by selecting the desired conditions that you want the policy to monitor. For this example, create a filter where **Device Tag Does Not Equal Compliant, Domain Joined**. Create a second filter where **App Equals Microsoft Exchange Online**. Create a third filter where **Activity Type Equals Print**. Refer to Figure 2-34 for an example of these settings.

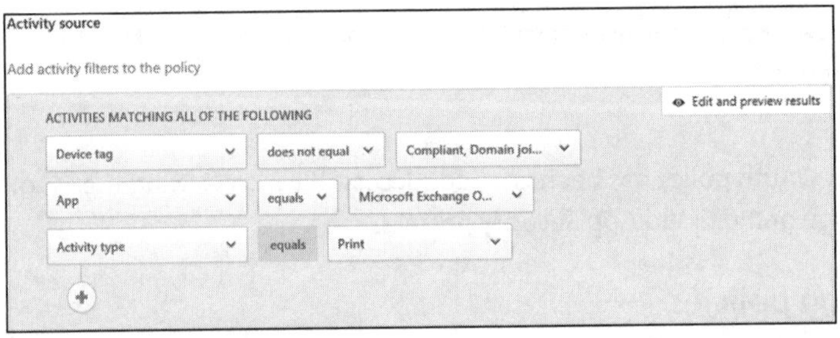

FIGURE 2-34   Session policy filter

   - **Actions**   Set to **Block**. Check the box to **Create An Alert For Each Matching Event With The Policy's Severity**.

5. Click **Create**.

Confirm your new session policy has been created successfully by reviewing the list of policies on the Policy page of the Cloud App Security portal.

EXAM TIP

After completing this skill section, take time to explore each of the available policies in the portal. Plan for exam items that present you with a scenario and ask which type of policy you need to deliver the desired outcome. Most policies are unique in behavior. Access policies and session policies have some similarities. Be sure to understand the different capabilities between these two. An access policy can block access to an app. A session policy can monitor access, block access to specific activities, or block access entirely.

Review and respond to Cloud App Security alerts

Cloud App Security is a solution designed to keep you informed about your organization's usage of cloud apps. Unusual behavior or possible security risks will generate alerts in the portal. As you establish your policy design, you will find that managing these alerts is an important task and something that you will be working on regularly. Your goal should be to understand why the alert is being generated. Then you can determine if it is a true concern or a sign that one of your policies needs to be reworked. In this section we will be looking at the alerts page in the portal and how to interpret and manage this information.

Manage Cloud App Security alerts

To begin managing your alerts, you can access the alerts page by clicking **Alerts** in the left navigation bar. You can also refer to the alert icon in the navigation bar for an at-a-glance count of any pending alerts that need attention. The number will remain over the icon until the alerts are dismissed or resolved.

In Figure 2-35 you can see an example of the alerts page in the Cloud App Security portal. In this example there are six pending alerts that need attention. From this interface you can manage your alerts and investigate issues.

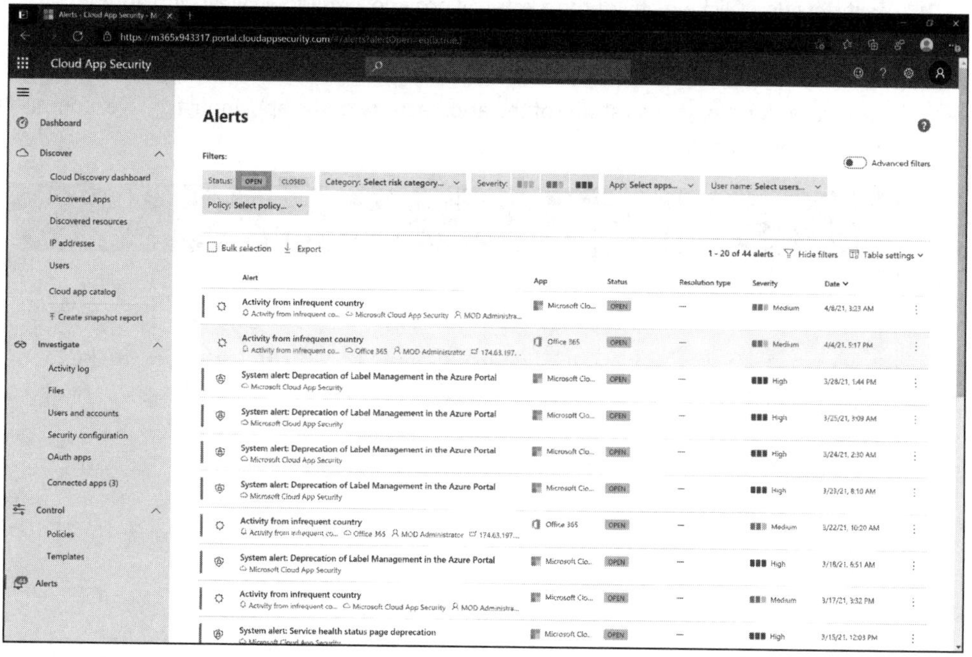

FIGURE 2-35 Cloud App Security - Alerts

The alerts page includes the following capabilities:

- **Filters** The filter bar at the top of the page includes multiple properties that you can use to narrow down the number of alerts you are viewing. These properties include: resolution status, category, severity, app, and user name. These controls are helpful when you start receiving alerts in high volume. For example, filtering on high severity alerts first is useful for addressing major issues quickly.

- **Bulk selection** On the Alerts table, the checkbox in the upper-left corner enables you to bulk select alerts for action. You can select all alerts, all alerts on the current page, or deselect alerts. This is helpful if you need to resolve or dismiss several alerts in one step.

- **Export** On the alerts table, the download icon in the upper-right corner enables you to export all alerts to a CSV file. This is helpful for offline review or sharing alerts with users that do not have access to the portal.

- **Dismiss/Resolve** Each alert has a More Options button to the far right. This button gives you the option to dismiss or resolve an alert individually. Alerts that are of little value can be dismissed. Alerts that have been worked on and resolved can be marked as resolved. Both actions will prompt you with a comment window to provide input as to why you are dismissing or resolving the alert.

- **Alert details** Clicking any of the alerts will provide a drilldown view with additional information about the discovered app. In Figure 2-36 you can see an example of the expanded view of an alert for the administatrive user account. The expanded view provides scores for the general status of the app, security of the app, industry-level compliance, and legal regulations.

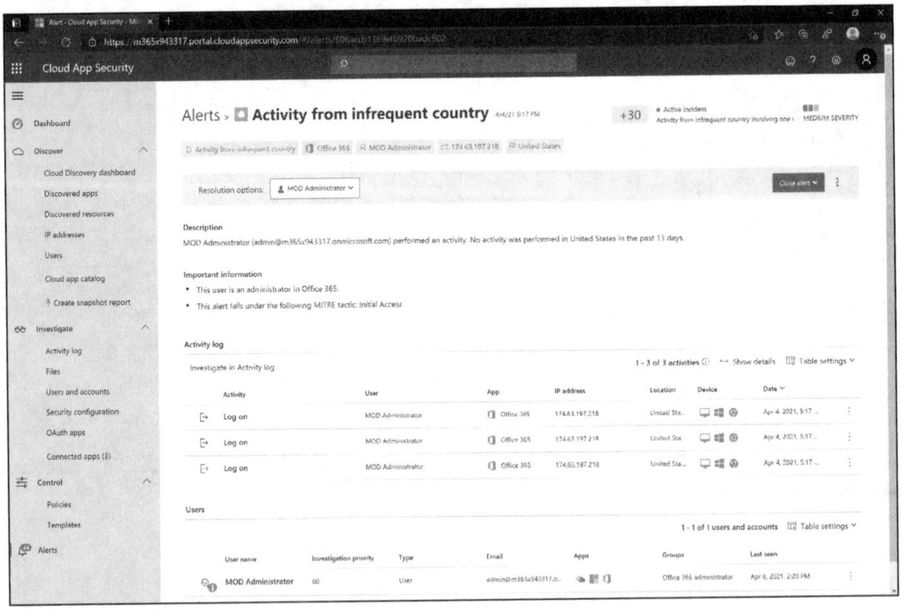

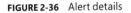

FIGURE 2-36 Alert details

Monitor for unauthorized cloud applications

The network appliances in your organization generate traffic logs that Cloud App Security can import. These traffic logs contain important information about your network and the cloud applications running in your environment. These logs can reveal suspicious events, security risks, shadow IT incidents, and much more. Once uploaded, this information can be analyzed and presented back to you in the portal for further investigation and action. In this section we are going to review the different methods available for uploading traffic logs to the Cloud App Security portal.

Managing traffic logs

There are two methods available for uploading logs to your Cloud App Security instance. The first method is accomplished through the snapshot reports feature. This feature is useful in situations where you need to review events that occurred on an isolated network where automatic uploads are not available, or at an earlier date in time.

The second method for uploading logs is through the automatic log upload feature. Automatic log upload enables you to configure a source server where Cloud App Security can connect and retrieve logs automatically. This feature is useful on networks where you need continuous monitoring and have approval from your cyber security partners to enable automatic uploads.

SNAPSHOT REPORTS

The snapshot reports feature is accessed by navigating to the **Cloud Discovery dashboard** page. From this page you can see all previous uploads and access the report data associated with each upload. In Figure 2-37 you can see an example of a snapshot report generated by uploading a static traffic log taken from a firewall.

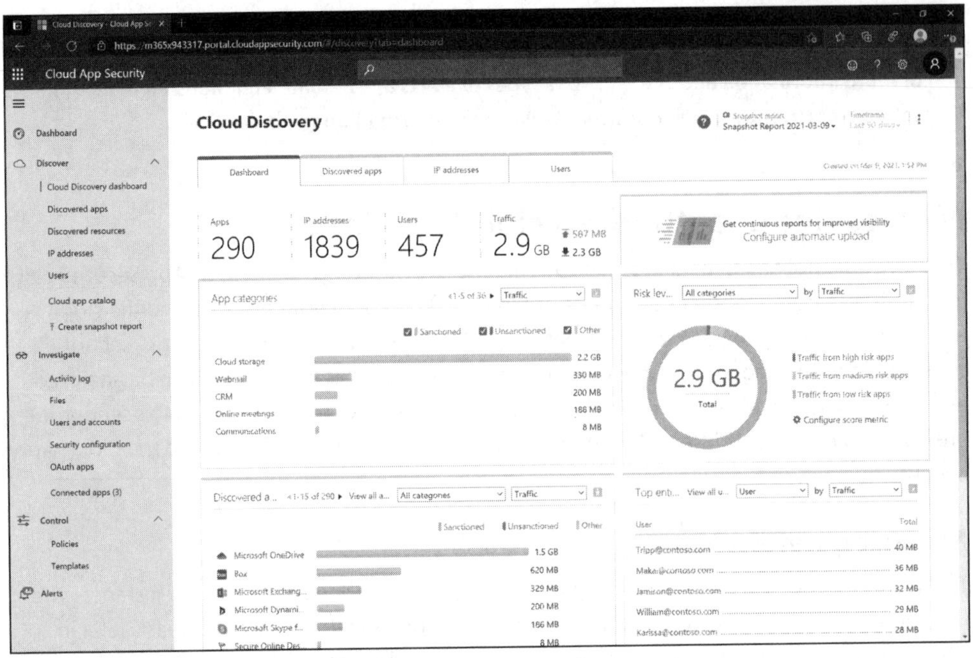

FIGURE 2-37 Cloud App Security - Snapshot Report

To upload a traffic log capture through the snapshot report interface, follow these steps:

1. Sign in to the Cloud App Security portal at: *https://portal.cloudappsecurity.com*.

2. From the navigation menu, expand Discover, and then click Cloud Discovery dashboard.

3. Click the elipses for the report, and then click **Create Cloud Discovery Snapshot Report**.

4. On the Create new Cloud Discovery snapshot report page, fill in the following information:

   - **Report Name**   Enter a name that clearly identifies the snapshot you are creating. In this example we named the snapshot report Cisco ASA Capture From November 2018.

   - **Description**   Enter a description for the snapshot report.

   - **Data Source**   Select the source appliance that you will be uploading your logs from. In this example we will be uploading logs from a **Cisco ASA Firewall**. After selecting the data source, you may see some additional notifications appear, as shown in Figure 2-38. In this example the tool is providing a link to verify the logs are formatted correctly. There is also a note that the Cisco ASA data source only contains partial information, with links for more information and alternative formats.

   - **Anonymize Private Information**   Leave this option unchecked for this example.

   - **Choose Traffic Logs**   Browse to the logs that you are going to upload and select them.

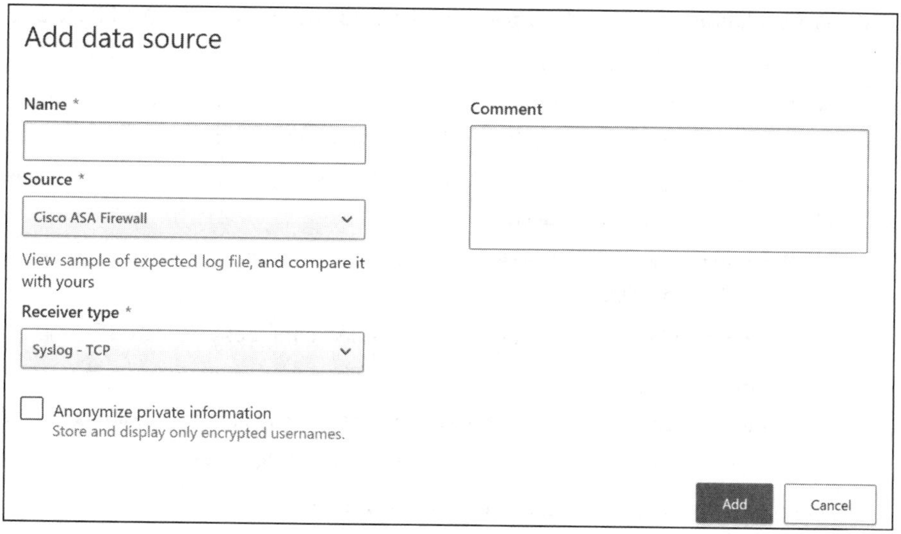

Add data source

Name *

Source *

Cisco ASA Firewall   ⌄

View sample of expected log file, and compare it with yours

Receiver type *

Syslog - TCP   ⌄

☐ Anonymize private information
   Store and display only encrypted usernames.

Comment

[Add]   [Cancel]

FIGURE 2-38   Snapshot Reports - Data Upload

5. Click **Create**.

Once uploaded, the logs will be processed and analyzed. Once complete you will receive a notification in the portal and the snapshot report will be available for viewing.

AUTOMATIC LOG UPLOAD

The automatic log upload feature is accessed by clicking the elipses and selecting **Configure Automatic Upload**. On this page there are two tabs available. The Data Sources tab is where you will manage your data sources, including the appliance that you are uploading logs from and the receiver, such as FTP or Syslog. The Log Collectors tab is where you will manage your log collector connections. A log collector runs as a Docker container. The log collector runs on your network, collecting logs from your firewall and/or proxy, processing them, compressing them, and uploading them to the Cloud App Security portal.

> **NEED MORE REVIEW?   DEPLOYING A LOG COLLECTOR**
>
> For more information about deploying a log collector in your environment, visit *https://docs.microsoft.com/cloud-app-security/discovery-docker*.

To configure automatic log upload in the Cloud App Security portal we will begin by creating the data source. Follow these steps to create a new data source:

1. Sign in to the Cloud App Security portal at: *https://portal.cloudappsecurity.com*.

2. From the menu bar, click the settings cog and select **Settings**.

3. On the Settings page, select **Automatic Log Upload**.

4. On the Automatic Log Upload page, on the Data Sources tab, click **Add Data Source**.

5. Fill in the following information:

   ■ **Name**   Enter a name representing the data source and receiver type. In this example we will enter **CheckPointSmartView-SyslogTLS**.

   ■ **Source**   Select the data source for your logs. In this example we will select **Check Point - SmartView Tracker**.

   ■ **Receiver Type**   Select the receiver type for the log source. In this example we will select **Syslog - TLS**.

   ■ **Anonymize Private Information**   We will leave this box unchecked for this example.

6. Click **Add**.

Our next step is to add the log collector. Follow these steps to add a new log collector:

1. On the Automatic Log Upload page, select the **Log Collectors** tab.

2. On the Log Collectors tab, click **Add Log Collector**.

3. On the Create Log Collector page, fill in the following information:

   ■ **Name**   Enter a name representing the log collector. In this example we will enter **ASH-LogCollector**.

   ■ **Host IP Address Or FQDN**   Enter the IP address or FQDN for the host machine that will be running the log collector.

   ■ **Data Source(s)**   Select the new data source that we created for our Check Point firewall.

4. Click **Update**.

After adding the log collector, follow the steps included on the creation page to deploy the log collector and configure it for automatic upload. Refer to Figure 2-39 for an example of the deployment instructions.

FIGURE 2-39   Create Log Collector

Once your log collector is deployed, traffic logs will start being processed and uploaded automatically into your Cloud App Security instance. If you need to edit or delete a data source or log collector, navigate back to the Automatic Log Upload page and click the More Options button for the corresponding item you need to update.

Thought experiment

In this thought experiment, demonstrate your skills and knowledge of the topics covered in this chapter. You can find the answer to this thought experiment in the next section.

You are an IT administrator for Contoso Electronics, supporting 1,500 users across the United States, Europe, and Japan. Contoso Electronics has two on-premises data centers. Most of their IT infrastructure resides in the data centers. The company recently adopted a "cloud first" strategy and has been aggressively looking to expand their cloud presence. The users you support are running laptops with Windows 10, version 1809. The company recently adopted Office 365 and is working toward cloud-based solutions for their applications and services to improve the capabilities of their workforce. Today you know several users are using non-approved cloud apps for collaboration and file sharing. Your information security department would like to start exploring Microsoft Cloud App Security as a solution for monitoring and addressing security risks within Contoso Electronics. Your manager has requested that you lead the effort. You need to address the following items:

1. Your organization has an Office 365 Business Premium subscription. You need the full capabilities of Microsoft Cloud App Security. What additional licensing do you need to deploy Cloud App Security?

2. Your organization has two domains, one for the point-of-sale devices and one for general employees. How do you add these domains to your Cloud App Security portal so all devices on the network are shown as internal?

3. You are still waiting for approval to deploy a log collector on your network. What other method can you use to upload traffic logs for analysis?

4. You want to create a policy that will generate an alert when a single user performs an unusual number of downloads in a short period of time. What type of policy should you apply?

5. You are preparing to deploy an access policy for Microsoft Exchange Online. What prerequisites do you need to address before you can complete this task?

Separately, a new project from the management team is to deploy cloud-based solutions whenever they meet the project requirements. The project has a code name of "Sky High." As part of the project, the company decides to enhance the security of the environment in two ways:

- **Reduce and or eliminate phishing** The company has had problems with phishing in the past. The company identified two key requirements: protecting specific individuals (such as high-ranking executives) and notifying users about potential phishing emails in Outlook.

- **Be notified about pass-the-hash and pass-the-ticket activity** The company has heard about the danger of pass-the-hash and pass-the-ticket and wants to be notified about activity as soon as it occurs.

You need to choose solutions for the Microsoft Cloud App Security project and to address the company's goals of enhancing their security. What should you do?

Thought experiment answers

This section contains the solution to the thought experiment. Each answer explains why the answer choice is correct.

1. You will need to procure Cloud App Security licenses, obtainable through an EMS E5 subscription.

2. These domains can be added to the Cloud App Security portal by navigating to the **Settings** page and selecting **Organization** details. Enter your domains in the **Managed** domains field.

3. You can do a static log upload through snapshot reports. To complete this task, navigate to the Settings page and select Snapshot reports. Create a new snapshot report, select the matching data source, and upload the corresponding log files in the verified format.

4. You can create an activity policy to achieve this behavior. You can also use the built-in policy template: Mass Download By A Single User.

5. You will need an active Azure AD Premium P1 subscription to support Conditional Access policies. Then you will need to create a Conditional Access policy for Microsoft Exchange Online that has Use Conditional Access App Control enabled.

For the "Sky High" project, you need two solutions: one solution to address phishing and the other to address pass-the-hash and pass-the-ticket. To address phishing, you should implement anti-phishing, which comes with Office 365 E5 or the Office 365 add-on for other enterprise subscriptions. Potentially, use the anti-phishing capabilities of Office 365, although that would reduce the features. One key feature that would be missing is the ability to add specific users to protect (and this is something the company wants to use). For the pass-the-hash and pass-the-ticket solution, you could implement Microsoft Defender for Identity. Both would notify you about pass-the-hash and pass-the-ticket.

Chapter summary

- You should have a good understanding on how to navigate the various configuration settings in the Cloud App Security portal. Remember that there is a search field at the top of the settings page. This is helpful as you explore the various settings. Keep in mind that some settings are specific to certain elements in the portal. For example, file policies will require that you enable file monitoring.

- You should have a good understanding of each Cloud App Security policy type, what purpose they serve, and how to create them.

- You should be familiar with how Cloud App Security operates and what benefits it delivers to an organization.

- You should be familiar with how to navigate alerts in the Cloud App Security portal and how to dismiss or resolve alerts based on your findings.

- There are different data upload options available in the Cloud App Security portal, such as using a snapshot versus continues uploads. You should be familiar with setting up a data source and log collector in the Cloud App Security portal, providing continuous log uploads.

- Defender for Identity is a cloud-based threat protection solution for your on-premises domain controllers.

- Defender for Identity integrates with other key technologies including Azure Security Center, Windows Defender for Endpoint, VPN solutions, and SIEM solutions (or syslog servers). Integrating with these other technologies enhances detection capabilities.

- Office 365 has built-in anti-phishing protection. For additional anti-phishing features, you need to deploy additional custom policies which offer more granular control and additional settings.

- Office 365 has built-in anti-spam protection. There is a myriad of anti-spam settings to control how aggressive the anti-spam protection is, what happens when spam is detected, and how users are notified about spam or potentially malicious messages.

- Office 365 provides multiple policies to combat spam. Each policy has a role in the overall protection. There is an anti-spam policy (where you find most of the anti-spam settings), a connection filter policy (to whitelist or blacklist IPs), an outbound spam filter policy (only for outbound email messages), and a spoof intelligence policy (which you can use to decide what to do in a situation where a user or domain was spoofed).

- You should test your anti-malware protection by using the EICAR.TXT file and sending it through email. EICAR.TXT should be picked up as malware although it is benign. The primary purpose of testing is to validate the notifications and end user experience, in addition to the protection itself.

- Office 365 includes built-in protection against phishing. You can extend that by creating your own anti-phishing policies.

- Office 365 Threat Intelligence, included with Office 365 Enterprise E5, provides additional tools to help secure your environment. Three key tools in Threat Intelligence are attack simulators for credential harvesting, attachments, and malware links.

- To troubleshoot email messages that might have been flagged as spam or as malware, you can use the Message Trace tool. The Message Trace tool can help you find out if an email message was dropped and will also tell you why it was dropped.

- You can configure Defender solutions to notify you via email about suspicious activities. Optionally, you can integrate these solutions with your SIEM solution and have your SIEM solution notify you instead. This is helpful if you want to have a single place for all IT alerts.

- You need to have Windows 10 Education or Enterprise E3 or E5 to obtain Windows Defender for Endpoint for your Windows 10 devices.

- All Windows Defender clients must be able to communicate with the service URLs over port 80 and port 443. Use of a proxy server is supported.

- You can configure your SIEM solution to get alerts from Windows Defender Security Center through a REST API.

- For enterprise environments, you should use role-based access permissions. This enables you to adhere to the principle of least privilege, which ensures that administrators only have the minimum permissions needed to do their jobs.

- If you want to ensure you have reporting when onboarding clients, use Intune or ConfigMgr for the onboarding process. Both have built-in reporting. Avoid Group Policy and scripts if reporting is required.

- Offboarding clients is like onboarding clients. You deploy an offboarding package through your preferred software distribution method. Data remains available for 6 months after onboarding.

- Windows Defender Antivirus (Windows Defender AV) is a built-in anti-malware solution that provides real-time protection, cloud-delivered protection, and automatic sample submission.

- You should be familiar with the Alerts dashboard, how to pin tiles to the home page, and how to navigate the drilldown reports.

- You should be familiar with the default alert policies and what events they alert on.

- You should be familiar with creating custom alert policies and what controls are available.

Manage Microsoft 365 governance and compliance

This chapter looks at the key technologies for governance and compliance in Office 365. When you complete this chapter, you should have a good understanding of which technologies are suitable based on a given scenario with specific requirements. You should also have a firm grasp of environment prerequisites, integration with other technologies, and common configurations. Although this chapter focuses on five key tools, you should familiarize yourself with complementary technologies to help solidify your knowledge for this area of the exam.

Skills covered in this chapter:

- 3.1: Plan for compliance requirements
- 3.2: Manage information governance
- 3.3: Implement Azure Information Protection
- 3.4: Plan and implement data loss prevention (DLP)
- 3.5: Manage search and investigation

Skill 3.1: Plan for compliance requirements

This section looks at built-in data-governance features in Office 365.

> **This skill covers how to:**
> - Plan compliance solutions
> - Assess compliance
> - Plan for legislative and regional or industry requirements and drive implementation

Plan compliance solutions

Microsoft 365 includes several services and features to help organizations achieve compliance and regulatory goals. Many of the features covered in the MS-101 exam, and included in this chapter, help you plan aspects of an overall compliance solution. You can manage many of these solutions through the Microsoft 365 compliance center at *https://compliance.microsoft.com*.

Key considerations of any compliance solution include managing the following:

- Insider risk
- Information protection
- Information governance
- eDiscovery
- Holds
- Auditing and alert policies
- Risks

You can use various Microsoft 365 features discussed in earlier chapters, such as the Secure Score, to gauge your organization's overall security and compliance posture. But one tool that brings all these features together, in terms of compliance, is the Microsoft 365 solution catalog.

The solution catalog is a one-stop location that contains information cards for compliance solutions like information protection, governance, insider risk management, discovery, and response. (See Figure 3-1.)

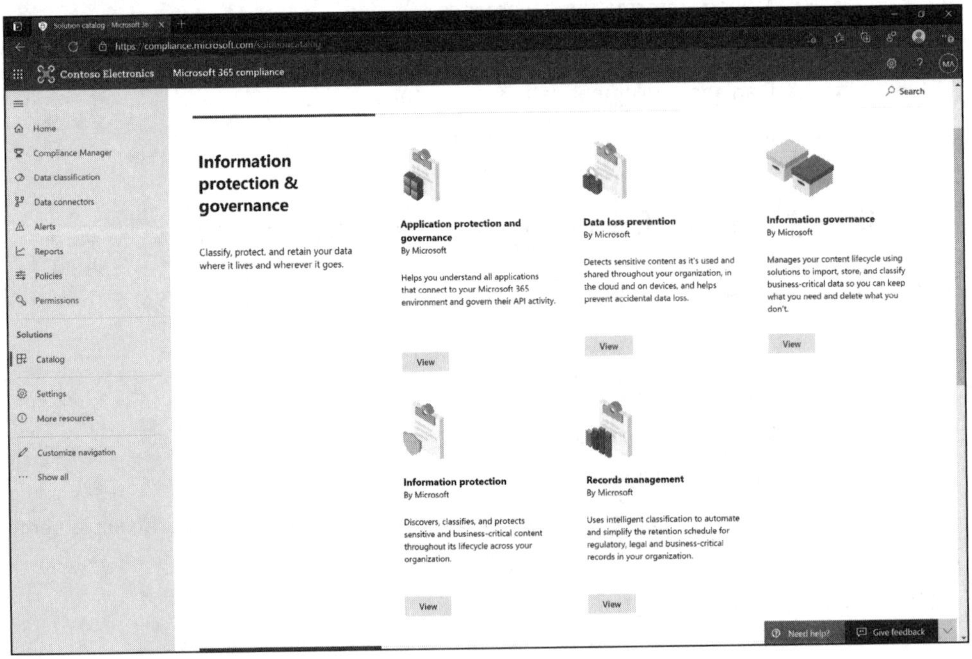

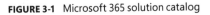

FIGURE 3-1 Microsoft 365 solution catalog

To access the solution catalog, click **Catalog** in the Microsoft 365 compliance center navigation bar on the left. To view the solution catalog, you must have one of the following roles assigned to your user account:

- Global administrator
- Compliance administrator
- Compliance data administrator

Assess compliance

The primary tool to assess compliance information for the Microsoft 365 tenant is the **Compliance Manager**. To access this tool, click **Compliance Manager** in the Microsoft 365 compliance center navigation bar. The Compliance Manager is similar to the Secure Score tool in that it has the following components:

- Compliance score
- Improvement actions
- Solutions
- Assessments
- Assessment templates

The compliance score and improvement actions work the same way the Secure Score does. The score is a representation of how many points the tenant configuration has relative to the compliance goals. The improvement actions are recommended changes that would increase the score.

To view the compliance score for your tenant, follow these steps:

1. Log in to the Microsoft 365 compliance center at *https://compliance.microsoft.com*.
2. In the navigation bar on the left, click **Compliance Manager**.
3. On the **Compliance Manager** page, review the overall compliance score. Figure 3-2 shows the compliance score for Contoso Electronics.

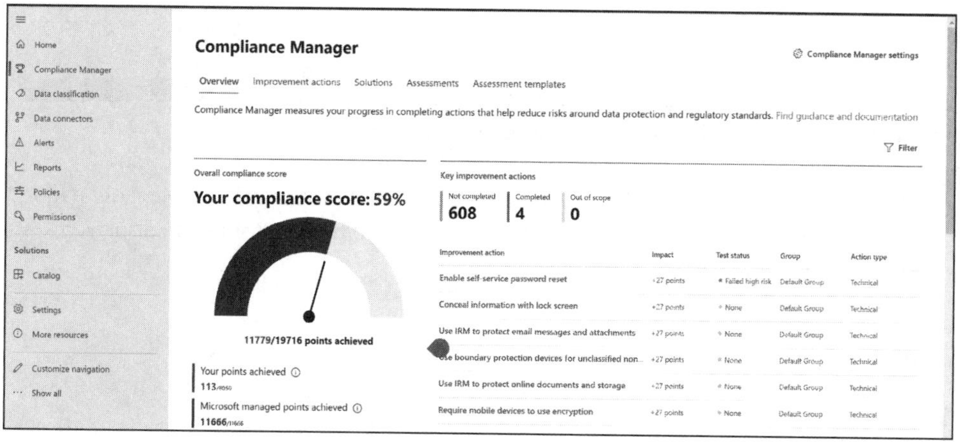

FIGURE 3-2 Microsoft 365 compliance score

The Compliance Manager page's Overview tab also breaks down the compliance score into different categories. (See Figure 3-3.) These include the following:

- Protect information
- Govern information
- Control access
- Manage devices
- Protect against threats
- Discover and respond
- Manage internal risks
- Manage compliance

Figure 3-3 shows the different categories with the score breakdown.

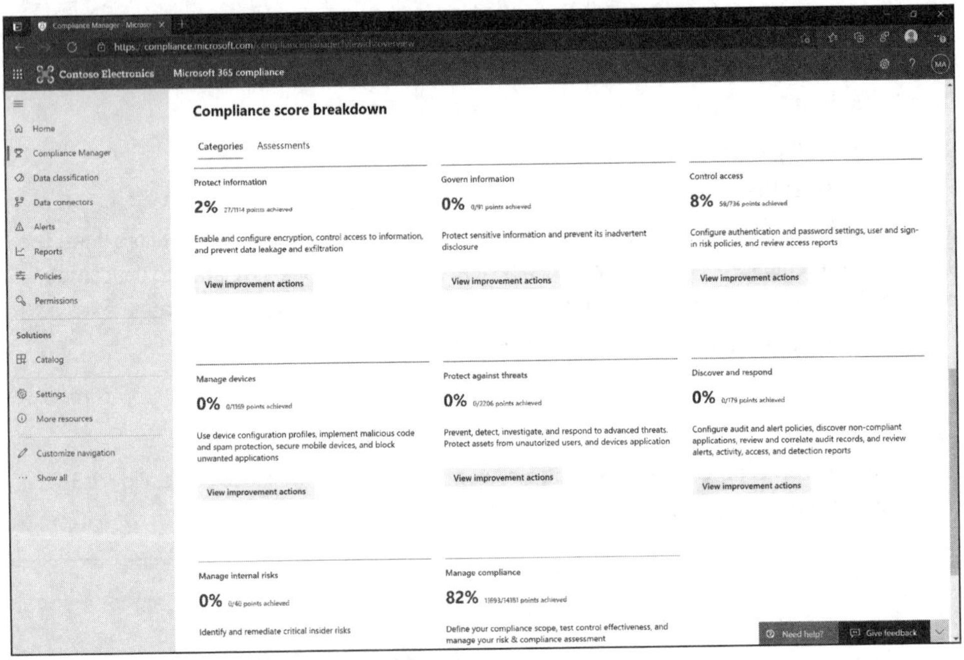

FIGURE 3-3 Microsoft 365 compliance score category breakdown

As with the Secure Score, the Improvement Actions tab of the Compliance Manager page shows actions you can take to improve compliance. The columns of information displayed are slightly different, however. They include the following:

- Points Achieved
- Regulations
- Solutions
- Assessments

- Test Status
- Action Type

Solutions as they relate to Compliance Manager are groupings of settings—not to be confused with categories, which are different—that relate to a solution. So the Solutions tab on the Compliance Manager page lists solution types and their current and potential compliance score. The built-in solutions include the following:

- Audit
- Azure
- Azure Active Directory
- Azure Information Protection
- Azure Security Center
- Cloud App Security
- Communication compliance
- Data classification
- Data loss prevention
- eDiscovery
- Exchange Online protection
- Information governance
- Insider risk management
- Intune
- Microsoft 365 Admin Center
- Microsoft Defender for Endpoint
- Microsoft Defender for Identity
- Microsoft Defender for Office 365
- Microsoft Information Protection
- Microsoft Teams
- OneDrive for Business
- Records management
- Compliance Center
- SharePoint
- Windows 10

With all these different solutions and the individual configurations that can be made in each area, there is a massive 19,716 possible points available. By default, Compliance Manager calculates your points by peering into these other solutions and capturing the current configuration.

You can change these settings by clicking the **Compliance Manager Settings** link in the upper-right corner of any **Compliance Manager** page, selecting either the **Turn On Per**

Improvement Action option button or the **Turn Off for All Improvement Actions** option button on the **Automated Testing** page, and clicking **Save**. Figure 3-4 shows the default settings for automatically collecting data about the tenant.

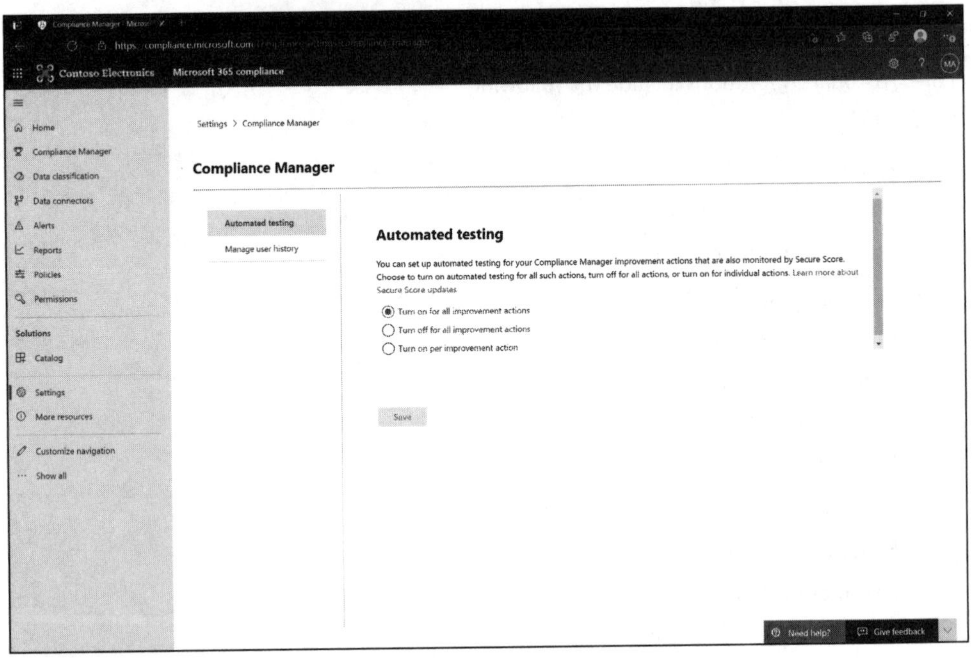

FIGURE 3-4 Microsoft 365 Compliance Manager settings

Plan for legislative and regional or industry requirements and drive implementation

The best way to plan for legislative, regional, and specific industry compliance requirements is to either use various built-in assessments or create a custom assessment for your specific organization. As of this writing, Compliance Manager offers more than 300 assessment templates. (Obviously, we won't look at every type of requirement or assessment here.)

Most organizations, depending on the type of license they have, will have access to the following assessment templates:

- Data Protection Baseline
- EU GDPR
- NIST 8 – 53 rev.4
- NIST 8 – 53 rev.5
- ISO 27001:2013

The other built-in templates must be purchased and renewed each year.

To use an assessment template, follow these steps:

1. Log in to the Microsoft 365 compliance center at *https://compliance.microsoft.com*.

2. In the navigation bar, click **Compliance Manager**.

3. On the **Compliance Manager** page, click the **Assessments** tab.

4. On the **Assessments** tab, click **Add Assessment**.

5. In the Create Assessment wizard's **Select a Template** page, click the assessment template you want to use—in this example, the **EU GDPR** template (see Figure 3-5)—and click **Next**.

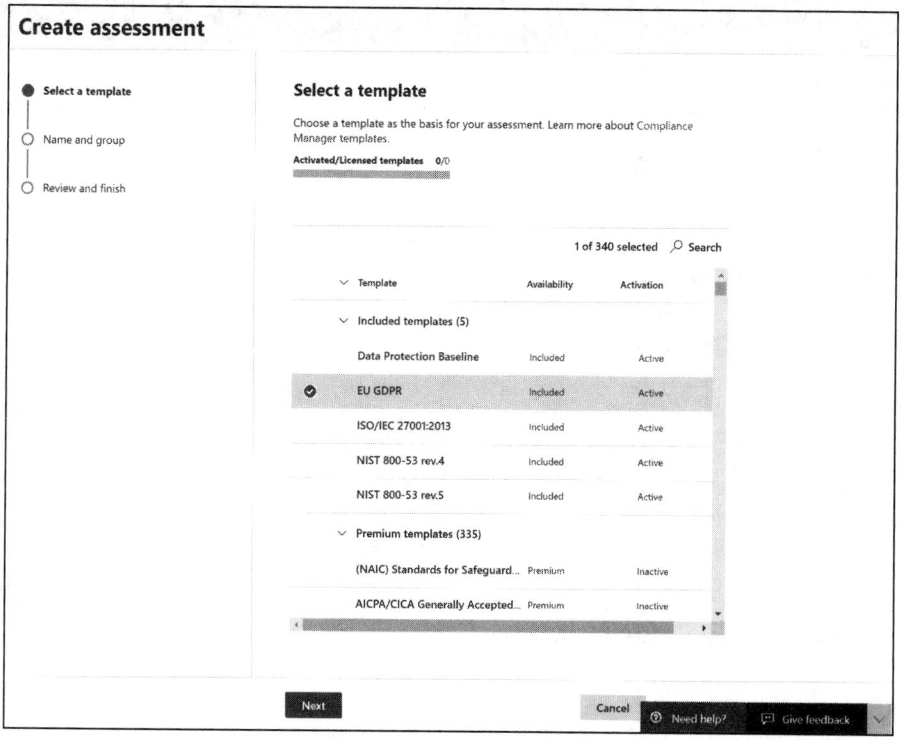

FIGURE 3-5 The Select a Template page of the Create Assessment wizard

6. On the **Name and Group** page, type a name for your assessment in the **Assessment Name** box.

7. To assign your assessment to a group, select **Use Existing Group**. Then select **Default Group** from the drop-down menu and click **Next**.

8. On the **Review and Finish** page, click **Create Assessment**.

9. Click **Done**.

After the assessment is created, your browser will display the progress of the assessment, a list of improvement actions, and the group of controls that relate to the compliance type you selected. (See Figure 3-6.) You can use this information to guide you in making any required changes in your organization. When you're finished, click the **Generate Report** button on the assessment to create and download an Excel spreadsheet that contains a line-by-line report of the current status of the environment as it relates to the selected compliance. For example, the Excel report created with regard to EU GDPR compliance is approximately 600 lines of individual technical, operational, and documentation requirements.

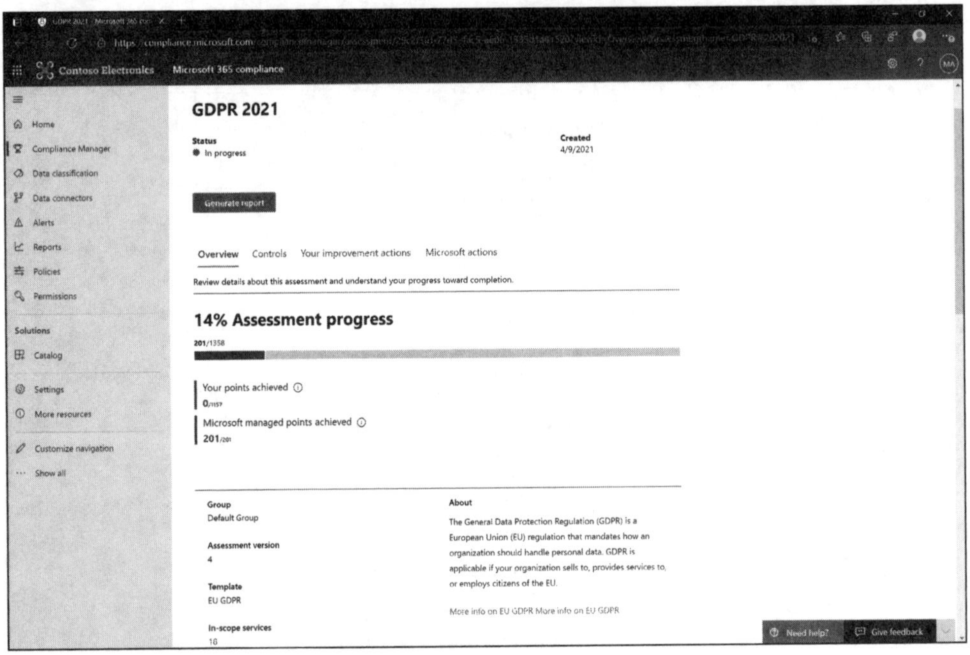

FIGURE 3-6 Microsoft 365 assessment in progress

Skill 3.2: Manage information governance

Organizations must manage their data by keeping it while it is needed, deleting it when it is no longer needed, and **labeling it to enable** any special handling requirements. These data-management tasks are often referred to as *data governance*.

In Office 365, data is spread across multiple services. So your **data governance** must be viable across these services. Historically, data governance has been handled within each individual service, such as Exchange Online. Now, data governance is moving toward a centralized model, which can be implemented across all Office 365 services. In this skill section, you will look at the built-in data governance features in Office 365.

Plan for data classification and labeling

Labeling is critical to the success of your Azure Information Protection (AIP) implementation. AIP enables you to control and secure email, documents, and other data with labels that you configure. Without proper labeling, sensitive data might be unprotected or leaked outside your organization. Too much complexity in your labeling, however, is difficult to manage, making it confusing for users and potentially leading to incorrect classifications (and by extension leakage of sensitive data).

Create a new label

In this section, you will go through the step-by-step process to create a new sensitivity label in the Microsoft 365 compliance center. For the purposes of this walk-through, you will mark the content of files. Follow these steps:

1. Use an administrator account to log in to the Microsoft 365 compliance center at *https://compliance.microsoft.com*.

2. In the navigation bar, click **Show All**, and then click **Information Protection**.

3. On the **Information Protection** page, click **+Create a Label**.

    The New Sensitivity Label wizard starts with the Name and Description page displayed.

4. In the **Label Name** and **Display Name** text boxes, type **HR Only**.

5. In the **Description** text box, type **This Data Is Limited to HR Team Members Only**. Then click **Next**.

6. On the **Scope** page, ensure that **Files & Email** is selected, and click **Next**.

7. On the **Files & Emails** page, select **Mark the Content of Files**, and click **Next**.

8. On the **Content Marking** page, enable the **Content Marking** toggle, and then click **Customize Text**.

9. A **Customize Watermark Text** panel opens. In the **Watermark Text** box, type **CONFIDENTIAL HR** (see Figure 3-7), and click **Save**.

10. Complete the remaining steps in the wizard and accept the default settings to create the label.

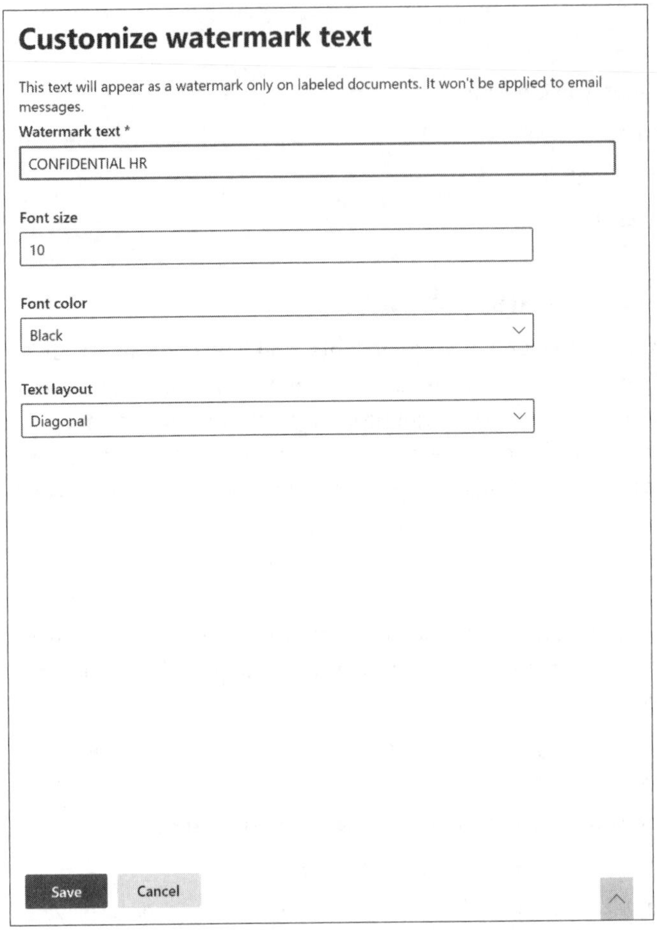

Customize watermark text

This text will appear as a watermark only on labeled documents. It won't be applied to email messages.

Watermark text *

```
CONFIDENTIAL HR
```

Font size

```
10
```

Font color

```
Black                                                          ∨
```

Text layout

```
Diagonal                                                       ∨
```

Save   Cancel

FIGURE 3-7 Creating a custom watermark label

After you create a label, it will appear in the list on the Labels tab of the Information Protection page. The list also indicates which labels have visual markings and protection.

For users to be able to apply a label you create, you must publish the label. When you publish a label, you essentially create a policy for applying that label. To publish a label, follow these steps.

1. Use an administrator account to log in to the Microsoft 365 compliance center at *https://compliance.microsoft.com*.

2. In the navigation bar, click **Show All**, and then click **Information Protection**.

3. On the **Information Protection** page, click **Publish Label**.

4. Choose the labels to publish—in this example, **HR Only**—and click **Next**.

5. Choose the users and/or groups to publish the label to—such as an HR group—and click **Next**.

6. On the **Policy Settings** page, accept the defaults, and click **Next**.

7. On the Name Your Policy page, type a name, like **HR File Policy**, and click **Next**.

8. Review your settings and click **Submit**.

After you publish the label, it appears in the Label Policies tab of the Information Protection page. (See Figure 3-8.)

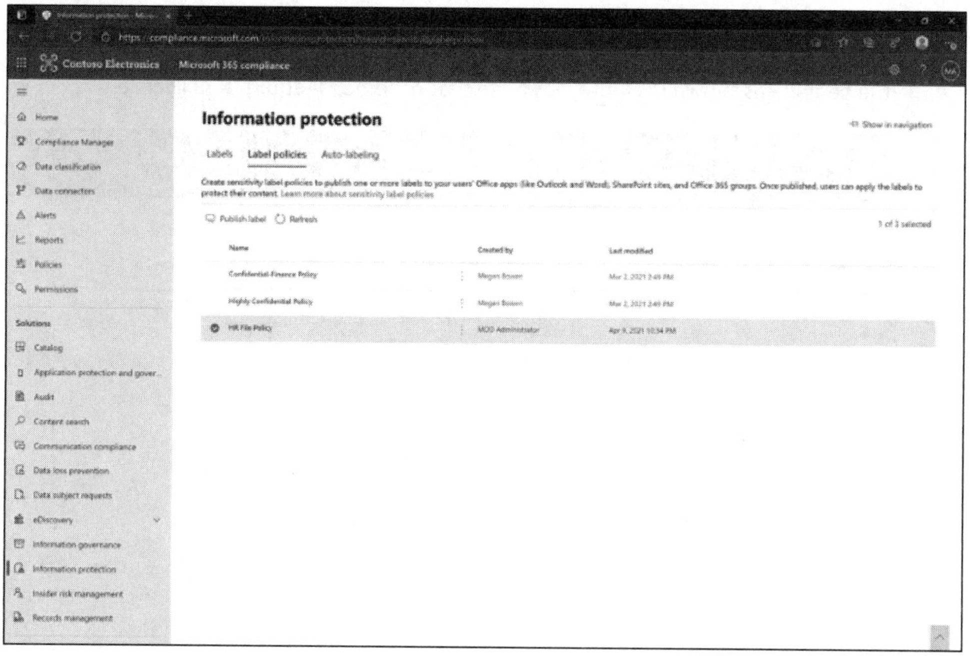

FIGURE 3-8 Published label policy

Understand label capabilities

Labels have certain capabilities, many of which are optional. At a minimum, labels provide a visual clue as to the sensitivity of the associated data. But you can configure other capabilities to enhance labels. Here are some of the key capabilities of labels, which you should be familiar with for the exam:

- **A label can automatically protect a document or email message** By default, a label does not protect data. However, you can configure a label to protect data, or to remove protection. Protection is applied (or not) by the label policy you create. You can define the specific permissions for users and groups—for example, one group can have view, open, and read permissions, while another group can have view, open, read, edit, and save permissions. Additionally, you can opt to use labels to expire content and enable offline access.

- **A label can mandate visual markings for a document** You can require a document header, footer, or watermark. In high-security organizations, you can have a label apply all three visual markings.
- **A label can have conditions** Using conditions with labels enables automatic classification. The available conditions are pulled directly from your configured sensitive information types. (These are covered in Skill 3.4.) For example, you could create a label that looks for Australian driver's license numbers in a document. When a condition is added to a label, you can have the label applied automatically or have it recommended (the default), as shown in Figure 3-9. Note that conditions require a P2 license.

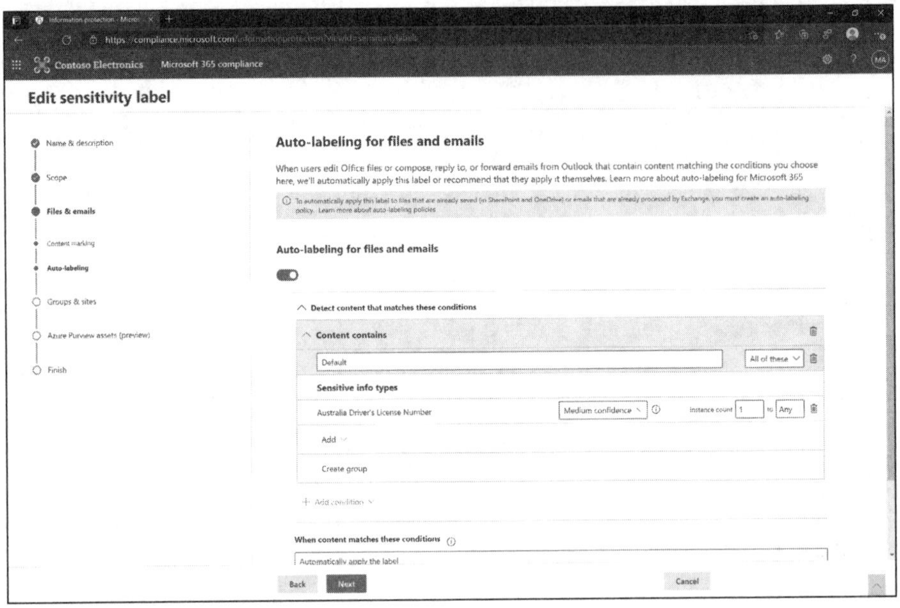

FIGURE 3-9 Custom label condition

Plan for restoring deleted content

As an administrator, you can restore deleted content in Exchange Online, SharePoint Online, and OneDrive for Business. This section looks at the restore process for all three of these technologies.

Restore deleted data in Exchange Online

You can restore deleted items by using the Outlook desktop app or Outlook on the web. This section looks at the options in the Outlook desktop app, which provides the same functionality as Outlook on the web.

RESTORE DELETED DATA IN OUTLOOK

To restore a deleted item in Outlook, follow these steps.

1. Launch Outlook.

2. In the left pane, click the **Deleted Items** folder.

   Items in the Deleted Items folder appear in list form to the right of the list of folders in the left pane.

3. Drag and drop an item from the **Deleted Items** list onto the desired folder in the left pane, such as the **Inbox** folder, to restore the item.

If the Deleted Items list is empty, follow these steps to restore a deleted item:

1. Click the **Recover Items Recently Removed from the Folder** link above the (empty) Deleted Items list.

2. In the **Recover Deleted Items** window, select the item you want to restore, make sure the **Restore Selected Items** option button is selected, and click **OK**.

> **TIP** To select multiple items, press the **Ctrl** key as you click each item.

You can also permanently delete items from the Recover Deleted Items window. To do so, simply select the **Purge Selected Items** option button instead of the **Restore Selected Items** option button.

CREATE A HOLD TO RECOVER PURGED ITEMS

Purged items are items that a user deleted and then purged using the Recover Deleted Items tool. Once an item is purged, only an administrator can recover it—if it is still recoverable. For example, with Exchange Online, you can configure the service to retain purged items for up to 30 days.

As an administrator, you can use the eDiscovery and Hold functions to recover purged items. eDiscovery is the process of identifying and delivering information that can be used as evidence in legal cases. As part of the eDiscovery process, you create an eDiscovery case; then, as part of the case you create holds. After you place a hold on a set of accounts, you can search existing and purged items for the content that might related to the case. These are part of the Content Search feature in the Microsoft 365 compliance center. To create an eDiscovery case for the purposes of restoring purged items, follow these steps:

1. Use an administrator account to log in to the Microsoft 365 compliance center at *https://compliance.microsoft.com*.

2. In the navigator bar, click **Show All**, click **eDiscovery**, and then click **Core**.

3. On the **Core eDiscovery** page, click **Create a Case**.

4. In the **New Case** window, type a name for the search, such as **Recovering Purged Items**, and click **Save**.

5. Click the **pop-out** icon to manage the case.

6. Click the **Holds** tab, and then click **Create**.

7. Type a name for the hold—for example, **Recover Purged Items**—and click **Next**.

8. On the **Choose Locations** page, for **Exchange Email**, click the **Choose Users, Groups, or Teams**. Then click **Choose Users, Groups, or Teams** again.

9. In the text box at the top of the **Edit Locations** page, type the name of a user, group, or team in your environment.

10. Choose a user, group, or team in the list that appears, and click **Choose**. Then click **Done**. This is the logical location(s) where the search will be performed.

    Figure 3-10 shows a search for **Sales**, with the **Sales Team** option selected.

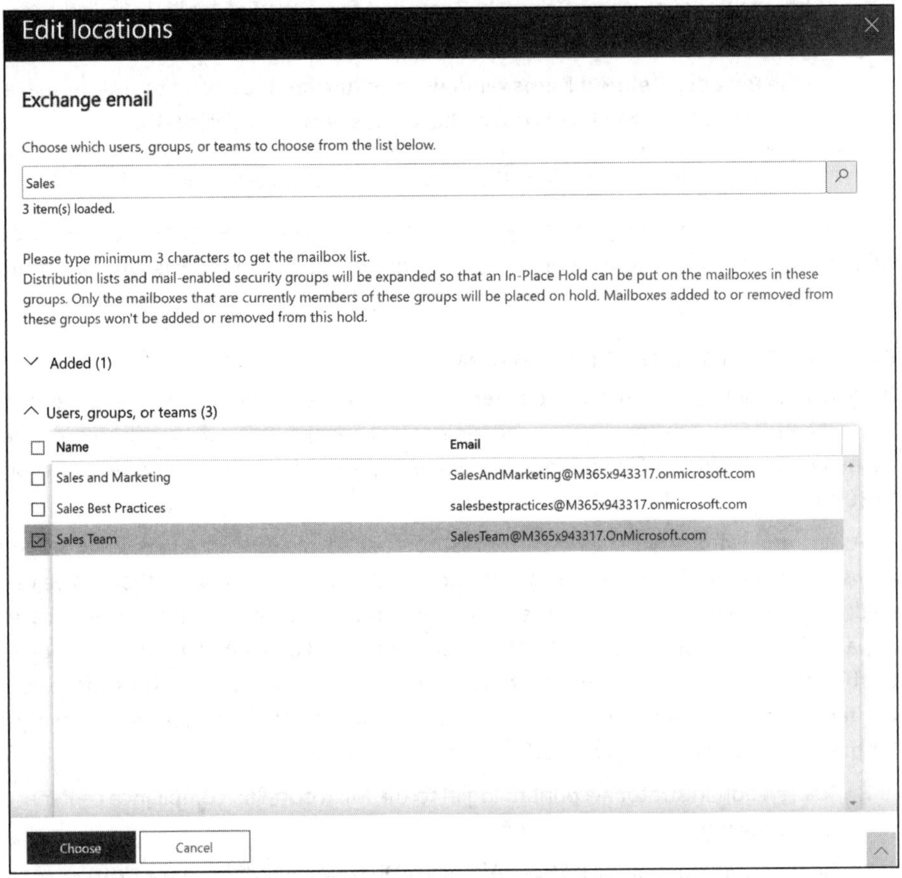

FIGURE 3-10 Custom label condition

11. On the **Query** page, add keywords to the query, such as **contact list**, and click **Next**. The keywords will be used to look through the locations that you selected earlier to return any results.

12. Click **Create This Hold**.

RECOVER PURGED ITEMS

After you create a case with a hold, you can use it to recover purged items. Follow these steps:

1. Use an administrator account to log in to the Microsoft 365 compliance center at *https://compliance.microsoft.com*.

2. In the navigation bar, click **Show All**, click **eDiscovery**, and then click **Core**.

3. Select the **Recovering Purged Items** check box and click **Open Case**.

4. On the case page, click the **Searches** tab, and then click **New Search**.

5. Type a keyword in the **Keywords** field, such as **contacts**, and click **Save & Run**. (See Figure 3-11.)

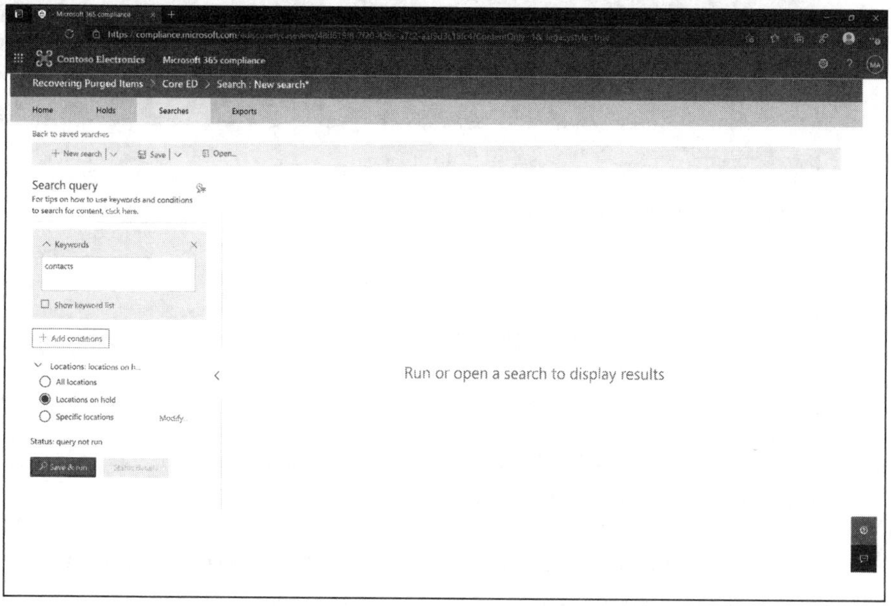

FIGURE 3-11   Searching an eDiscovery case

6. Type a name for the search and then click **Save & Run**.

   Search results are displayed in the pane on the right side of the page.

7. On the **Actions** menu, click **Export Results**. You can export all messages to a PST file or export individual messages.

Restore deleted data in SharePoint Online

You can restore data from a SharePoint Online site's Recycle Bin or, if it has been purged from the Recycle Bin, from the site's collection Recycle Bin.

To restore data from a SharePoint site's Recycle Bin, follow these steps:

1. Sign in as an administrator to the SharePoint site where you want to restore deleted items.

2. In the left pane, click **Recycle Bin**.

    The **Recycle Bin** page displays a list of deleted items. (See Figure 3-12, which shows the Recycle Bin for a Contoso Electronics SharePoint site.)

3. Click the item you want to restore; then click the **Restore** button.

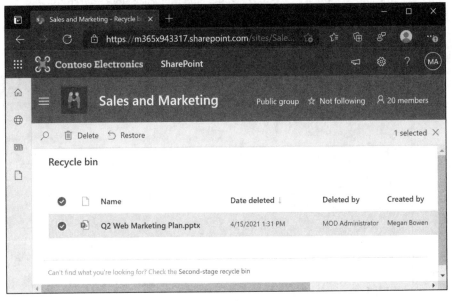

FIGURE 3-12 Restoring content from a SharePoint site

To restore data from a site collection's Recycle Bin, follow these high-level steps:

1. Sign in as an administrator to the SharePoint admin center.

2. Navigate to the **Site Collections** page.

3. Click the site collection that has the data you want to restore.

4. Navigate to the site collection's Recycle Bin.

5. Restore the desired data.

Restore deleted data in OneDrive for Business

For OneDrive for Business, there are three scenarios in which you might need to restore data:

- If data was deleted
- If a user was deleted
- If you need to restore all OneDrive data to a specific date—for example, if all data was accidentally deleted

RESTORE ONEDRIVE DATA FROM THE RECYCLE BIN

To restore items that were deleted from your OneDrive but are still in the Recycle Bin, follow these steps:

1. Using a web browser, sign in to your OneDrive account.

> **NOTE** The URL for your OneDrive is *https://<SiteName>-my.sharepoint.com*, where *<SiteName>* represents your individual site name. This will redirect to *https://<SiteName>-my.sharepoint.com/personal/<User_UPN>/_layouts/15/onedrive.aspx*, where *<SiteName>* is the individual site name and *<User_UPN>* is the user's user principal name (UPN) with underscores (such as charles_pluta_com for charles@pluta.com).

2. In the left pane, click **Recycle Bin**.

   Files in the Recycle Bin are listed in the right pane.

3. Click the file you want to restore.

4. Click **Restore**. (See Figure 3-13.)

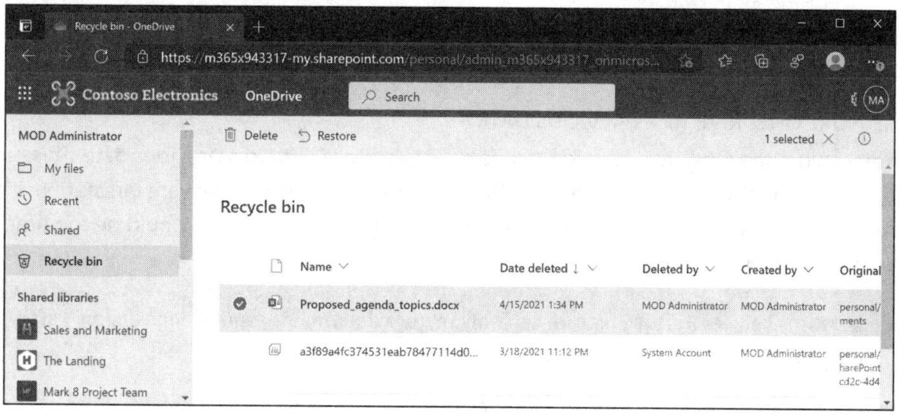

FIGURE 3-13 Restoring content from a SharePoint site

RESTORE A DELETED USER'S ONEDRIVE

If a user account was recently deleted (within the last 30 days, by default), you can restore that user account and all its OneDrive data from the Microsoft 365 admin center. Simply navigate to the **Deleted Users** page and restore the user.

If a user account has been deleted for too long and no longer appears on the Deleted Users page in the Microsoft 365 admin center, you can use PowerShell to restore the user, as shown here. This example uses a fictitious user named Kari Tran within the Contoso Electronics organization.

To connect to SharePoint Online via PowerShell as Kari, run the following commands:

```
$adminUPN=kari@contosoelectronics.com
$orgName="karitran"
$userCredential = Get-Credential -UserName $adminUPN -Message "Type the password."
Connect-SPOService -Url https://$orgName-admin.sharepoint.com
-Credential $userCredential
```

To restore the deleted user with OneDrive content, follow these steps:

1. From the PowerShell prompt, run the following command:

   ```
   Get-SPODeletedSite -IncludeOnlyPersonalSite | FT url
   ```

   If the site appears in the output, you can restore it.

2. Run the following command to obtain the site URL. Substitute your tenant name at the beginning of the resulting URL and Kari's UPN at the end.

   ```
   Get-SPOSite -IncludePersonalSite $true -Limit all -Filter "Url -like '-my.
   sharepoint.com/personal/" |select Url
   ```

3. Run the following command, where <URL_of_deleted_site> is the site URL you obtained in step 2:

   ```
   Restore-SPODeletedSite -Identity <URL_of_deleted_site>
   ```

RESTORE ONEDRIVE TO A PREVIOUS DATE

You can use the OneDrive Files Restore feature to restore data to a previous date. This is handy if you must restore all the data on the drive—for example, after a malware infestation. It's also helpful if you need to restore a large number of individual files, which would be too time consuming to restore one-by-one.

> **NOTE** The Files Restore feature can only restore data that is available in version history, the Recycle Bin, or the site collection Recycle Bin.

Follow these steps to restore your OneDrive to a previous date:

1. Using a web browser, log in to your OneDrive account.

2. In the upper-right corner of the page, click the **Settings** button (it features a picture of a gear), and select **OneDrive (Restore your OneDrive)** in the menu.

3. On the **Restore Your OneDrive** page, select a date from the drop-down menu.

4. Click **Restore**.

Plan for Microsoft 365 backup

Although many administrators are familiar with backing up their data when it is on-premises, they are not familiar with backups in the public cloud. Many on-premises backup solutions don't work for cloud-based services or feel like quickly developed add-ons that lack critical features. This section looks at the planning considerations for backing up data in Microsoft 365/Office 365.

Understand backup capabilities and limitations

Many organizations simply use the built-in backup capabilities of Office 365, which allow for basic data recovery in specific scenarios. However, some organizations enhance and/or extend these built-in capabilities with third-party tools to meet all their disaster-recovery and business-continuity needs. This section outlines the capabilities and limitations of these capabilities, separating Exchange from SharePoint and OneDrive.

EXCHANGE ONLINE

Microsoft uses database availability groups (DAGs) to protect the Exchange Online service. In this scenario, your data is stored in multiple data centers that are geographically dispersed. These backups are used only in case of a service outage, however. You still need a way to back up your data in case you need to access it for some other reason.

Exchange Online backup capabilities focus on email data and public folder data. This is like what you find with Exchange Server on-premises. Outside of email, key data also exists in Active Directory (if you are syncing users and groups from on-premises) or in Azure Active Directory (if your users and groups are in Azure Active Directory but not in an on-premises Active Directory environment). The key capabilities are as follows:

- **Recovering deleted items**   Deleted items are stored in the Deleted Items folder and are recoverable by users. After items are permanently deleted, they are stored in the Recoverable Items/Deletions folder for 14 days by default, although you can extend this to a maximum of 30 days. Administrators can recover permanently deleted items.

- **Archiving email data forever**   In Office 365, you can create archive mailboxes for users. Archive mailboxes store older email data and are configurable based on time or size. Initially, the archive mailbox had a maximum size of 100 GB, although you could contact Microsoft to increase the size. Today, archive mailboxes have an unlimited size. They also automatically increase in size as needed, although this is an optional feature. An Exchange Online Plan 2 license, Exchange Online Archiving license, or Office 365 E3/Microsoft 365 E3 license is required for unlimited archiving.

- **Maintaining email for legal purposes**   During a lawsuit or similar legal issue, organizations are often required to preserve email data that is specifically related to the matter. Historically organizations have relied on two specific Office 365 features to preserve this type of data:
  - **In-Place Hold**   This enables you to place a hold specific data, such as data based on a query for keywords or similar, such that it cannot be deleted or archived. In-Place Holds can be used for both private and public folders.
  - **Litigation Hold**   When you place a Litigation Hold on a mailbox, all mailbox data is maintained. Again, you cannot delete or archive it. Litigation Holds cannot be used for public folders.

> **NOTE**   Items on hold do not count against a mailbox quota.

Following are the key limitations of the backup features in Exchange Online:

- **You cannot restore mailboxes to a specific point in time**   Imagine a mailbox is flooded with malware or spam or becomes corrupt in some way. With many technologies, you could restore the mailbox to a point in time just before the issue started. This capability is commonly found in on-premises solutions for Exchange Server. It is not, however, offered with Exchange Online.

- **Archive mailboxes have limits in some plans**   Archive mailboxes are limited to 50 GB for Office 365 Business Essentials, Office 365 Business Premium, and Office 365 Enterprise E1. For more information about the capabilities of different plans, see *https://docs.microsoft.com/en-us/office365/servicedescriptions/exchange-online-service-description/exchange-online-limits*.

SHAREPOINT ONLINE AND ONEDRIVE FOR BUSINESS

In SharePoint Online, Microsoft backs up the environment every 12 hours and retains that data for 14 days. Additionally, your SharePoint Online instance is available in two geographically dispersed datacenters. This is helpful from a SharePoint Online service perspective. But you still need a way to maintain your own data. Following are the key capabilities for maintaining data:

- **SharePoint document versioning**   With document versioning, each time a document is updated, a new version is created. You can store up to 50,000 major versions (such as 1.0, 2.0) and 511 minor versions (such as 2.1, 2.2). Versioning is configurable—you can turn it off, set it to only create major versions, or set it to configure major and minor versions. Versions take up space in your tenant. For example, if you have 5 MB Excel file and it has 10 versions, then it takes up 50 MB in your tenant.

- **The SharePoint site's Recycle Bin keeps data for 93 days**   After 93 days, the data is permanently deleted.

- **The SharePoint site collection Recycle Bin maintains data for up to 93 days**
  The time is based on how much time the data spent in the site's Recycle Bin. For example, if data is kept in the site's Recycle Bin for 40 days and is then deleted, it will be stored in the site collection Recycle Bin for 53 days. Data is maintained for up to 93 days, no matter which Recycle Bin is used.

- **OneDrive offers the OneDrive Files Restores feature**   This feature enables users to restore data from up to 30 days ago.

- **OneDrive offers a Recycle Bin**   The Recycle Bin maintains data for up to 93 days.

Remember the Microsoft backups we talked about at the beginning of this section? You can request a restore from those backups. You can, however, only request a restore of an entire site collection or sub-site with all of its content. Consider this as a last resort if you are unable to get the data elsewhere, as the restores can take as long as a few days.

Back up Exchange Online data

This section walks through configuration items for maintaining your Exchange Online data. This isn't a traditional backup, whereby you use software to make backup copies of your Exchange databases. Rather, Exchange Online offers retention policies and retention tags, which are service-specific and apply only to Exchange Online. Policies and labels in the Microsoft 365 compliance center protect content across services and are the recommended method to use.

CONFIGURE HOW LONG TO RETAIN DELETED ITEMS

You must use Exchange Online PowerShell to work with the settings for retaining deleted items in your mailbox. By default, deleted items are maintained for 14 days. You can change the period, although 30 is the maximum number of days. Run the following commands to connect to Exchange Online PowerShell.

```
$Creds = Get-Credential
$Session = New-PSSession -ConfigurationName Microsoft.Exchange
-ConnectionUri https://outlook.office365.com/powershell-liveid/
-Credential $Creds -Authentication Basic  - AllowRedirection
Import-PSSession $Session -DisableNameChecking
```

As an example, the following command looks at the retention settings for Charles Pluta's mailbox:

```
Get-Mailbox -Identity "Charles Pluta" | select RetainDeletedItemsFor
```

To individually set Charles's mailbox to retain deleted items for 30 days, run the following command:

```
Set-Mailbox -Identity "Charles Pluta" -RetainDeletedItemsFor 30
```

If you want to set all mailboxes to retain data for 21 days, run the following command:

```
Get-Mailbox -ResultSize unlimited -Filter {(RecipientTypeDetails -eq
'UserMailbox')} | Set-Mailbox -RetainDeletedItemsFor 21
```

CREATE ARCHIVE MAILBOXES

By default, archive mailboxes are not created for new mailboxes. To archive mail, you must create archive mailboxes. Follow these steps to create an archive mailbox:

1. Log in to the Security & Compliance Center as an administrator at *https://protection.office.com*.

2. In the left pane, click **Data Governance**, and then click **Archive**.

    A list of your mailboxes is displayed in the right pane. Entries in the **Archive Mailbox** column indicate whether there is an archive mailbox associated with your mailbox.

3. Click the mailbox you want to configure for archiving.

4. Click **Enable** in the **Archive Mailbox** column.

   You'll see a warning that items older than two years will be moved to the archive mailbox. (This is based on the archiving policy.)

5. Click **Yes**.

You can also use PowerShell to enable archiving as well as to view the current archiving configuration. First, connect to Exchange Online PowerShell. Then enter the following commands:

```
$Creds = Get-Credential
$Session = New-PSSession -ConfigurationName Microsoft.Exchange
-ConnectionUri https://outlook.office365.com/powershell-liveid/
-Credential $Creds -Authentication Basic  - AllowRedirection
Import-PSSession $Session -DisableNameChecking
```

To check **all mailboxes for their current archiving status,** run the following command:

```
Get-Mailbox -Filter {ArchiveStatus -Eq "None" -AND RecipientTypeDetails
-eq "UserMailbox"} | Select Name,*ArchiveSt*
```

To enable archiving for a single mailbox (Charles's mailbox, in this example), run the following command:

```
Enable-Mailbox -Identity "Charles Pluta" -Archive
```

To enable archiving for all user mailboxes, run the following command:

```
Get-Mailbox -Filter {ArchiveStatus -Eq "None" -AND RecipientTypeDetails
-eq "UserMailbox"} | Enable-Mailbox -Archive
```

Back up SharePoint Online and OneDrive for Business data

This section walks through some of configuration options for maintaining your SharePoint Online and OneDrive for Business data. This doesn't involve a traditional backup procedure, whereby you use software to back up your SharePoint databases. Rather, it involves using tools like document versioning (SharePoint) and adjusting backup settings (OneDrive) to retain and recover data.

CONFIGURE DOCUMENT VERSIONING FOR SHAREPOINT

In this section, you will configure SharePoint Online document versioning settings. Follow these steps:

1. Sign in as an administrator to the SharePoint site whose settings you want to change.

2. Click the **Settings** button (it features a picture of a gear) and select **Library Settings**. (See Figure 3-14.)

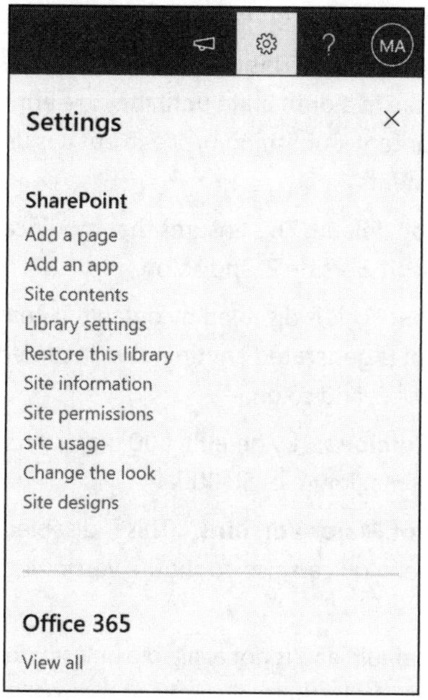

FIGURE 3-14 The SharePoint Settings menu

3. On the **Settings** page (see Figure 3-15), click **Versioning Settings**.

FIGURE 3-15 SharePoint library settings

The **Versioning Settings** page opens, where you can configure several versioning settings:

- **Require Content Approval for Submitted Items** This is off by default. When enabled, items that are new or edited remain in a draft state until they are approved. Enabling this setting can slow down the content-publishing process, but it is useful in highly regulated or high-security environments.

- **Create Major Versions** This is enabled by default. This ensures that modifications are saved to a major version, such as version 1, version 2, and so on.

- **Create Major and Minor (Draft) Versions** This is disabled by default. If enabled, a major and minor version of the document is generated anytime the document is changed—for example, version 1.1, version 1.2, and so on.

- **Keep the Following Number of Major Versions** By default, 500 major versions are kept. You can increase the number to a maximum of 50,000.

- **Keep Drafts for the Following Number of Major Versions** This is disabled by default. If you enable content approval, then you can also configure versioning for drafts.

- **Draft Item Security** This is disabled by default, and is not available unless you require content approval. You can configure drafts so that only users who can edit drafts are allowed read them; any user can read them; or only the author and approvers can read them. This is useful for highly regulated industries or high-security organizations.

- **Require Check Out** This is disabled by default. If you enable it, users must check out a file before editing it. When a file is checked out, other users cannot edit the document.

4. Choose the desired versioning settings and click **OK**.

EXAM TIP

If you plan to use document co-authoring, you must disable the Require Check Out option. Otherwise, multiple people will be unable to work on a document at the same time.

CONFIGURE ONEDRIVE DATA RETENTION FOR DELETED USERS

By default, OneDrive content is retained based on SharePoint retention settings. For deleted users, OneDrive retains the user data 30 days by default. Follow these steps to change the retention period for deleted users:

1. Sign in as an administrator to the OneDrive admin center at *https://admin.onedrive.com/*.

2. In the left pane, click **Storage**.

3. On the **Storage** page, type the number of days to retain files for deleted users in the text box, and then click **Save**.

NOTE Days are counted from the time the user is deleted.

When users are deleted, access to the OneDrive content is automatically enabled for the user's manager (if configured). This is controlled in the SharePoint settings through the Enable Access Delegation feature, which is enabled by default. Optionally, you can manually designate a secondary owner, which is useful if the user doesn't have a manager. Managers will be notified by email with instructions to access the deleted user's data.

Configure information retention

Office 365 retention policies apply to your SharePoint, email, and Skype/Teams content. To retain data, you must configure retention policies. The policies will be based on your company requirements and which services you use. For the exam, you should be familiar with the capabilities across all the services and understand the limitations of the built-in retention capabilities.

Sometimes, retaining information is required for compliance or legal reasons. Other times, it is merely a way to help employees work more efficiently. For example, suppose you are trying to locate a document in your organization. Instead of searching through only the last year of documents, you might have to search every document ever produced (for example, in a company that keeps all data indefinitely). Obviously, that is not efficient.

Many organizations retain data for compliance, legal, and efficiency reasons. There are also organizations that maintain data "just in case," or "because they aren't sure if they will need it sometime in the future." This often points to immature information retention policies or a non-existent information retention strategy.

The exam covers two ways to retain data:

- **Information retention policies** These can be used to retain data for a specific period of time, delete data after it has been retained for a set period of time (optional), or delete data when it reaches a certain age. You choose the location(s) for the policy, including Exchange Online, SharePoint Online, and OneDrive. You can look at all of the locations later in this section.

- **Retention labels** These are displayed in apps such as Outlook and OneDrive. Users can opt to use them to retain or delete data. One downside is that users choose whether to use labels and if so which ones. To avoid this, you can apply labels automatically based on conditions you dictate. (This requires an E5 license.) Labels can be used across Exchange, SharePoint, OneDrive, and Office 365 groups, but not across other services such as Teams, which is supported by retention policies.

Beyond retention policies and labels, this section also covers built-in features to manage data, such as the In-Place Hold in Exchange Online and the SharePoint Recycle Bin. Some of these built-in features, like the In-Place Hold, are deprecated or are no longer being developed, and will be replaced by retention labels and retention policies.

Before you implement information retention, you should have a good understanding of the prerequisites, capabilities, and limitations of the Office 365 information-retention policies.

Retention prerequisites

When using retention policies for Exchange Online and SharePoint Online, there are licensing prerequisites that must be met. These include:

- **Exchange Online** Mailboxes must be tied to an Exchange Online Plan 2 license, an Office 365 E3 or Office 365 E5 license, or a Microsoft 365 E3 or E5 license. Anything less than that requires a separate Exchange Online Archiving license.
- **SharePoint Online (by way of the preservation hold library)** You need SharePoint Online Plan 2, Office 365 E3 or E5, or Microsoft 365 E3 or E5.

Retention capabilities

Retention policies work across several areas of Office 365. While the focus here is on the major services of Office 365 (Exchange Online, SharePoint Online, and OneDrive for Business), you should be familiar with applicable locations for the smaller services. The following services are supported locations for retention policies:

- **Exchange email** With Exchange email, you target mailboxes. Although you can use a distribution group or a mail-enabled security group as a target, the groups are expanded at the time of use and not dynamic. So, for example, if you add Group1 to a retention policy, and that group contains nine members, only those nine members will be the target of the retention policy—even if you add 10 more people to the group later on. Note that in addition to including mailboxes, you can also exclude mailboxes.
- **SharePoint sites** For SharePoint Online, you target the site level. You just need the site URL. Alternatively, you can select the site from a list.
- **OneDrive accounts** For OneDrive, you can add accounts individually using the account URL or by selecting a site from a list.
- **Office 365 groups** Office 365 groups can be targets of retention policies. You can search for a group or select groups from a list.
- **Skype for Business** For new policies, this is off by default. If you enable it, you can choose individual users.
- **Exchange public folders** For new policies, this is off by default. You can enable this, which automatically retains all public folders.
- **Teams channel messages** For Teams, you can target channel messages for select teams and exclude specific teams.
- **Teams chats** For Teams chats, you can include or exclude individual users.

Retention policies begin the retention period based on the age of the content or the last modification date. In contrast, retention labels can be used to start the retention period at the time of labeling. Additionally, labels can be used to launch a disposition review after the retention period has passed. This simply means the SharePoint or OneDrive document must be reviewed before it can be deleted.

Retention limitations

Microsoft is rapidly enhancing its services. As such, although the limitations listed here existed when the exam was developed, and even at the time of this writing, some of them may have been resolved by the time you read this.

Typically, the exam will reference limitations, especially long-term (or permanent) limitations. However, the exam often avoids short-term limitations. Be aware of the following limitations for the exam:

- When you create a retention policy for Teams (Teams channel messages or Teams chats), all other retention locations are turned off. To retain Teams data, you must have a dedicated retention policy.

- Teams does not support advanced retention. Therefore, you cannot create a retention policy to apply to data that meets specific conditions.

- Advanced retention does not apply to Skype for Business or Exchange Online public folders. This is because public folders and Skype for Business do not support sensitive information types (which is one of the options for advanced retention).

- Retention labels are not valid for Teams channel messages, Teams chats, or Skype for Business.

- Only one retention label can be applied at a time.

Design data retention labels

There are two types of labels: sensitivity labels and retention labels. These cannot be used interchangeably. Sensitivity labels are for classifying documents to a certain level and retention labels prevent the data from being deleted before a certain amount of time. If you want to use a label for retention, it must be a retention label.

After you decide on a design for your data retention labels—whether it's a sensitivity label or a retention label, and what settings you want to apply (discussed in the next section), you can create these labels. Once the labels are in place, you must monitor how effective they are.

Create a data retention label

In this section, you will go through the process of creating a data retention label and explore the available options. Follow these steps:

1. Use an administrator account to log in to the Microsoft 365 compliance center at *https://compliance.microsoft.com*.

2. In the navigation bar, click **Show All**, and then click **Information Governance**.

   The Information Governance page opens with the Labels tab displayed by default. This tab contains a list of existing sensitivity labels. (See Figure 3-16.)

Information governance

Labels   Label policies   Retention   Import   Archive

When published, retention labels appear in your users' apps, such as Outlook, SharePoint, and OneDrive. When a label is applied to email or docs based on the settings you chose. For example, you can create labels that retain content for a certain time or ones that simply delete content whe

+ Create a label   ⊃ Publish labels   ↑ Import   ↓ Export   ○ Refresh   7 items

Name		Retention duration
Medical Records Retention Policy	⋮	7 years
Private	⋮	5 years
Public	⋮	5 years
Confidential	⋮	7 years
Personal Financial PII	⋮	3 years
Product Retired	⋮	10 years
PII Retention Policy	⋮	7 years

FIGURE 3-16   The Information Governance page with the Labels tab displayed

3.   Click the **Retention** tab.

4.   Click **+Create A Label**.

The Create Retention Label wizard starts.

5.   On the **Name Your Label** page, type a name for the label—for this example, **Tax Data – 7 Years**.

6.   Optionally, type a description for admins and a description for users. Then click **Next**.

> **NOTE**   It is recommended that you enter both of these descriptions. Although you might know what the label is for, others might not, and the label usage might not be so obvious, say, three years from now.

7.   On the **Define Retention Settings** page (see Figure 3-17), select a retention option— in this case, **Retain Items for a Specific Period**.

> **NOTE**   Your other options here are to retain items forever, only delete items when they reach a certain age, or to *not* retain or delete items. Be aware that if you opt to delete items when they reach a certain age, that will apply to all items, not just items with retention labels applied.

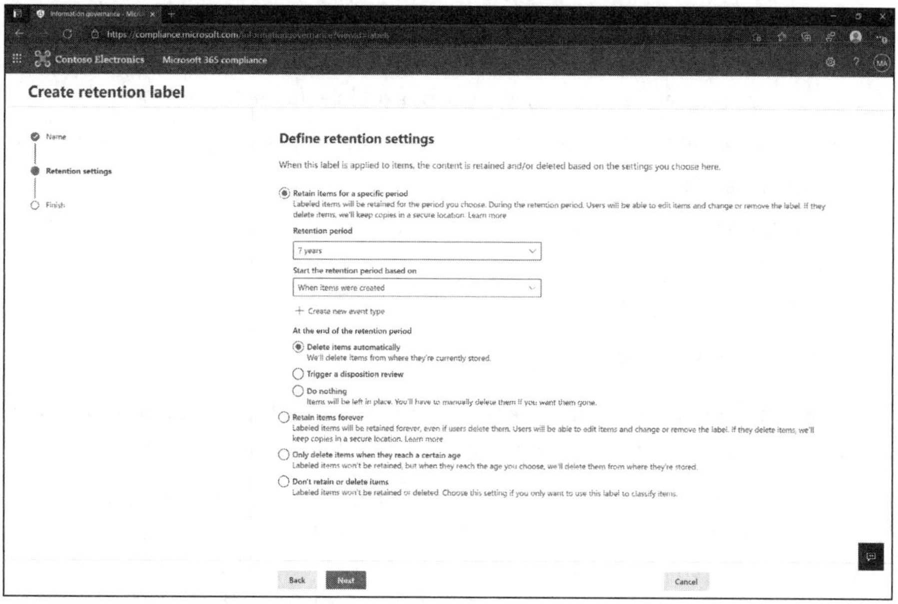

FIGURE 3-17   Defining retention settings

8. Leave the **Retention Period** drop-down list at the default setting (**7 Years**).

9. Leave the **Start the Retention Period Based On** drop-down list at the default setting (**When Items Were Created**).

10. Under **At the End of the Retention Period**, choose one of the following, and then click **Next**:

    ■ **Delete Items Automatically**   Any item with the retention label applied will be deleted automatically when the retention period ends.

    ■ **Trigger a Disposition Review**   Reviewers will receive an email to review the data when the retention period expires.

    ■ **Do Nothing**   Choose this to leave the content as is when the retention period expires.

11. On the **Review Your Settings** page, click **Create This Label**.

12. On the **Tax Data – 7 Years** workspace, click **Close**.

Now that you have a retention label, you can use it to retain data—but first, it must become available for use. Remember, you create labels from the Microsoft 365 compliance center. After that, labels must sync to the applicable services such as Exchange Online and SharePoint Online. For SharePoint and OneDrive, the sync might take up to one day. For Exchange Online, the sync might take up to seven days.

NEED MORE REVIEW?   DIGGING INTO LABELS

To find out more about the label sync process and timing, along with other details of how labels work, see *https://docs.microsoft.com/office365/securitycompliance/labels*.

Monitor data governance

After you implement data governance, you need a way to find out if it is effective. You must also track usage rates and see whether any gaps exist in your implementation.

The Data Governance dashboard enables you to review key data-governance data at a glance:

- Top five labels
- Labels trend over the past 90 days
- Top label users/policies
- Risky labels activity
- How labels were applied

> **NOTE** Data-governance data is available for up to 90 days. If you need to maintain data longer, you should plan to capture the data before it becomes unavailable.

One option for monitoring data governance is to use supervision policies. These enable you to capture organizational communications that can then be examined. Supervision is often used for individual employees or to monitor communications between specific groups in your organization. During the communication examination, an examiner classifies items as Compliant, Non-Compliant, Questionable, or Resolved. The examination takes place in Outlook on the web (via an add-in) or in the Outlook desktop app (also via an add-in).

Skill 3.3: Implement Azure Information Protection

Azure Information Protection (AIP) helps organizations protect data by using encryption, data classification, and labels. It was built from Active Directory Rights Management Services (AD RMS) and various acquisitions that Microsoft has made over the last few years.

AIP provides everything that AD RMS provides, plus much more. Where AD RMS is an on-premises service that is often restricted to internal use only, AIP is cloud-based and enables you to easily interoperate and share data with people at other organizations—even if they don't have AIP.

This skill covers how to:

- Plan information protection solution
- Implement Azure Information Protection policies
- Monitor label alerts and analytics
- Deploy Azure Information Protection unified label client
- Configure Information Rights Management (IRM) for workloads
- Plan for Windows Information Protection (WIP) implementation

Plan information protection solution

The first step in an AIP implementation project is to plan the implementation. To maximize your chances of a successful implementation, you must identify prerequisites, licensing requirements, and integration fundamentals before you start the implementation process.

Understand AIP prerequisites

Although AIP is a cloud-based service, there are prerequisites that you must be able to meet before you can use AIP. Following are the key prerequisites:

- **Azure Active Directory (Azure AD)**   Although many organizations have Azure AD for other reasons (for example, to support Office 365 or other cloud-based apps), some organizations don't. Azure AD requires its own planning (for example, for Azure AD security, syncing from on-premises, and so on) but that isn't part of this exam.
- **Client computers**   AIP clients must run Windows 7 or later or macOS 10.8 (Mountain Lion) or later.
- **Mobile devices**   Android phones must run Android 6.0 or later, while iOS devices must run iOS 11.0 or higher.
- **On-premises applications**   To integrate Exchange Server with AIP, you need a minimum of Exchange Server 2010. For SharePoint, you need a minimum of SharePoint 2010. To integrate with Windows file servers (specifically, with the File Classification Infrastructure), you need servers that run Windows Server 2012 or later. You can protect data on Windows Server 2008 R2 by using PowerShell, but not by using a file-management task like you can in Windows Server 2012 and later.

License AIP

You must license AIP before you can use it. Although you can consume AIP content without a license—for example, if a licensed AIP user protects data and sends it to you—you can't protect content. To protect content, you need a license.

You have three options for AIP licensing:

- **Azure Information Protection Premium P1**   AIP P1 is included with Enterprise Mobility + Security E3 and Microsoft 365 E3.
- **Azure Information Protection Premium P2**   AIP P2 is included with Enterprise Mobility + Security E5 and Microsoft 365 E5.
- **Azure Information Protection for Office 365**   AIP for Office 365 is included with Office 365 Enterprise E3 or higher plans.

Table 3-1 shows the key feature differences between versions of AIP. Note that this is not an exhaustive list of features.

TABLE 3-1 AIP features

Feature	AIP P1	AIP P2	AIP O365
On-premises connectors	Yes	Yes	No
Track and revoke shared documents	Yes	Yes	No
Automated classification	No	Yes	No
Recommended classification	No	Yes	No
Labeling	No	Yes	No
Bring your own key (BYOK)	Yes	Yes	Yes
Hold your own key (HYOK)	No	Yes	No

Plan for AIP

Before deploying AIP, you must plan for the implementation. Now that you understand the prerequisites, the licensing, and the features available, you must figure out how your organization will use AIP and what you'll need to do to prepare your environment for AIP.

USERS AND GROUPS

Earlier in this section, we noted that a prerequisite for AIP is to have a sync between your on-premises AD DS environment and Azure AD. To license users with AIP, they must be in Azure AD. You can create users manually; however, it is a good practice to sync users from AD DS instead, because this reduces administrative overhead.

Along with users, you also must account for AD DS groups. You can use groups to delegate administration of AIP, to control the use of AIP, or for document access. As part of your planning, you should figure out which users and groups need to be synced. In many organizations, you should sync your user accounts for your users, but not for your on-premises service accounts, or other non-human accounts.

ASSIGN LICENSES

After you have users and groups synced (or created) in Azure AD, you must assign licenses. Each user who uses AIP must be licensed.

You can assign licenses individually, but this is tedious for organizations with more than a few users. You can also assign licenses to groups, such as an AIP Users group. This is especially effective for large organizations.

If you plan to do a phased implementation of AIP (for example, where the IT department is the first department to use AIP), you can create multiple groups and use them for licensing.

CHOOSE AN AIP KEY

The AIP key is an important planning consideration. You can choose the Microsoft-managed key (the default configuration) or bring your own key (BYOK).

CONFIGURE CLASSIFICATION AND LABELING

Labels identify data based on sensitivity. For example, marketing materials used on your website might be labeled Public, while documents outlining a product strategy for the future might be labeled Sensitive.

When you apply a label to data, it can automatically encrypt data or adjust user access. Classification is the act of labeling data. For example, you might classify a Word document as Confidential (with Confidential being a label).

You can manually classify data or use automatic classification. Additionally, you can opt for classification tips, or recommendations. In this scenario, you enter a condition—for instance, "If a document contains X, then..."—and recommendations are displayed in supported applications such as Microsoft Word. As an example, Word might detect a condition in a document and recommend that the document be labeled Confidential. The user can then accept that recommendation by clicking **Change Now** or dismiss it by clicking **Dismiss**.

Some organizations might already use classification and labeling—for example, if they use data loss prevention (DLP), or if they use AD RMS with on-premises file servers. But for many organizations, classifying and labeling documents is a new concept. To start, these organizations might consider using a built-in AIP policy that provides various default labels, such as Confidential and Highly Confidential and build up from there. Most organizations will need more than the default labels.

As part of your classification and labeling strategy, you must train end users on the proper labeling of data. At some point, you might also want to take advantage of advanced features such as enforced labels, customization, and conditions. You will look at labeling in more detail later in this chapter.

Implement Azure Information Protection policies

With information protection, you publish policies to apply to a set of users or to all users. These policies contain various default labels (such as Public and Confidential) as well as some optional ones, most of which are turned off.

Although the default policies might work for some organizations, many will need to customize them or create new ones. When you publish a policy, you essentially indicate how the labels that comprise that policy should be used.

View existing policies

To view existing policies, follow these steps.

1. Log in to the Microsoft 365 compliance center at *https://compliance.microsoft.com*.

2. In the navigation bar, click **Show All**, and then click **Information Protection**.

3. On the **Information Protection** page, click the **Label Policies** tab.

   You will see any existing policies. Figure 3-18 shows three policies.

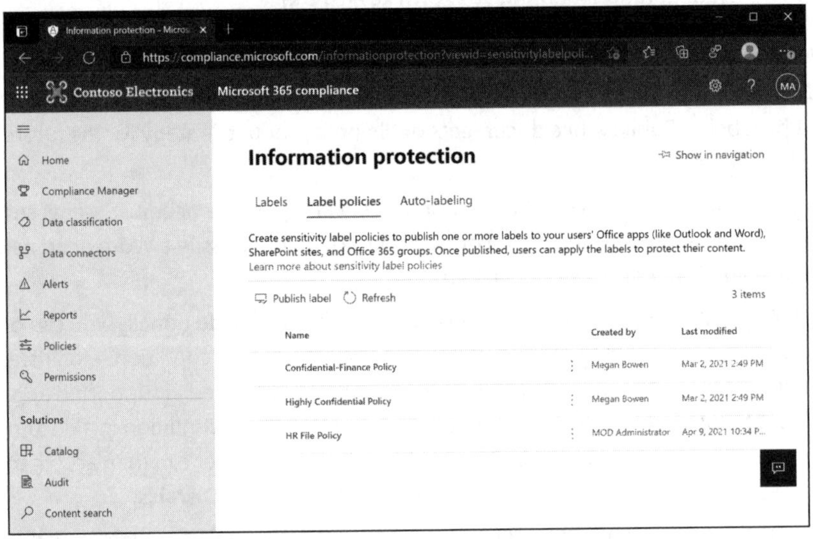

FIGURE 3-18 Information protection policies

Create and configure a policy

When you create a policy, you essentially publish how the labels in that policy should be used. For example, the HR department might have its own scoped policies.

The primary end-user settings that you can define in a policy are as follows:

- **Require Users to Apply a Label to Their Email or Documents** This setting is turned off by default. If you turn it on, users will be prompted to label a document or email when they save or send it, respectively. Optionally, you can automatically label a document or email based on a condition or automatically assign a default label.

- **Users Must Provide Justification to Set a Lower Classification Label, Remove a Label, Or Remove Protection** This setting is turned off by default. If you turn it on, and a user tries to lower the label classification, remove protection, or remove a label, they will be prompted to provide an explanation. This explanation is saved to the local event log (called the Applications and Services Logs/Azure Information Protection log). This log is not usually captured by log archiving or SIEM solutions, so consider capturing it as part of your AIP deployment.

- **Provide Users with a Link to a Custom Help Page** This setting is turned off by default. If you turn it on, you will be prompted to include a URL that users can visit to learn more about the labels and policies within the organization.

In a scoped policy, you can implement departmental settings that override the global policy settings. Follow these steps to create a new scoped policy:

1. Log in to the Microsoft 365 compliance center at *https://compliance.microsoft.com*.
2. If necessary, click **Show All** on the navigation bar. Then click **Information Protection**.
3. On the **Information Protection** page, click the **Label Policies** tab.
4. Click **Publish Label.**
5. On the **Create Policy** page, click **Choose Sensitivity Labels to Publish**.
6. Select a label that you created in skill section 3.2 and click **Next**.
7. On the **Publish to Users and Groups** page, click **Select Which Users or Groups Get This Policy**.
8. In the Azure AD **Users and Groups** pane, search for the email-enabled group to which you want to apply the policy, select it, and click **Done**.

> **NOTE** **You can apply this policy only to groups that are email-enabled.**

The group will be displayed below the name and description, as shown in Figure 3-19.

9. Click **Next**.

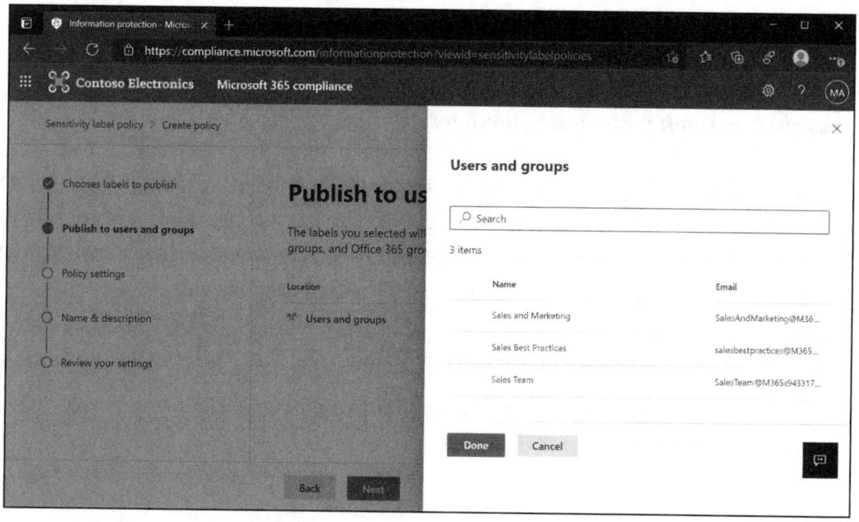

FIGURE 3-19 New scoped policy configuration settings

10. In the **Policy Settings** page, select the **Require Users to Apply a Label to Their Email or Documents check box**, and click **Next**.

11. In the **Name & Description** page, type a name for the policy, and click **Next**.

12. Review your settings and click **Submit**.

> **NOTE** If you have multiple policies, they are applied in order. In other words, the last policy in the list is applied.

When using custom policies, it is a good practice to use sub-labels. This enables departments to use more precise labels than the default ones such as Public and Confidential. The following steps show you how to create a new sub-label for the Highly Confidential label:

1. On the Microsoft 365 compliance center **Information Protection** page, click the **Labels** tab. (See the preceding series of steps for help accessing this page.)

2. Click the ellipsis (**...**) on the right side of the **Highly Confidential** label entry and choose **Add Sub-Label** from the menu that appears.

3. On the **New Sensitivity Label page**, type a name for the sub-label, such as **HR PII**.

4. Type a description for the label—for example, **HR PII Data – Automatic Headers**—and click **Next**.

5. On the **Scope** tab, specify how the label should be applied within the organization, and click **Next**.

6. On the **Files & Email** page, specify the encryption and content-marking settings, and click **Next**.

7. Click Next on the **Groups & Sites** and **Azure Purview Assets** pages.

8. On the **Review & Finish** page, click **Create Label**.

   Figure 3-20 shows the label added as a sub-label under Highly Confidential.

> **NEED MORE REVIEW?   LEARN MORE ABOUT POLICY SETTINGS AND LABELS**
>
> To learn more about policy settings and creating new labels, see the how-to guides at *https://docs.microsoft.com/en-us/azure/information-protection/how-to-guides*.

After an organization has established policies, labels, and clients (discussed later), the next task it often takes on is protecting data. For this, Microsoft offers an Azure Information Protection scanner. The scanner runs as a service on a Windows server and can scan and protect local files on the server, UNC paths, and on-premises SharePoint libraries and sites.

> **NEED MORE REVIEW?   AIP SCANNER**
>
> For more information about the AIP scanner, see *https://docs.microsoft.com/en-us/azure/information-protection/tutorial-install-scanner*.

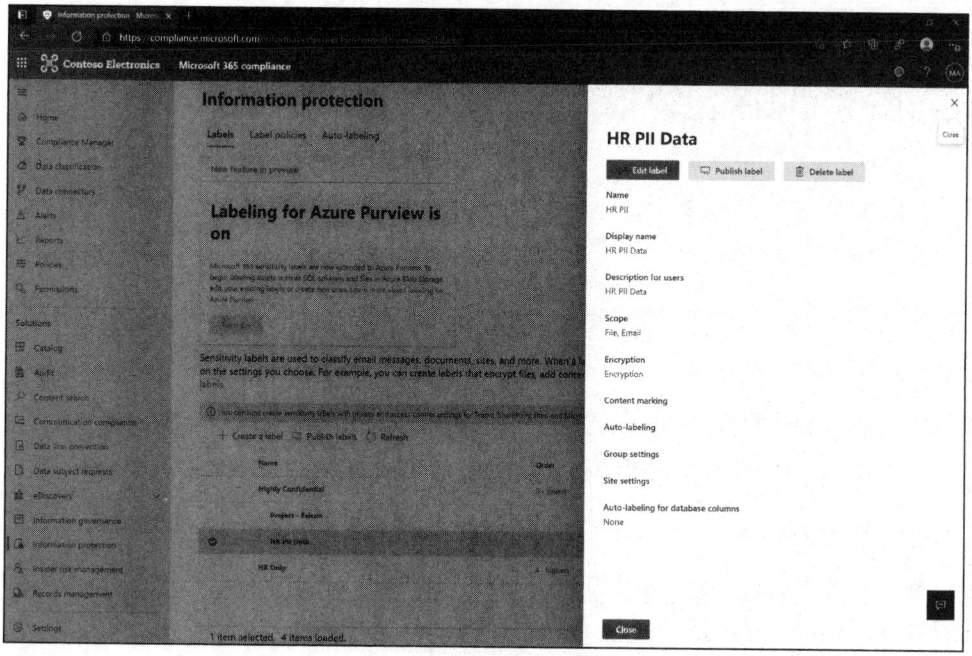

FIGURE 3-20 The Highly Confidential label with sub-labels

Monitor label alerts and analytics

The Microsoft 365 compliance center has built-in reporting and analytics for the labels that you have configured in the organization. To access this information, click **Reports** in the navigation bar on the left. The Reports page contains the following information cards (see Figure 3-21):

- **How Labels Were Applied** Shows how many labels were applied manually and how many were applied automatically
- **Labels Classified as Records** Shows how many labels are records and how many are non-records
- **Labels Trend Over the Past 90 days** Shows the use of labels across SharePoint, OneDrive, and Exchange
- **Top 5 Labels** Shows the top five labels used over the last 90 days
- **Retention Label Usage** Shows the top labels applied for SharePoint, OneDrive, and Exchange
- **Sensitivity Label Usage** Enables you to configure analytics using a Log Analytics workspace in Microsoft Azure

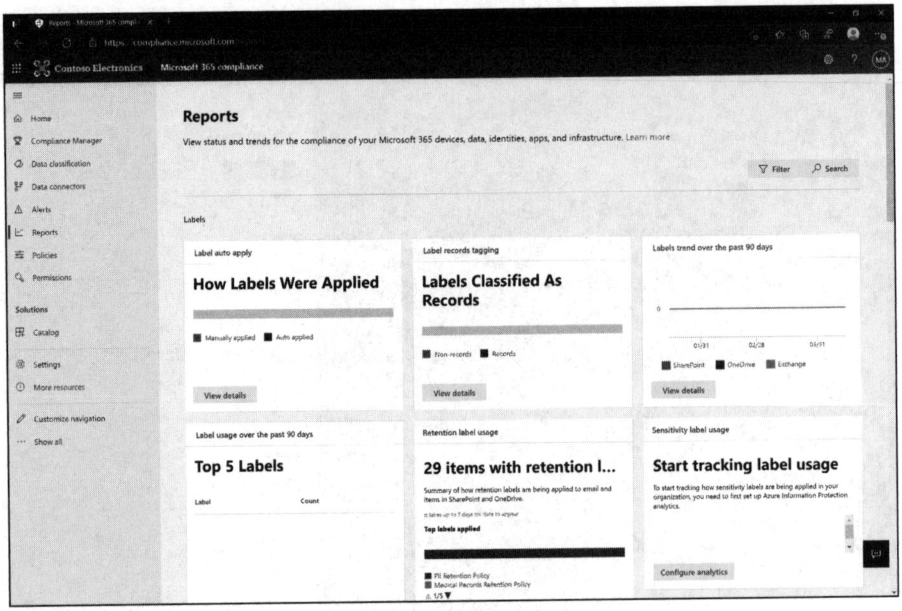

FIGURE 3-21 The Microsoft 365 compliance center Reports page

Reporting in Azure Information Protection

Azure Information Protection offers centralized reporting. The following reports are available.

Usage report

Activity logs

Data discovery report

Recommendations report

As of this writing, using centralized reporting with Azure Information Protection is in preview. For more information, see *https://docs.microsoft.com/en-us/azure/information-protection/reports-aip*.

Deploy Azure Information Protection unified labeling client

The unified labeling client is a local installation that allows users to work with documents that have been marked with sensitivity labels, even if those users do not have an AIP license. There are two options to deploy the unified labeling client:

- **Executable**   The EXE version checks for and can install many prerequisites.
- **Windows Installer**   The MSI version can be used with Intune, Configuration Manager, or group policies for large deployments. This version does not automatically install any missing prerequisites.

You can perform the executable version of the installer silently by running the following command from a command prompt or script:

```
AzInfoProtection_UL.exe /quiet
```

If you plan to use the MSI version, you must manually install the prerequisites, depending on which version of Office the client will be running. Table 3-2 outlines the dependencies required on the client based on Office version.

TABLE 3-2   Unified labeling client prerequisites

office version	operating system	software
All versions except Office 365 1902 or later	Windows 10 version 1809 only	KB 4482887
Office 2016	All supported versions	KB 3178666
Office 2013	All supported versions	KB 3172523
Office 2010	All supported versions	Microsoft Online Service Sign-in Assistant v2.1
Office 2010	Windows 8.1 and Windows Server 2012 R2	KB 2843630
Office 2010	Windows 8 and Windows Server 2012	KB 2843630

For a default installation, you can also install the unified labeling client from the command prompt or script by running the following:

```
AzInfoProtection_UL.msi /quiet
```

Configure Information Rights Management (IRM) for workloads

AIP is functional when used with Microsoft Office. However, you can enhance its capabilities and increase its benefits by extending the functionality to other supported applications.

Earlier, you looked at integration with on-premises technologies such as file servers, Exchange Server, and SharePoint. In this section, you examine the process of integrating IRM with Office 365.

AIP integrates with some Office 365 applications. You should be familiar with these applications and the integrations. Additionally, there are some specific implementation details that you should know for the exam.

Here are the supported integrations with Office 365:

- **Exchange Online**   Integration with Exchange Online enables users to protect individual email messages. For example, you can prevent recipients from forwarding emails and protect attachments by encrypting them. Optionally, you can enable only the HR department to view specific attachments. On the back end, email administrators can use mail flow rules to automatically apply protection to email messages based on recipient, subject, or content (based on keywords or phrases).

> **NOTE**   AIP is useful for DLP policies because when something sensitive is being sent outbound, it can automatically be protected with AIP.

- **SharePoint Online**   When SharePoint Online is integrated with AIP, admins can protect SharePoint lists and document libraries with IRM. As users download files, those files will be protected based on the configured protection settings. When unprotected files are uploaded, they will be automatically protected upon download.
- **OneDrive for Business**   After integration, users can configure their OneDrive for Business library for IRM. Note that OneDrive integration relies on the SharePoint Online integration with AIP. Optionally, admins can use PowerShell to configure IRM on behalf of users.

There are different capabilities offered with the integrations:

- **Protection**   You need a subscription that includes AIP to enable protection capabilities. All AIP levels (AIP for Office 365, AIP P1, and AIP P2) offer protection capabilities. AIP for Office 365 is included with Office 365 Enterprise E3 and above. AIP P1 is included with Microsoft 365 E3 and Microsoft Enterprise Mobility + Security E3. AIP P2 is included with Microsoft 365 and Enterprise Mobility + Security E5.
- **Classification and labeling**   To enable classification and labeling, you must have a subscription that includes AIP P1 or AIP P2. AIP for Office 365 does not include classification and labeling. Automatic labeling and classification is included only with AIP P2.

Plan for Windows Information Protection (WIP) implementation

Windows Information Protection (WIP) is a data-protection technology that focuses on data residing on client computers running Windows 10. WIP combines mobile device management (MDM), AppLocker, and Encrypting File System (EFS). WIP isn't a direct competitor of AIP. Instead, it focuses on a different kind of protection—protecting local data on devices—whereas AIP focuses on protecting shared data or protecting data in Exchange, on SharePoint, and on file servers.

Understand WIP

WIP relies on data encryption through EFS to encrypt data based on an organization's WIP MDM policies. These policies dictate if and when data is encrypted and if and when it can be accessed.

WIP allows organizations to obtain the following benefits:

- **Encrypt corporate data** By using EFS, WIP encrypts corporate data across all enrolled devices.

- **Wipe corporate data from devices** When users use their own devices, it can be challenging to manage those devices and to ensure that corporate data isn't lost on them. WIP enables administrators to wipe only corporate data on these devices.

- **Enable personal devices to access corporate data** Some organizations prohibit the use of personal devices to access corporate data. With WIP, organizations can safely enable such access while providing data protection.

- **Specify the list of apps that can access corporate data** WIP enables you to specify a whitelist of applications that can access corporate data.

WIP relies on Windows 10 (version 1607 and later) and an MDM solution. At the time of this writing, the supported MDM solutions are Microsoft Intune and System Center Configuration Manager. You can also use a third-party MDM, although you might not be able to take advantage of a GUI for the configuration. Instead, you might have to use the EnterpriseDataProtection cloud solution provider (CSP).

WIP categorizes apps into two categories:

- **Enlightened apps** These apps can figure out the difference between corporate data and personal data.

- **Unenlightened apps** These apps consider all data to be corporate data. Therefore, they encrypt all data instead of just encrypting corporate data.

You can convert an unenlightened app to an enlightened app by using code and the WIP API. Note, however, that if an app is intended to work only with corporate data, you might not need to enlighten it.

At the time of this writing, the following Microsoft apps are enlightened:

- Microsoft 3D Viewer
- Microsoft Edge

- Internet Explorer 11
- Microsoft People
- Mobile Office apps, including Word, Excel, PowerPoint, OneNote, Outlook Mail, and Calendar
- Office 365 Professional Plus apps, including Word, Excel, PowerPoint, OneNote, and Outlook
- OneDrive app
- OneDrive sync client (OneDrive.exe, the next generation sync client)
- Microsoft Photos
- Groove Music
- Notepad
- Microsoft Paint
- Microsoft Movies & TV
- Microsoft Messaging
- Microsoft Remote Desktop
- Microsoft To Do

WIP has some limitations that you should know about (this isn't an exhaustive list):

- **WIP is suited for single-user devices** If two or more people use the same computer, there might be app-compatibility issues when using WIP. So, if you want to use WIP, you should limit each device to a single user.
- **Sharing data with USB drives doesn't work** If you use WIP, you can copy data to a USB drive, and it stays encrypted. The data, however, will be is inaccessible on other devices or for other users. Instead, you should share files through your internal file servers or authorized cloud data repositories.
- **WIP is limited to a select set of apps** WIP can't cover all use cases because it is limited to a specific set of apps. Although you can add more apps, not all apps will support WIP integration.

Implement WIP

To apply a WIP policy to an enlightened app, follow these steps:

1. Log in to the Microsoft Endpoint Manager admin center at *https://endpoint.microsoft.com*.
2. Click **Apps** in the navigation bar. Then click **App Protection Policies.**
3. In the **App Protection Policies** page, click **Create Policy** and choose **Windows 10** from the menu that appears. (See Figure 3-22.)

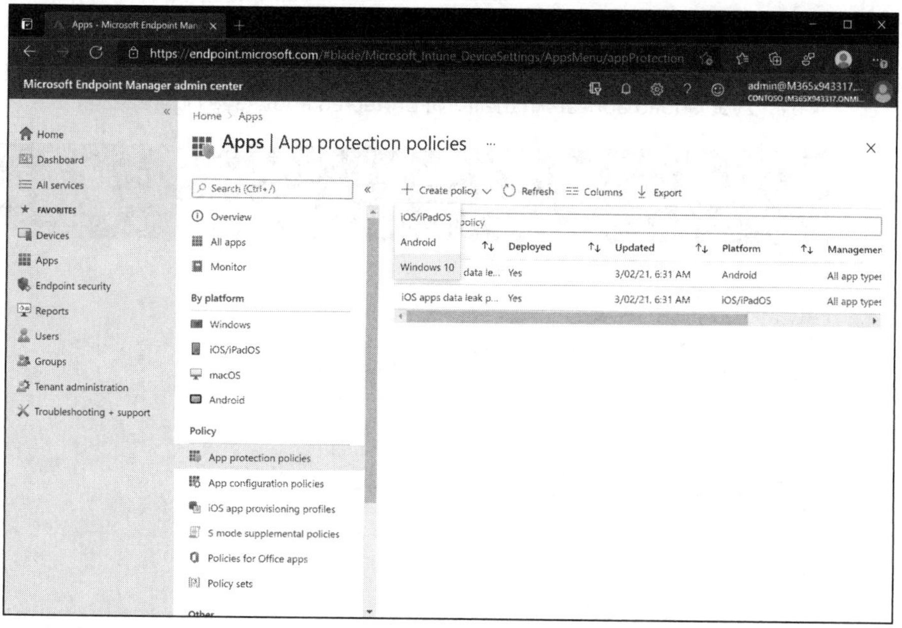

FIGURE 3-22 Creating an app protection policy

The **Create Policy** wizard starts with the **Basics** tab displayed.

4. Type a name for the policy in the **Name** box—in this case, **BYOD – WIP Policy**.

5. Select the desired platform—here, **Windows 10**.

6. Open the Enrollment State drop-down list and choose **With Enrollment**. (See Figure 3-23.) Then click **Next**.

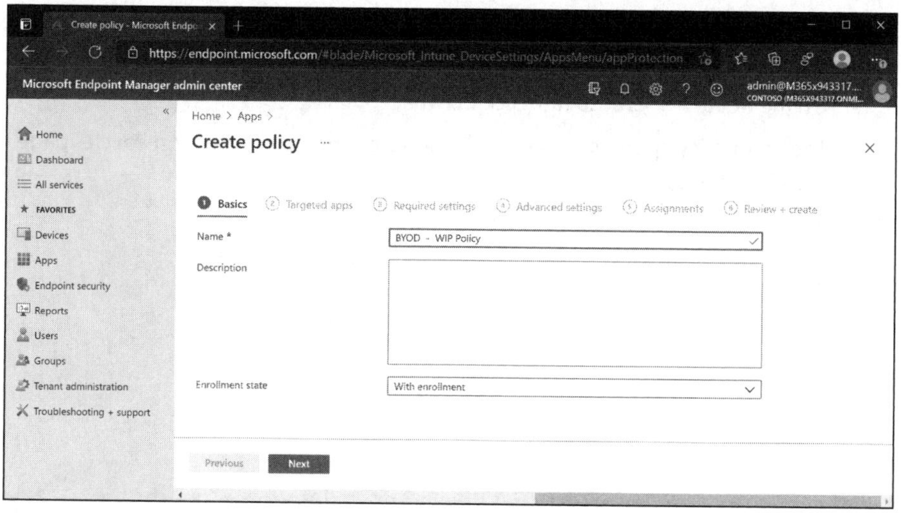

FIGURE 3-23 The Basics tab on the Create Policy wizard

7. In the **Targeted Apps** tab, click the **Add** link under **Protected Apps**.

8. Select the **Word Mobile** check box and click **OK**.

   The app you added appears in the list of protected apps. (See Figure 3-24.)

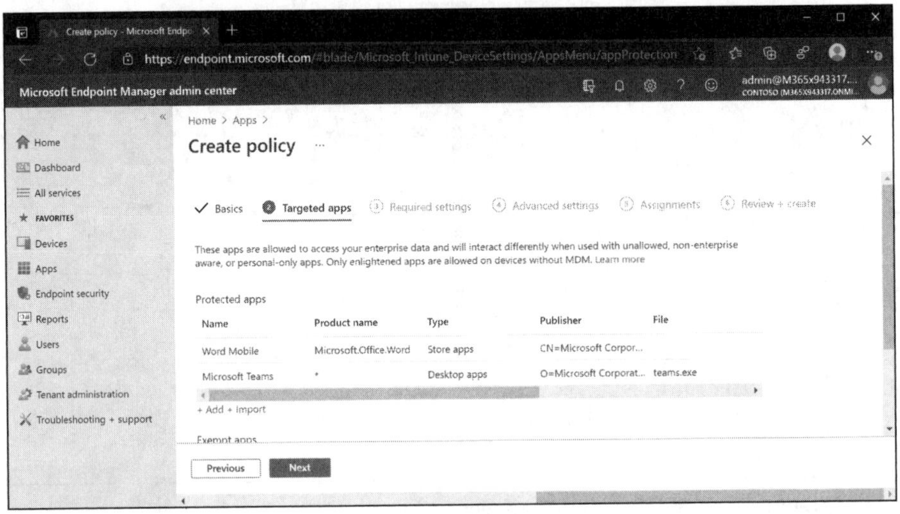

FIGURE 3-24   The Protected Apps list in the Targeted Apps tab of the Create Policy wizard

9. Optionally, add more apps. When you're finished, click **Next**.

10. In the **Required Settings** tab, set the **Windows Information Protection** mode to **Block**. Then click **Next**.

11. On the **Advanced Settings** tab, click the **On** button under **Show the Enterprise Data Protection Icon**. Then click **Next**.

12. On the **Assignments** tab, add groups to which the policy should be assigned. Then click **Next**.

13. On the **Review + Create** tab, click **Create**.

    The new policy appears in the list of policies on the App Protection Policies page. (See Figure 3-25.)

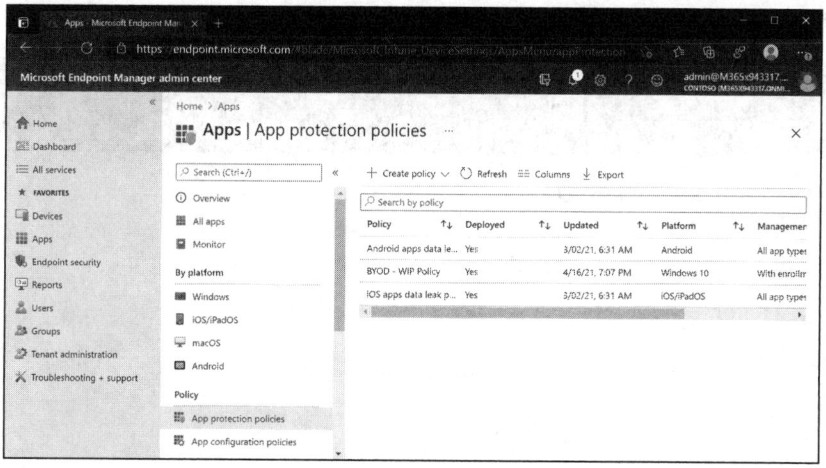

FIGURE 3-25   WIP policy list

Whereas adding recommended apps is easy, adding desktop and store apps to the list of protected apps isn't as intuitive. The following steps walk you through the process of adding a desktop app (in this case, Microsoft Word).

1. On a computer that has the desktop app you want to add installed, open a **Power-Shell** prompt.

2. Run the following command:

```
Get-AppLockerFileInformation -Path C:\Program Files\Microsoft Office\root\
Office16\WINWORD.EXE' | FL
```

3. Copy the publisher value to the clipboard.

4. Log in to the Microsoft Endpoint Manager admin center at *https://endpoint.microsoft.com.*

5. Click **Apps** in the navigation bar. Then click **App Protection Policies.**

6. In the **App Protection Policies** page, click **Create Policy** and choose **Windows 10** from the menu that appears.

   The **Create Policy wizard** starts.

7. Click the **Targeted Apps** tab. Then click the **Add** link under **Protected Apps**.

8. Click **Protected Apps** in the left pane and then click the **Add Apps** button in the right pane.

9. Click the drop-down menu at the top of the right pane and then click **Desktop Apps**.

10. Enter the following information:

    - **Name**   Microsoft Word
    - **Publisher**   Publisher value from PowerShell command output
    - **Product Name**   Microsoft Word
    - **File**   WINWORD.EXE
    - **Min Version**   15.0

11. Finish the Create Policy wizard to add the policy. Figure 3-26 shows the result.

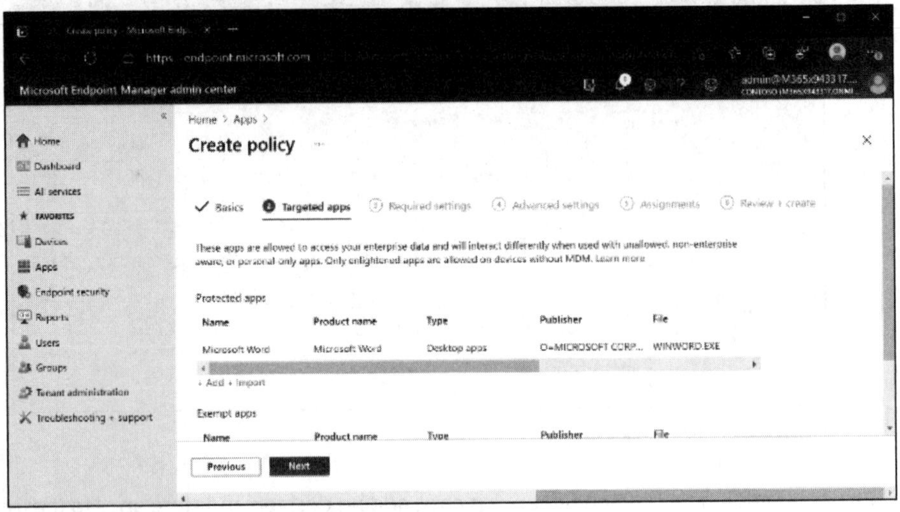

FIGURE 3-26 Add a desktop app to the policy.

When it comes to the policy, be aware of the following:

- The filename for protected apps is the executable file of the application.
- The min version specifies the minimum app version. Be sure to account for the lowest version in use at your organization.
- There are four WIP modes you can use in a policy:
  - **Block**   Enterprise data is blocked from being copied or moved to an unprotected app.
  - **Allow Overrides**   Users are prompted if they try to copy or move data from a protected app to an unprotected app. They can override and perform the copy or move, but the action will be logged.
  - **Silent**   Users can copy or move data from protected apps to unprotected apps, but the actions are logged. Think of this as an auditing mode.
  - **Off**   Users can copy or move data from protected apps to unprotected apps, but the actions are not logged.

Here, you created a basic policy. However, there are additional advanced options that you should be aware of. These are covered in the following list. Each bulleted item represents an optional advanced setting.

- **Add Network Boundary**   Network boundaries are locations from which clients can get enterprise data. For example, you can add cloud resources (such as SharePoint), protected domains, network domains, proxy servers, IPv4 or IPv6 ranges, and other resources.
- **Enterprise Proxy Servers List Is Authoritative (Do Not Auto-Detect)**   Windows auto detects proxy servers. Turn on this setting if you want to define an authoritative list of proxy servers.

- **Enterprise IP Ranges List Is Authoritative (Do Not Auto-Detect)** Instead of having Windows auto detect IP address ranges, you can define them manually.

- **Data Protection** You can upload an EFS Data Recovery Agent (DRA) certificate so that you can recover encrypted data. While this is optional, it is highly recommended. Without a DRA, if anything happens to your EFS encryption key, your encrypted data is unrecoverable.

- **Prevent Corporate Data from Being Accessed By Apps When the Device Is Locked** This setting prevents data from being accessed while a device is locked. (Note that this setting applies only to Windows 10 Mobile.)

- **Revoke Encryption Keys on Unenroll** If a device unenrolls from your policy, then the encryption keys are revoked. This is turned on by default.

- **Show the Enterprise Data Protection Icon** The Data Protection icon indicates to users that they are working with enterprise data. It is helpful for users, especially during the early stages of a WIP deployment.

- **Use Azure Rights Management Service (RMS) for WIP** Azure RMS can be used for WIP encryption—specifically to protect data when it leaves a device. This is an enhancement that extends data protection beyond just using WIP by itself.

- **Allow Windows Search Indexer to Search Encrypted Items** This is turned on by default. It enables Windows Search to index encrypted items. In high-security environments, you should turn this off.

- **Add Encrypted File Extensions** You can specify that files with certain file extensions be encrypted automatically when they are copied to a file server in your corporate boundary.

> **NEED MORE REVIEW? CREATE AN EFS DRA**
>
> You should familiarize yourself with the process of creating an EFS DRA. See *https://docs. microsoft.com/previous-versions/tn-archive/cc512680(v=technet.10)* for more information.

Skill 3.4: Plan and implement data loss prevention (DLP)

Data loss prevention (DLP) is a technology made up of hardware and software to prevent, minimize, or protect against data loss or unauthorized access to data. Specific to Microsoft 365 and Office 365, DLP is a security feature to protect against data loss, data leakage, and unauthorized viewing of data in Exchange Online, SharePoint Online, and OneDrive for Business. In some cases, DLP is used to enable a company to meet compliance or adhere to government regulations. In other cases, DLP is used to enhance the security of an organization (from intellectual property loss, for example). DLP is one technology, and is intended to be layered with other security technologies, such as data encryption, threat management, and anti-malware.

This is a hands-on skill section. Your goal should be to understand how to create, configure, and manage DLP policies with an emphasis on the configuration. In this section, you will learn how DLP works, create a DLP policy, configure a DLP policy, and monitor DLP policy matches.

EXAM TIP

On the exam, be prepared for questions related to different DLP policy settings. DLP policies are a key element of DLP, enabling you to implement protection mechanisms for your data.

This skill covers how to:

- Plan for DLP
- Configure DLP policies
- Monitor DLP policy matches

Plan for DLP

Data loss prevention (DLP) is a technology that enables you to minimize the leakage of sensitive data. In Office 365, DLP is integrated with Exchange Online (and thus Outlook on the web and Outlook), SharePoint Online, and OneDrive for Business. Additionally, it helps protect information in the desktop versions of Excel, PowerPoint, and Word.

DLP relies on content analysis to detect information you have defined as sensitive. The content analysis includes the following methods:

- **Dictionary matches** DLP scans your dictionaries (if you have any) for matches. You can create optional dictionaries containing lists of sensitive information. A single dictionary supports as many as 100,000 terms. When adding multiple keyword terms, you can opt to use keyword lists. These are available as a way to manage smaller sets of keywords.

- **Keyword matches** DLP scans documents and emails for keywords that you define in keyword lists. You do this by modifying a built-in sensitive information type.

- **Regular expression matches** Sometimes, you need to protect company-specific sensitive information, such as internal project names or numbers. You can create a custom sensitive information type and use regular expressions to define the criteria. DLP will scan using the defined regular expressions.

- **Internal functions** DLP uses many internal functions to facilitate built-in functionality. For example, the func_expiration_date function looks for date formats often used by credit cards such as 12/25 (for December of 2025) to identify credit card information.

Understand the DLP policy sync process

By default, there are no DLP policies. You must create them. You can use built-in templates to cover common use cases, such as protecting health information and financial information. Because these policies are used across multiple technologies, you must sync them after creating or modifying them. Figure 3-27 shows an overview of the sync process.

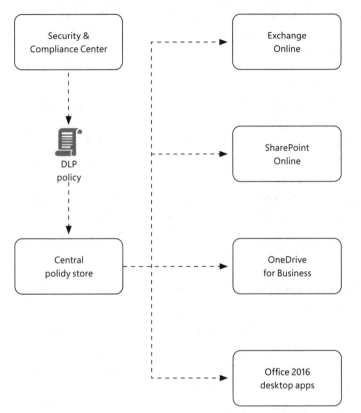

FIGURE 3-27 DLP policy sync process

The following steps describe the general DLP policy sync process:

1. You create a new DLP policy in the Security & Compliance Center. Note that all new policies are created there.

2. The DLP policy syncs to the central policy store.

3. From the central policy store, the DLP policy syncs to Exchange Online (and from there, Outlook on the web and Outlook), SharePoint Online, OneDrive for Business, and Office desktop apps (Word, Excel, and PowerPoint).

4. After the syncing process is complete, DLP begins to evaluate content in each of the services, based on the DLP policies.

DLP policies have the following characteristics:

- **A location to indicate where to protect content**   This could be Exchange Online, SharePoint Online, or OneDrive for Business.

- **Conditions to indicate when to protect content**   For example, you might have a condition that requires a driver's license number to be shared with people outside your organization. Conditions are stored in rules.

- **Actions to indicate how to protect content**   You use actions to specify what action should be taken when matching content is discovered. For example, you can configure an action to restrict access or notify a user. Actions are stored in rules.

Create DLP policies

You can create DLP policies from the Security & Compliance Center or by using PowerShell. You should be familiar with both methods for the exam.

Let's look at the procedure for creating a new DLP policy in the Security & Compliance Center. Follow these steps:

1. Log in to the Microsoft 365 compliance center at *https://compliance.microsoft.com*.

2. Click **Data Loss Prevention** in the navigation bar on the left.

3. On the **DLP** page, click the **Create Policy** button.

   A DLP wizard launches and presents you with categories of built-in templates. Alternatively, you can choose to create a custom policy from scratch. (See Figure 3-28.)

4. Click the **Privacy** category and choose the **U.S. Personally Identifiable Information (PII) Data** template. Then click **Next.**

5. Use the default name or type a new name for the policy. For this demonstration, we'll use the default name.

6. Optionally, type a description of the policy. Then click **Next**.

   By default, all DLP policies protect content in all supported locations (such as email, OneDrive, and SharePoint). If you are creating a policy for a particular platform, you can opt to choose specific services instead.

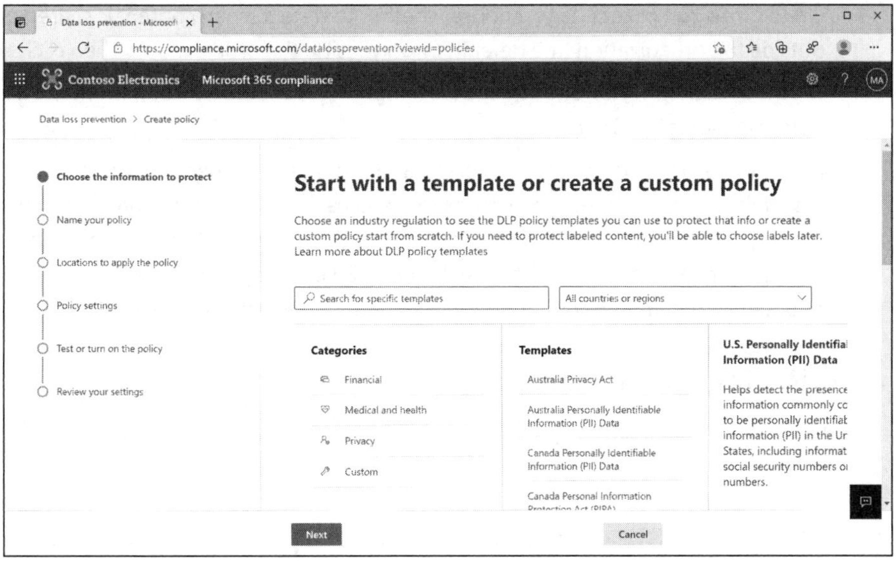

FIGURE 3-28 DLP policy templates

7. In this example, you will protect content in all locations, so simply click **Next**.

    In this template, the policy is configured to look for specific information and to dictate
    how aggressively data is labeled (using a match accuracy number).

8. On the **Define Policy Settings** page, choose the **Review and Customize Default
    Settings from the Template** option button (see Figure 3-29) and then click **Next**.

    The template's default settings are to detect when content that contains personally
    identifiable information (PII) is shared only with people outside your organization. How-
    ever, you can change the policy to detect when data is shared only with people *inside*
    your organization. (Note that if you want to detect both scenarios, you will need to cre-
    ate two policies.) Alternatively, you can select the **Create or Customize Advanced DLP
    Rules** option button to add more conditions or exceptions to the configuration.

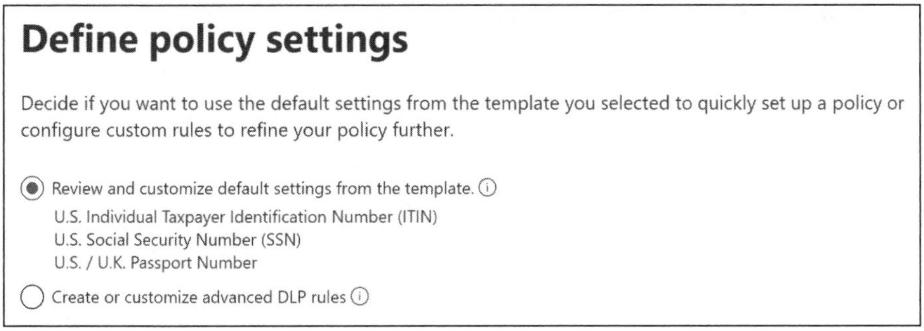

Define policy settings

Decide if you want to use the default settings from the template you selected to quickly set up a policy or
configure custom rules to refine your policy further.

◉ Review and customize default settings from the template. ⓘ
  U.S. Individual Taxpayer Identification Number (ITIN)
  U.S. Social Security Number (SSN)
  U.S. / U.K. Passport Number

◯ Create or customize advanced DLP rules ⓘ

FIGURE 3-29 DLP policy content-detection configuration

9. On the **Info to Protect** page, choose whether to detect when content is shared only outside the organization (the default) or only inside the organization. Then click **Next**.

10. On the **Protection Actions** page, choose how users should be notified when PII is detected, and click **Next**.

   By default, a policy tip is shown to users, and users get an email notification. You can customize the tip and the email, if desired. You can also change the number of times sharing sensitive data must occur before the action is deemed a violation. Finally, you can opt to restrict access to the data if there is PII or encrypt the data (such as with Azure Information Protection). Figure 3-30 shows the available options.

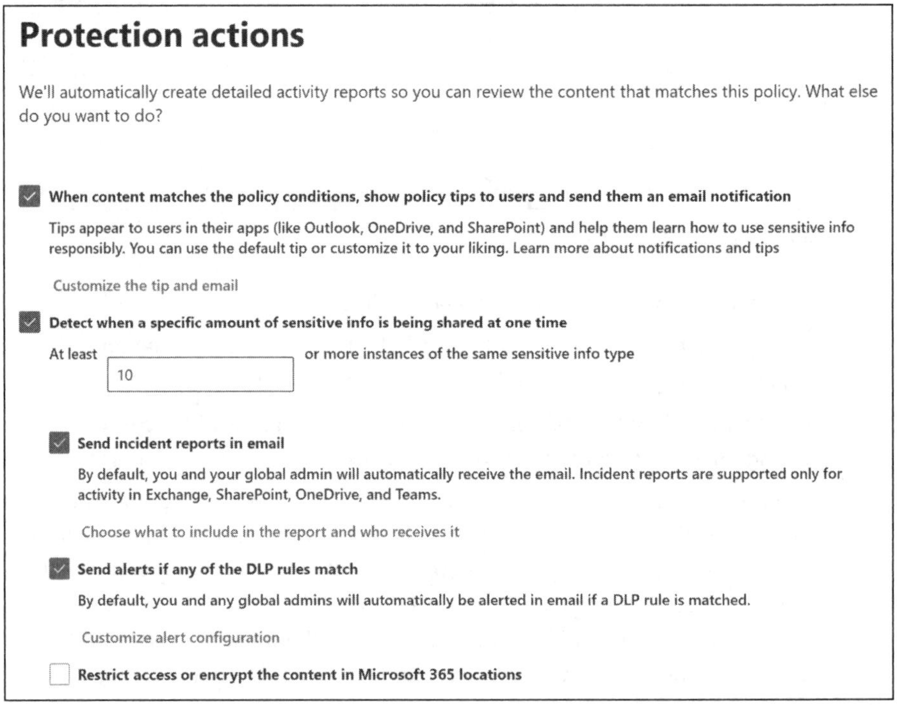

FIGURE 3-30 DLP policy protection actions

11. On the **Customize Access and Override Settings** page, specify whether to restrict access or encrypt content, audit or restrict various device actions, restrict third-party apps, and/or restrict access to on-premises file servers. Then click **Next**. Figure 3-31 displays some of the settings that can be configured at the device level.

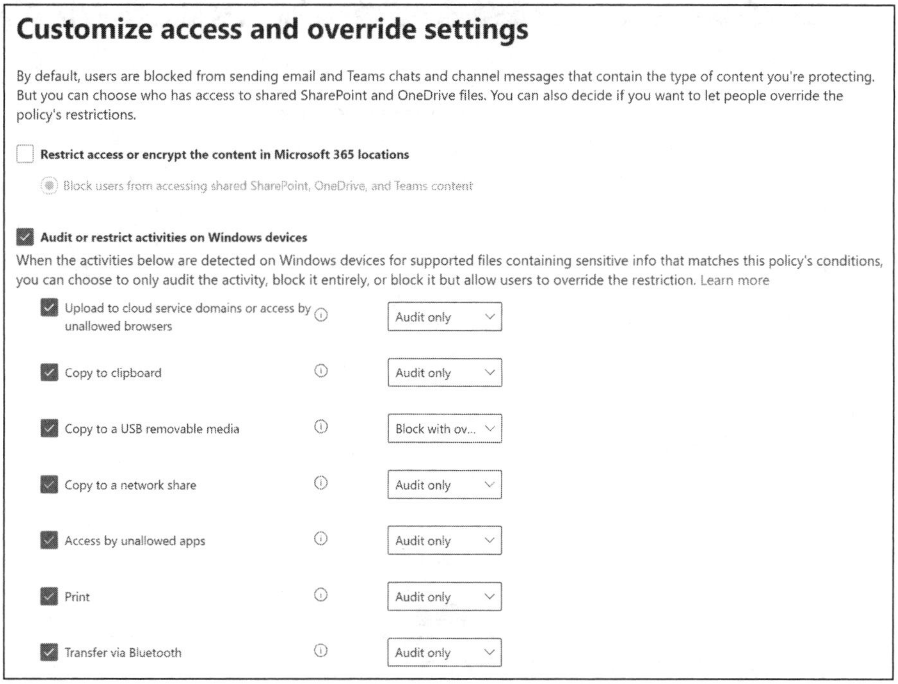

Customize access and override settings

By default, users are blocked from sending email and Teams chats and channel messages that contain the type of content you're protecting. But you can choose who has access to shared SharePoint and OneDrive files. You can also decide if you want to let people override the policy's restrictions.

☐ **Restrict access or encrypt the content in Microsoft 365 locations**

  ◉ Block users from accessing shared SharePoint, OneDrive, and Teams content

☑ **Audit or restrict activities on Windows devices**

When the activities below are detected on Windows devices for supported files containing sensitive info that matches this policy's conditions, you can choose to only audit the activity, block it entirely, or block it but allow users to override the restriction. Learn more

☑ Upload to cloud service domains or access by unallowed browsers	ⓘ		Audit only ⌄
☑ Copy to clipboard	ⓘ		Audit only ⌄
☑ Copy to a USB removable media	ⓘ		Block with ov... ⌄
☑ Copy to a network share	ⓘ		Audit only ⌄
☑ Access by unallowed apps	ⓘ		Audit only ⌄
☑ Print	ⓘ		Audit only ⌄
☑ Transfer via Bluetooth	ⓘ		Audit only ⌄

FIGURE 3-31 Customizing access for restricted content

12. On the **Test or Turn On the Policy** page, indicate whether you want to turn on the policy now, keep the policy turned off, or test it (the default). In this case, accept the default setting, and click **Next.**

> **NOTE** It is a good practice to test new policies before turning them on.

13. On the **Review Your Policy and Create It** page (see Figure 3-32), check the settings to ensure they are correct, and click **Submit.**

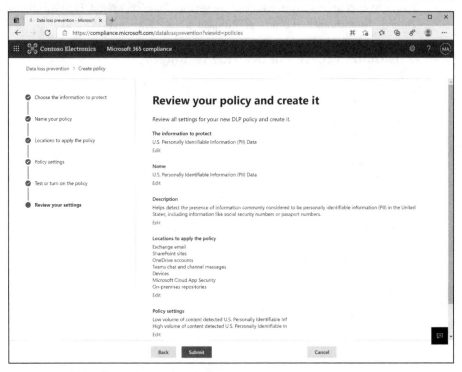

FIGURE 3-32 DLP policy settings review page

The console displays the policy and status. Note that it can take as long as an hour before the policy takes effect, as shown in Figure 3-33.

If you have more than one DLP policy, then policies are ordered, with each policy having an order number. The order number is shown when you view policies in the portal. When you get information about policies from PowerShell, however, you use the term *priority*. An order of 3 is the same as a priority of 3.

The first policy you create has an order or priority of 1; the second one has an order or priority of 2; and so on. You can't change the order, and the lower the number, the higher the priority. When you have multiple policies with conflicting rules, the most restrictive action is enforced. Here is an example of how priority works in action:

- **Rule 1 (priority/order 1)** Restricts access, allows user overrides
- **Rule 2 (priority/order 2)** Restricts access, notifies users, does not allow user overrides
- **Rule 3 (priority/order 3)** Notifies users, does not restrict access
- **Rule 4 (priority/order 4)** Restricts access, does not notify users
- **Rule 5 (priority/order 5)** Restricts access, notifies users, does not allow user overrides

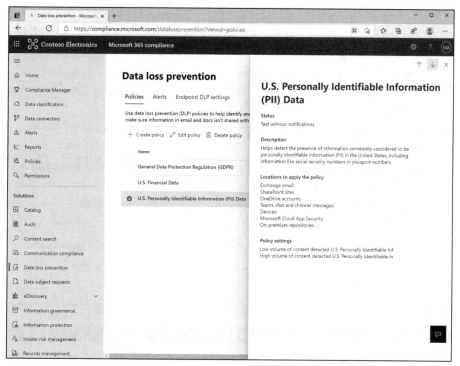

FIGURE 3-33 DLP policy overview

If you send an email that matches all of the rules (rule 1, 2, 3, 4, and 5), then rule 2 is enforced. That's because rule 2 is the most restrictive and highest priority. Notice that rule 2 and rule 5 have the same restrictions. However, rule 2 is higher priority, so it ends up being the rule enforced.

Configure DLP policies

In this section, you will first look at some key settings. After that, you'll walk through some of the policy settings.

You can configure DLP policies when you create them, after you create them, or both—for example, tweaking settings to enhance the outcome. Each policy can have three states.

- **Turned on**   When a policy is on, it evaluates content and takes actions, as configured.
- **Turned off**   When a policy is off, it does not evaluate content or take any action. Sometimes, administrators prefer to leave newly created policies turned off, have a peer review the policies, and then turn the policies on during a maintenance window.
- **In test mode**   You can test a rule before turning it on by using test mode. Optionally, you can have policy tips shown in test mode. It is a good practice to use test mode, run DLP reports, and then make necessary tweaks before turning on a policy.

Rules can have two states:

- **Turned on**   By default, rules in a policy are turned on. Turning off rules is useful for troubleshooting.

- **Turned off**   If you are troubleshooting a policy or find an issue with a rule in a policy (for example, it's too restrictive), you can temporarily turn off the rule. After making changes, you can turn the rule back on.

Policies can protect information in three locations. Inside of each location, you have additional options, as follows:

- **Exchange Online**   You can specify specific distribution groups to be included for protection. You can also specify distribution groups to be excluded from protection.

- **SharePoint Online**   You can specify specific SharePoint sites to be included or opt to exclude specific SharePoint sites.

- **OneDrive for Business**   You can include or exclude specific accounts.

Next, let's review policy conditions in a rule. Figure 3-34 shows the conditions for content within documents or emails.

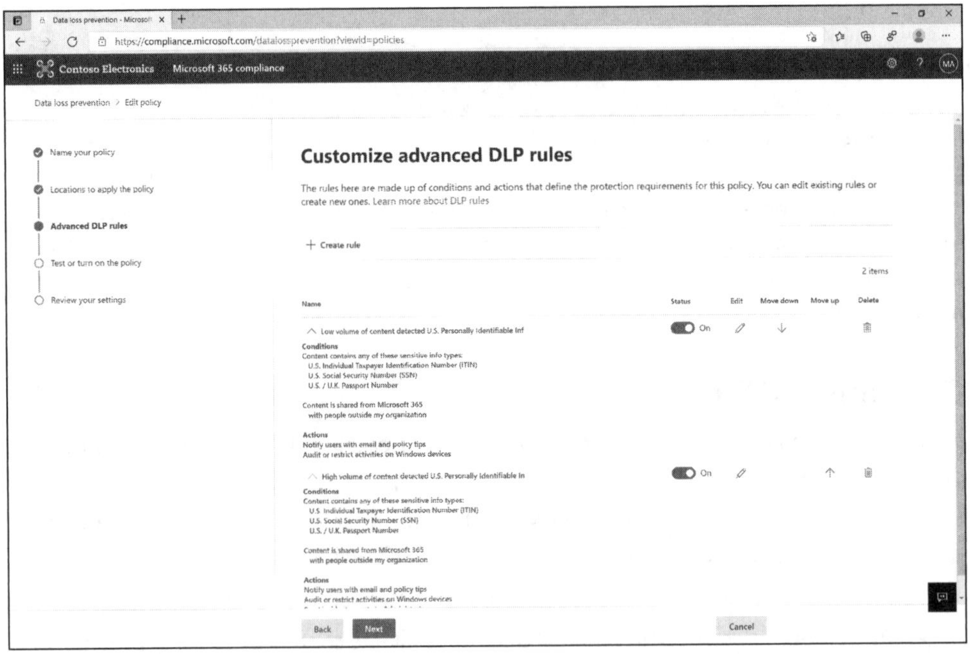

FIGURE 3-34   Customizing DLP rules

In this policy, there are two rules defined. These include a low-volume rule, which is triggered if there are between one and nine instances of the sensitive info types, with a match accuracy between 75 and 100. You can change the minimum and maximum instance counts and the minimum and maximum match accuracy numbers. For example, you could change the **Max Instance** count to **5** and handle everything above that in a high-volume rule.

As part of conditions, you can dictate whether a rule applies to content shared within your organization or outside your organization. You can add other conditions, too. The list of conditions you can add is:

- **Sender IP Address Is** Detect content sent from a specific IP address or range of IP addresses.

- **Any Email Attachment's Content Could Not Be Scanned** Flag email with attachments that cannot be scanned.

- **Any Email Attachment's Content Didn't Complete Scanning** Flag email with attachments that did not finish scanning.

- **Attachment Is Password Protected** Message an attachment that is password protected (and thus can't be opened to be scanned).

- **Recipient Domain Is** Detect when content is sent to a specific domain(s).

- **Attachment's File Extension Is** Detect email messages with attachments that have a specific file extension(s). For example, you might specify .exe as one file extension.

- **Document Property Is** Match data that has document properties. Document properties are used in Windows Server File Classification Infrastructure (FCI), SharePoint, and other third-party systems. Some organizations already use document properties to classify content (for example, sensitive data). In such organizations, it can be very efficient to reuse the document properties for DLP.

A rule has actions that dictate how to protect the content. The following actions are available:

- **Block People from Sharing and Restrict Access to Shared Content** When you block someone, it means they can't send email with the content, and can't access the content in SharePoint or OneDrive for Business. You can block people who are outside of your organization, or block everybody (excluding the content owner, the last person to modify the content, and the site admin).

- **Encrypt Email Messages** This action is only applicable to Exchange Online. It encrypts email messages using Azure Information Protection.

Each rule has user notification settings. You can opt to notify users or not, based on your goals. It is a good practice to notify users because it helps them understand the sensitivity of the data and to think about proper data usage.

In addition to notifying the user who sent, shared, or last modified the offending content, you can also email the SharePoint site owner, the owner of the OneDrive account or content, and additional people as designated by you. You can also enable users to override a policy if they see a policy tip. However, in most cases, this isn't a good practice when dealing with sensitive data; it adds risk to your organization by enabling users to bypass a DLP policy.

Manage DLP exceptions

So far, you've learned how DLP works and how a policy and a set of rules prevent or minimize data leakage. Next, you will look at exceptions. Exceptions are conditions that dictate when a

DLP rule *won't* apply to content. For example, you might have a DLP rule to protect tax data. However, you might have an exception if a document has a specific property and value (for example, a property named *Description* with a value of *Personal*).

Understand DLP exceptions

Before you implement exceptions, you should have a good understanding of their capabilities. Thereafter, you will have a better idea how to create and modify exceptions.

In a perfect world, you wouldn't need any exceptions. Your DLP configuration would be simple and easy to work with. Often, however, exceptions are required to meet your goals. Even so, you should try to keep your configuration as simple as possible while also meeting your requirements.

The available exceptions are:

- **Except If Content Contains Sensitive Information**   This exception enables you to specify sensitive information types or specific labels. In such scenarios, the content will not be subject to the rule.
- **Except If Content Is Shared**   This exception enables you to specify content shared internally or externally and to ensure such content will not be subject to the rule.
- **Except If Sender IP Address Is**   If you want to whitelist a specific IP address or IP address range, you can use this exception.
- **Except If Any Email Attachment Content Could Not Be Scanned**   This exception applies if an email message has an attachment that cannot be scanned.
- **Except If Any Email Attachment Content Didn't Complete Scanning**   This exception applies if an email message has an attachment that does not finish scanning.
- **Except If Attachment Is Password Protected**   This exception applies if an email attachment has a password (and thus can't be scanned).
- **Except If a Recipient Domain Is**   If you want to whitelist a domain(s), you can use this exception. For example, imagine that you use DLP for external communication. You acquire a company, and after the acquisition closes, you must ensure that email going to the acquired company's domain is not part of DLP.
- **Except If Attachment's File Extension Is**   If you want to whitelist specific file extensions for attachments, you can use this exception.
- **Except If Document Property Is**   Use this exception to check document properties for specific property values. In this scenario, you can exclude specific content based on the values.

Some settings are service specific. For example, exceptions that pertain to recipient domains are limited to use with Exchange/email.

As with most DLP settings, you should test them before you implement them in production. Otherwise, you might end up with undesirable behavior because it can be hard to understand the ramifications of an exception without seeing it work with production data.

Create DLP exceptions

You can establish exceptions during your initial DLP rule creation. However, you'll often find that you must create exceptions *after* a policy and rule are deployed, when the need for an exception becomes obvious. You can create DLP exceptions after a policy and rule are deployed by editing the rule in the portal. For example, Figure 3-35 shows a rule set up to protect the PII information you configured earlier in this skill section. Configuring an exception might be useful if you have a vendor or partner who handles your customer-service or tech-support department and you will routinely send IP addresses to them via email (such as in trouble tickets or support email).

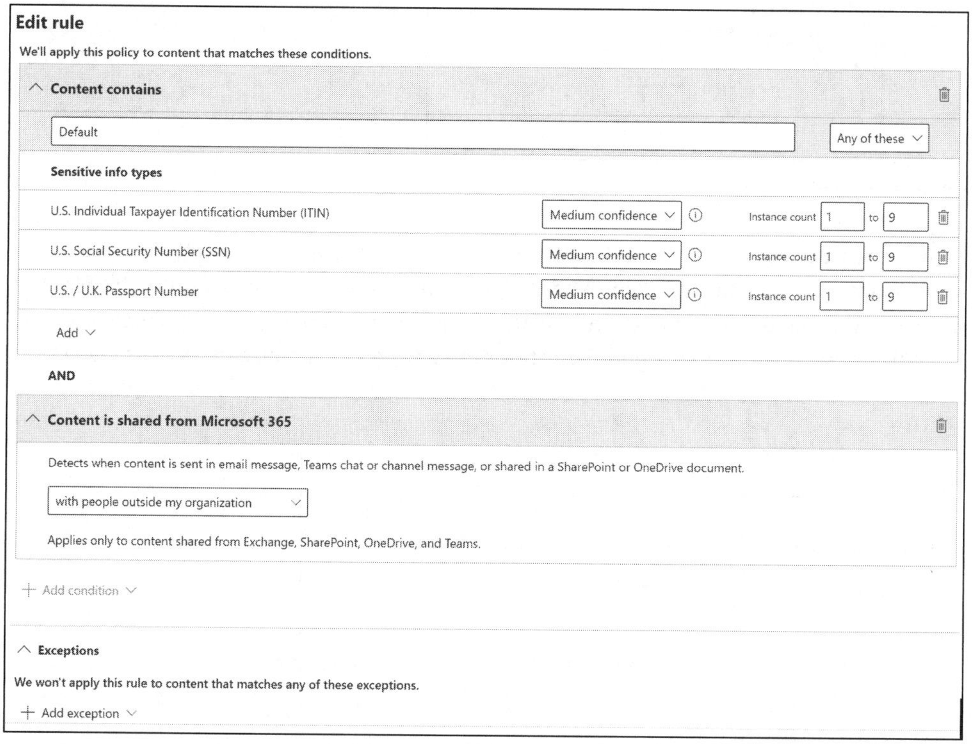

Edit rule

We'll apply this policy to content that matches these conditions.

∧ **Content contains**

| Default | | Any of these ∨ |

Sensitive info types

U.S. Individual Taxpayer Identification Number (ITIN)	Medium confidence ∨ ⓘ	Instance count 1 to 9
U.S. Social Security Number (SSN)	Medium confidence ∨ ⓘ	Instance count 1 to 9
U.S. / U.K. Passport Number	Medium confidence ∨ ⓘ	Instance count 1 to 9

Add ∨

AND

∧ **Content is shared from Microsoft 365**

Detects when content is sent in email message, Teams chat or channel message, or shared in a SharePoint or OneDrive document.

| with people outside my organization ∨ |

Applies only to content shared from Exchange, SharePoint, OneDrive, and Teams.

+ Add condition ∨

∧ **Exceptions**

We won't apply this rule to content that matches any of these exceptions.

+ Add exception ∨

FIGURE 3-35   DLP condition and exception

> **NOTE**   When you create exceptions, always use test mode to understand the impact of the exceptions on the policy's detection behavior.

Monitor DLP policy matches

After you deploy DLP policies, you need a way to find out whether they are working and how effective they are. You also need a way to pinpoint problems or unexpected behavior. Monitoring is an effective way to understand how DLP is functioning in your environment.

Use policy tips

Policy tips are small informational messages displayed in a web page or a client (such as Outlook). Often, tips are used to provide information to users. For example, if a user is composing an email message that violates a DLP policy, a policy tip can notify the user. The user then has a chance to rectify the violation before sending the email. Figure 3-36 shows a policy tip in Outlook. In this scenario, Brian is sending Bob a message, and there is a conflict with a DLP policy.

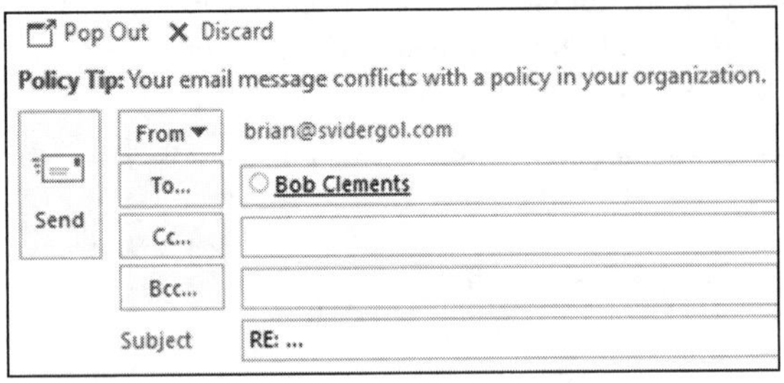

FIGURE 3-36   Policy tip in Outlook

The policy tip shown in Figure 3-36 is the default text. There are other default policy tips (such as when access to an item is blocked). Notice that the default text does not indicate which DLP policy was violated or provide much information for the user. Optionally, you can customize the text. Customization is per rule. Figure 3-37 shows the setting to customize the policy tip text.

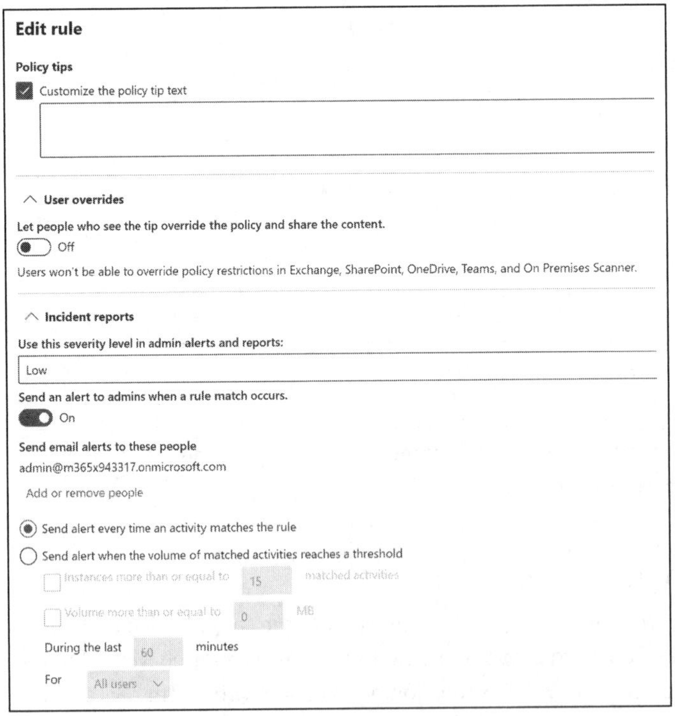

FIGURE 3-37   Customizing a policy tip

When you use policy tips, you have an option to enable users who have seen the policy tip to override the DLP policy. You can also require them to report false positives or enter a business justification for the override.

Use the DLP Incidents report

The DLP Incidents reports show you DLP policy matches by date and service (Exchange, SharePoint, and OneDrive for Business). You view this report in the Reports section of the Microsoft 365 compliance center dashboard. Figure 3-38 shows the DLP Incidents report. You can click the graph for this report or the **View Details** button to see a more detailed dedicated page.

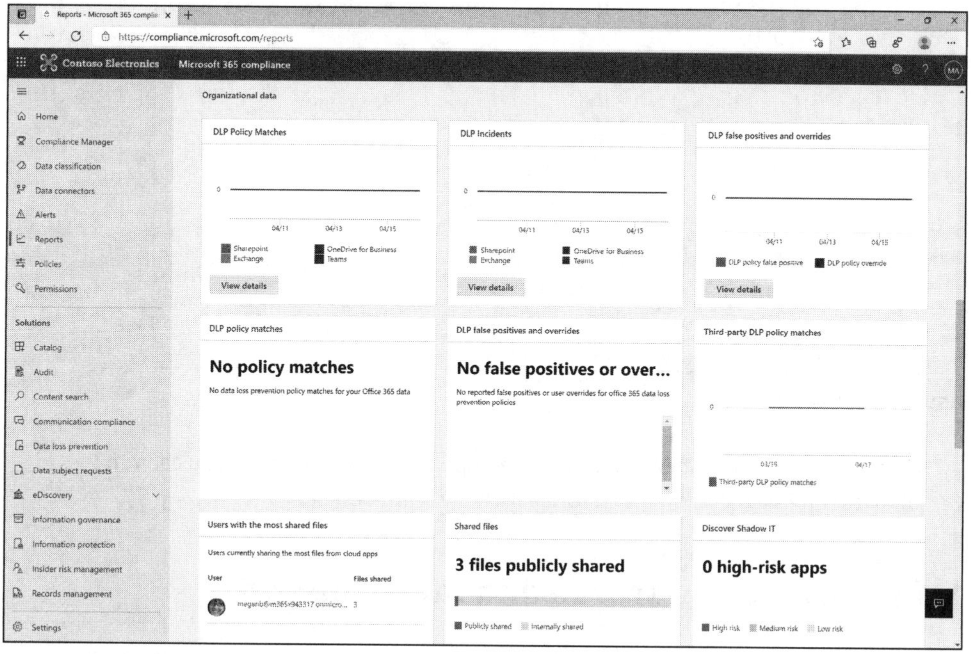

FIGURE 3-38   Reports dashboard

Use DLP reports

In addition to DLP Incident reports, you can use other reports to help you understand how your organization is complying with your DLP policies. The following reports are available in the Reports section of Microsoft 365 compliance center:

- **DLP Policy Matches**   This report shows the number of policies that matched in the last week. Although the default view is a graph, you can customize the output to view the data as a table. It also shows the breakdown of policy matches per service: Exchange, SharePoint, and OneDrive for Business.

- **DLP False Positive and Override**   If you enable users to report false positives and override a policy, this report will show you when and how often it is happening.

Figure 3-39 shows the DLP Policy Matches graph. You access this graph by clicking the corresponding graph or **View Details** button in the Reports section of the dashboard.

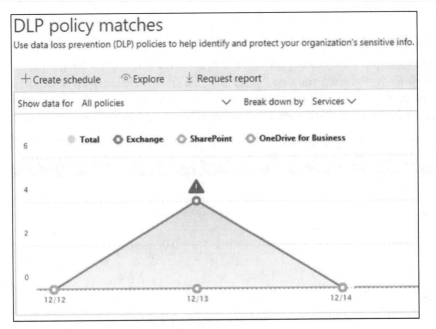

FIGURE 3-39   DLP policy match graph

You can also use PowerShell to obtain some report data. For example, you can run the `Get-DlpDetectionsReport` command to see a list of recent detections.

Skill 3.5: Manage search and investigation

Historically, auditing has been a decentralized feature available in each of the Office 365 services. You individually configured each service for auditing and individually searched each service for items.

Microsoft is moving to a more centralized approach to data governance. Today, while you can still configure each services individually for auditing, you can also search the audit logs across all services from the same place. This skill section looks at the auditing feature and configuration.

This skill covers how to:

- Plan for auditing
- Plan for eDiscovery
- Implement insider risk management
- Design Content Search solution

Plan for auditing

Office 365 audits many activities by default. From an administrative perspective, there isn't much to do to configure audit log retention. This section covers default auditing settings and additional auditing you can enable.

Understand prerequisites

Although auditing is enabled by default, you might need to check your licensing, permissions, and other settings before you start looking at audit logs. The following items are the key prerequisites you must know about:

- **Permissions** To have complete control over auditing settings, you must be assigned the organization management or compliance management role or be a global administrator in Office 365. Other roles cannot turn auditing on or off. To search and view audit logs, you can use the view-only audit logs or audit logs role.

- **Licensing** The Office 365 E3 license offers up to 90 days of audit log retention. The Office 365 E5 license offers up to 365 days of audit log retention. You can, however, use any Office 365 subscription and add on the Office 365 Advanced Compliance license to get up to 365 days of audit log retention. Today, you can bundle Office 365 Advanced Compliance with Azure Information Protection in a package named Information Protection & Compliance. Expect package names and offerings to change. For the exam, just be aware of the Office 365 Advanced Compliance add-on to gain additional days of retention.

Understand auditing

Office 365 audits several areas across various services by default. For some organizations, the default auditing is enough to meet company requirements. The following activities are audited by default:

- Admin activity in Azure Active Directory
- Admin activity in Exchange Online
- Admin activity in SharePoint Online
- User activity in SharePoint Online and OneDrive for Business
- User and admin activity in Dynamics 365
- User and admin activity in Microsoft Flow
- User and admin activity in Microsoft Stream
- User and admin activity in Microsoft Teams
- User and admin activity in Power BI
- User and admin activity in Sway
- User and admin activity in Yammer
- eDiscovery activities in the Office 365 Security & Compliance Center

Monitor unified audit logs

Before unified audit logs, admins had to search logs in each service. For example, the admin might search in the Exchange Online logs and then search through the SharePoint Online logs. With unified audit logs, admins can search in one place: the Microsoft 365 compliance center. This chapter offers an overview of the unified audit log and walks through various search scenarios.

> **NOTE** Auditing is turned on by default, but you must have appropriate permissions to search logs.

Verify that audit logging is enabled

Before you start using unified audit logs, assuming all the prerequisites are in place, you must verify that audit logging is enabled. As mentioned, audit logging is enabled by default, but it might have been disabled somewhere along the way.

To make sure audit logging is enabled, follow these steps:

1. Run the following PowerShell command.

   ```
   Get-AdminAuditLogConfig | FL UnifiedAuditLogIngestionEnabled
   ```

   If this command returns True, then audit logging is already enabled.

2. If the previous command returned False, run the following PowerShell command to turn audit log search on:

   ```
   Set-AdminAuditLogConfig -UnifiedAuditLogIngestionEnabled $true
   ```

> **NOTE** If logging is enabled and you want to disable it, run the following command:
> Set-AdminAuditLogConfig -UnifiedAuditLogIngestionEnabled $false

> **EXAM TIP**
>
> Watch for troubleshooting scenarios in the exam in which audit logs don't deliver the data you expect or you aren't getting audit data at all. If any of the answer choices relate to turning on auditing or adjusting permissions, you might have found your answer!

Perform searches in unified audit logs

You can search unified audit logs in the Microsoft 365 compliance center or through Power-Shell. You can search for all activities, very specific activities, or activities in a specific service, such as Exchange Online.

The following steps walk you through searching unified audit logs in the Microsoft 365 compliance center:

1. Use an administrator account to log in to the Microsoft 365 compliance center at *https://compliance.microsoft.com.*

2. In the navigation bar, click **Audit.**

   The **Audit** page opens with the **Search** tab displayed. (See Figure 3-40.)

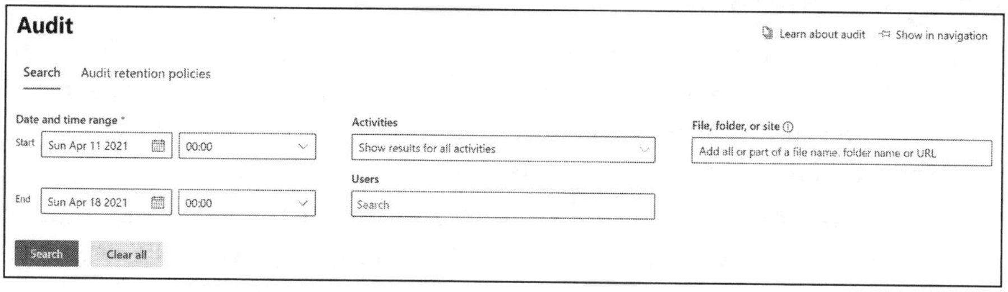

FIGURE 3-40 Unified audit log search interface

3. In the **Date and Time Range** section, use the **Start** and **End** settings to choose a start date, start time, end date, and end time.

   > **NOTE** If you are licensed with E3 or equivalent, audit logs can be retained for 90 days. If you are licensed for E5 or equivalent, audit logs can be retained for 365 days. (This option is currently in preview, but likely to become generally available soon.)

4. In the **Activities** section, leave the default settings.

5. In the **Users** section, search for the user or users you want to include in the search. You can specify one user, multiple users, or all users (by leaving the box blank).

6. In the File, Folder, or Site section, specify the file, folder, or site that you want to search for. This is optional and is relevant for some services.

   Figure 3-40 shows a search for all activities from April 11, 2021 to April 18, 2021, for any user, without a specific file, folder, or site.

7. Click **Search**.

   Search results will be displayed in the right pane. You can click an entry to bring up the details for that entry.

As mentioned, you can also use PowerShell to search unified logs. You do this by using the `Search-UnifiedAuditLog` command.

Design Content Search solution

You can use the Content Search tool to quickly search your Office 365 services for material matching targeted criteria. The results can be used to determine scope, impact, and next steps in the event additional action is required, such as a legal hold. You can save search queries for reuse and export search results for offline review.

In the following steps, you will create a search query for a fictitious company named Contoso Electronics. The legal department needs to know if any documents were shared in the last 30 days related to the Mark 8 Project.

1. Use an administrator account to log in to the Microsoft 365 compliance center at *https://compliance.microsoft.com*.

2. In the navigation bar, click **Show All**, and then click **Content Search**.

3. On the **Content Search** page, click **+Guided Search**.

   This option provides a guided experience for creating a new search query. Once you are comfortable with creating queries, you can click **+New Search** and create your own queries from scratch.

4. On the **New Search** panel, in the **Name Your Search** box, type a name for your new search query—in this example, **Mark 8 Project**.

5. Optionally, type a description to help differentiate this search query from other search queries. Then click **Next**.

6. On the **Choose Locations** tab, click the **All Locations** option button. Then click **Next**.

   This enables your search to find data across Office 365 services. If you intend to only search a specific service, such as Exchange Online, you can opt to specify that location instead.

7. On the **Create Query** tab, in the **Keywords** box, type the following keywords:

   - **project**
   - **mark 8**
   - **mark 8 project**

8. Below the search query, click **+Add Conditions**.

9. In the **Add Conditions** panel, select the **Date** and **File Type** check boxes, and click **Add**.

10. In the **Date** section, specify the desired dates—in this example, configure the date representing the last 30 days.

11. In the **File Type** section enter the following file types:

- **docx**
- **xlsx**
- **pptx**
- **pdf**

12. Click **Finish**.

You will return to the Content Search page and the query will run automatically. Any results from the query will be displayed in the main window.

You can update search queries and save your changes from the search results page for the specific query. For example, if there are too many results returned for the Mark 8 Project query, you can open the results for that search query and update the list of keywords or add more conditions.

Results for search queries can also be exported. To access export options for Content Search, select the project whose query results you want to export and click **More**. A panel opens containing options to export results or reports. As shown in Figure 3-41, these options are as follows:

- **View Results**   This outputs a copy of all discovered results. Exchange content can be exported as a PST file or as individual emails. Individual messages and SharePoint content can be exported as a compressed ZIP file.

- **Export Report**   This outputs a report in CSV format. The report contains properties such as sender, recipient, attachments, and date received.

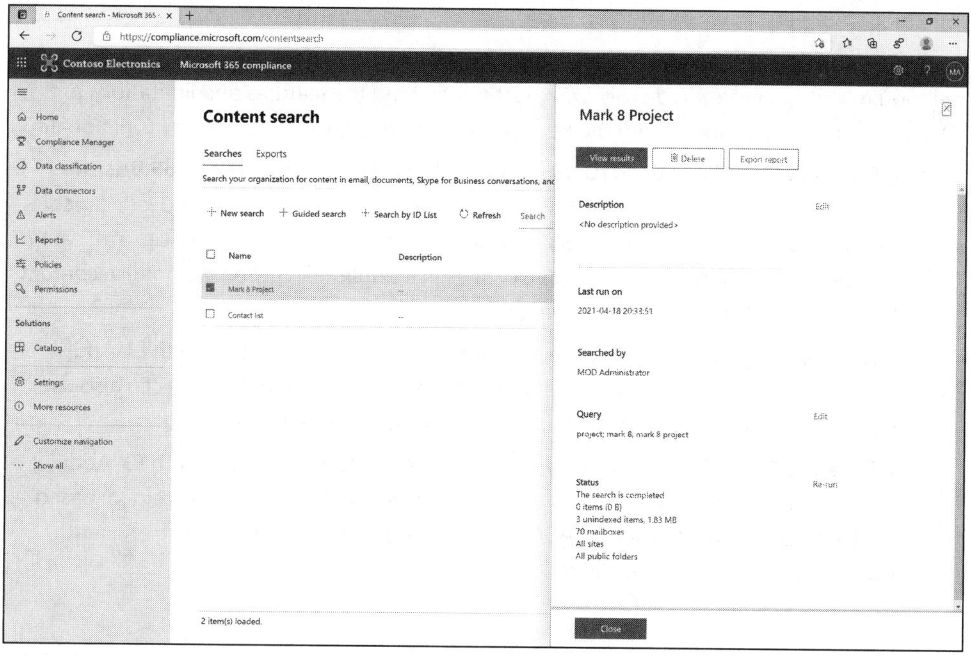

FIGURE 3-41   Content Search export options

Plan for eDiscovery

The eDiscovery tools in Microsoft 365 give you the ability to create electronic discovery cases when required for legal issues. With eDiscovery, you can create either Core or Advanced cases, both of which enable you to create in-place or litigation holds. You then combine this with the Content Search to find data relative to the eDiscovery case.

Often, the first step an administrator will take before creating an eDiscovery case will be to use the Content Search tool. Content Search is part of the eDiscovery solution. Content Search enables administrators to quickly search for content across various services in Office 365. Content Search and eDiscovery generate the same results, including data from email messages, Skype for Business conversations, documents in SharePoint Online or OneDrive for Business, Microsoft Teams, and Office 365 groups. However, they offer different capabilities, such as exporting reports and assigning an in-place hold.

Understand prerequisites

This section looks at the prerequisites for working with eDiscovery and Content Search. These prerequisites include licensing considerations and permissions required to perform various tasks. As mentioned, Content Search is part of the eDiscovery solution, so licensing and permissions are similar for both tools. You must have a clear understanding of these prerequisites for the exam.

LICENSING CONSIDERATIONS

The licensing options for Content Search are tied to eDiscovery. As you move up in licensing, you unlock more eDiscovery features.

When it comes to licensing, you want to acquire the license that provides all the features you require, but not more. To do this, you must understand the features and limitations of eDiscovery licensing. Following are the key license types that include eDiscovery functionality.

- **Office 365 E1/Office 365 F1/Office 365 Business Essentials/Office 365 Business Premium** The E1 license is the lowest license that provides some eDiscovery capabilities. With an E1 license, you can perform searches across Office 365 services. You can also search across multiple mailboxes or sites in a single search. You cannot use content holds or export results from the searches.

- **Office 365 E3** With an E3 license, you get the same functionality as with E1. Additionally, you can export data from the search and use content holds. You can also use eDiscovery cases, which enable you to organize and segment searches.

- **Office 365 E5** With an E5 license, you get the same functionality as with E3. Additionally, you gain access to the Advanced eDiscovery feature, which uses cloud-based analytics to analyze your searches. Advanced eDiscovery provides a more efficient eDiscovery process, potentially reducing costs.

EXAM TIP

If you have Office 365 E3 and want to use Advanced eDiscovery, you can purchase the Advanced Compliance add-on instead of upgrading to the E5 license. However, users who are targeted by Advanced eDiscovery must have an E5 license. Thus, this is something you can do for some admins, but not across your entire user population.

PERMISSIONS

To enable administrators to perform eDiscovery or use Content Search, you must assign the necessary permissions. By default, nobody has permissions—even your existing Office 365 administrators.

The Microsoft 365 compliance center provides several built-in role groups. One such role group, eDiscovery manager, has two role groups inside of it. You assign these to administrators who need to work with eDiscovery.

- **eDiscovery manager** An eDiscovery manager can create, view, and edit cases that they have access to. By default, they only have access to cases they create. You can add users or groups to this role group.

- **eDiscovery Administrator** An eDiscovery administrator can view and edit all cases. By default, they only have access to cases they create. They can, however, add themselves to any other case. You can only add users, not groups, to this role group.

The eDiscovery Manager role group is assigned roles. The roles give the permissions needed to perform eDiscovery tasks. The default roles for the eDiscovery manager role group are:

- **Export** With this permission, you can export data from a search.
- **RMS decrypt** You can decrypt RMS-protected content so you can export the data from a search.
- **Review** This permission enables you to work with advanced eDiscovery features, such as analyzing results.
- **Preview** You can view the list of items returned from a search.
- **Compliance Search** You can search across multiple mailboxes.
- **Case management** You can create, edit, and delete eDiscovery cases. You can also adjust permissions for cases you own.
- **Hold** This permission enables you to place a hold on content.

You can edit the roles included in the role group. However, this isn't necessary unless you have a specific requirement to enable more functionality or restrict some eDiscovery tasks.

In addition to eDiscovery role groups, there are certain roles that can perform some eDiscovery tasks:

- **Reviewer**   A reviewer can use advanced eDiscovery functions for existing cases that they are a member of.
- **Organization management**   Members of this role can create, edit, and delete eDiscovery cases, search across multiple mailboxes, place content on hold, and perform search and purge tasks—that is, perform a search and then delete data in bulk based on that search.
- **Compliance administrator**   A compliance administrator can create, edit, and delete eDiscovery cases; search across multiple mailboxes; and place content on hold.

Understand legal holds

At any point, your organization could be required to preserve content in Office 365. With eDiscovery, you accomplish this by placing the content on an in-place hold.

An administrator can place content on hold across all Office 365 services. Content holds offer granular controls that leverage the same query interface seen in Content Search and eDiscovery. In this skill, you are going to look at how holds work and how to configure them in the Microsoft 365 compliance center.

HOW HOLDS WORK

Holds focus on preserving data. Sometimes, holds are for a defined period. Other times, holds are indefinite (or the hold requirements are not finalized yet). Holds are invisible to users and cannot be bypassed. Holds are available for the following areas:

- **Exchange Online mailboxes**   Although you can target groups too, the mailboxes that are members are placed on hold, not the actual group.
- **Exchange Online public folders**   While you can place holds on public folders, you cannot specify individual public folders. Instead, you have to place a hold on all public folders if you want to hold items in any of the folders.
- **SharePoint Online sites**   You can choose individual SharePoint Online sites to hold data. You just need the URL for the sites you want to target for holds.

When you place holds on mailboxes, the data is preserved in the Recoverable Items folder, which isn't viewable with the default view in Outlook. The Recoverable Items folder also holds permanently deleted items, such as when users delete items from the Deleted Items folder. A dedicated subfolder named DiscoveryHold is used to store held items.

For the exam, be sure to know some of the details around holds, such as:

- Items in the Recoverable Items folder don't count toward a user's mailbox quota. Instead, the Recoverable Items folder has its own quota, which is 30 GB by default.
- When a hold is placed on a mailbox, the quota for the Recoverable Items folder is automatically increased to 100 GB. You can enable the archive mailbox and use auto-expanding archiving if you need more space.

- A minimum license of Exchange Online Plan 2 or Office 365 E3 is required for a mailbox to be placed on hold.

- Deleting a mailbox on hold will convert it to an inactive mailbox. Inactive mailboxes can no longer receive messages and are not listed in the global address list. The contents of the mailbox will be retained for the duration of the hold.

NEED MORE REVIEW?   WORKING WITH OFFICE 365 HOLDS

To find out more about holds, see *https://docs.microsoft.com/exchange/security-and-compliance/in-place-and-litigation-holds*.

CONFIGURE HOLDS

The following steps show the process to create a hold for all email items for one mailbox. To create a hold, you must have created a case and defined a search.

1. From your existing case, click the **Holds** tab.

2. On the **Holds** tab, click **+Create**.

3. On the **Create a New Hold** panel, type a name for the hold—for example, **Recover Purged Items**. Then click **Next**.

4. On the **Choose Locations** tab, click **Choose Users, Groups, or Teams**. Then, click **Choose Users, Groups, or Teams**.

5. In the search text box, type the name of the person you are targeting for the hold. A search will be performed dynamically. If it is not, click the **search** (magnifying glass) icon.

6. In the results, click the checkbox next to the target mailbox and then click **Choose**.

7. Click **Done**. Then click **Next** to continue.

8. On the **Create Query** tab, type a keyword or list of keywords, such as a configuration referred to as a *query-based hold*. This limits the search results to the keyword(s) that you specify. Or, if you want to hold everything, do not enter anything. This is called an *indefinite hold*. Optionally, add conditions. Then click **Next**.

9. On the **Review Your Settings** tab, click **Create This Hold**.

    Figure 3-42 shows a sample hold status panel. In this example, a hold named Recover Purged Items has been created.

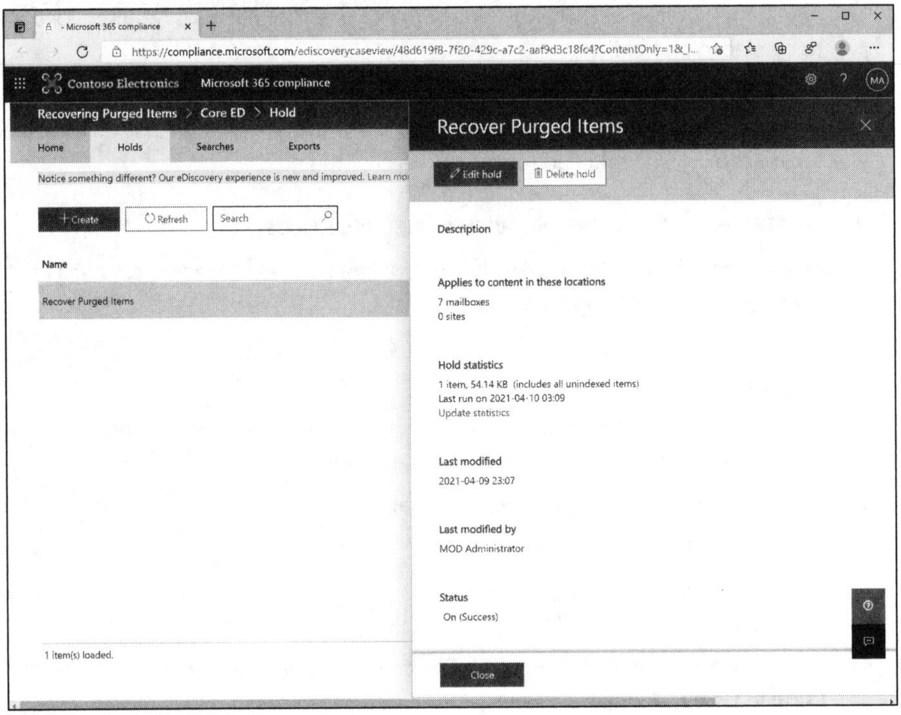

FIGURE 3-42 eDiscovery hold details

10. Click **Close**.

> **NEED MORE REVIEW?   MANAGING CONTENT HOLDS**
>
> To find out more about configuring and managing holds, read through
> *https://docs.microsoft.com/office365/securitycompliance/ediscovery-cases#step-4-*
> *place-content-locations-on-hold.*

Configure eDiscovery

In this skill, you will work with eDiscovery. eDiscovery extends the capabilities of Content Search. With eDiscovery, administrators can create cases for ongoing events. Cases offer an extra layer of permissions, enabling you to control who has access to a case and what level of access they have. You will also work with advanced eDiscovery, an enhancement that enables additional analysis of the eDiscovery results.

Work with eDiscovery cases

You can use eDiscovery cases to organize your eDiscovery searches, preserve content, and export data from your searches. Cases help organize your eDiscovery work. You create and manage cases from the Microsoft 365 compliance center.

In the following steps, you create and configure an eDiscovery case based on a fictitious company named Contoso Electronics that needs to uncover information about a broken part. As part of a case, you essentially create a search query and a hold that retains any data returned by that query.

1. Use an administrator account to log in to the Microsoft 365 compliance center at *https://compliance.microsoft.com*.

2. In the navigation bar, click **Show All**, choose **eDiscovery**, and click **Core**.

3. On the **Core eDiscovery** page, click **Create a Case**.

4. On the **New Case** page, type a name for the case, such as **Recovering Purged Items**, and then click **Save**.

5. Click the **Pop-Out** icon to manage the case.

6. Click the **Holds** tab, and then click **Create**.

7. Provide a name for the hold, such as **Recover Purged Items**, and click **Next**.

8. On the **Choose Locations** page, click **Choose Users, Groups, or Teams** for Exchange email, and then click **Choose Users, Groups, or Teams** again.

9. In the search box, search for a user, group, or team in your environment. When you find the one you're looking for, click **Choose**, and then click **Done**.

10. On the **Query** page, add keywords to the query, such as **broken**, and click **Next**.

11. Click **Create This Hold**.

ADJUST AND EXPORT

After previewing the results, you can adjust your search query, similar to a Content Search. For example, you can add more conditions, change the locations, or add more keywords. To export the results from a search, follow these steps:

1. From the search results, click the **More** button and then click **Export Results** in the drop-down menu that appears.

2. In the **Export Results** panel, configure the export options:

   - **Output Options** You can export all items that are in a usable format, all items regardless of whether they are in a usable format, or just items that are in an unusable format.

- **Export Exchange Content Options** You can export all Exchange content in a single PST file for each mailbox where data was found, in a single PST file for all messages found, in one PST file with a single folder for all messages found, or individual messages.
- **De-Duplication** Optionally, you can enable de-duplication. For example, if your search found results in 53 mailboxes, you can use de-duplication so that you don't get the same message from all 53 mailboxes. (Instead, you get a single message.)

3. Click **Export**. Then click **Generate Report**.

4. Click the **Exports tab**. Then, in the list of completed exports, click the export you just ran.

5. In the panel that appears, copy the export key.

   The export key is sensitive, so you should protect it like a password or secret. It can be used by anybody to download the search results.

6. Click **Download Report**.

   You must use Microsoft Edge or Internet Explorer to perform the download.

7. If this is your first time downloading results, you will be prompted to install the Microsoft Office 365 eDiscovery Export Tool. This tool is required to download results. Click **Install**.

8. In the **eDiscovery Export Tool** pop-up box, paste the export key, browse to the location where you want to save the data, and click **Start**.

9. When the status shows that the process is complete, click **Close**.

   The exported data will be saved to a folder. Inside, you will find a summary CSV file along with the data. The data is separated into folders by service.

USE ADVANCED FEATURES

By default, the Core eDiscovery functionality is used when working with eDiscovery cases. You can switch to advanced eDiscovery to unlock additional functionality, such as analyzing your search results. As discussed, you must have the right licensing for the advanced functionality.

Follow these steps to create an advanced case and analyze the results:

1. Use an administrator account to log in to the Microsoft 365 compliance center at *https://compliance.microsoft.com*.

2. In the navigation bar, click **Show All**, choose **eDiscovery**, and click **Advanced**.

3. Type a name for the case.

4. Select the **No, Just Go to the Home Page. I'll Use the Default Case Settings for Now** option and click **Save**.

5. After the case loads, click the **Settings** tab. (See Figure 3-43.) This is where you manage information, access and permissions, and search and analytics for the case.

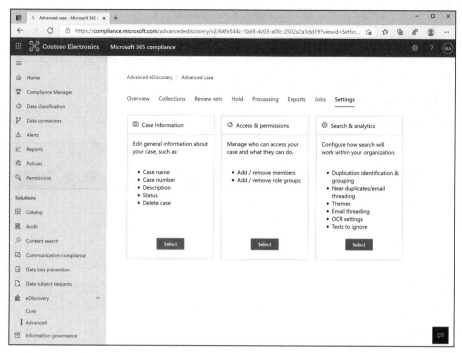

FIGURE 3-43 Advanced case settings

6. In the **Search & Analytics** section, click **Select**.

7. Configure the desired settings in the Search & Analytics panel. (See Figure 3-44.) For example, select the **Enable OCR** check box to enable optical character recognition. Then click **Save and Exit**.

Search & analytics

☑ Near duplicates/email threading

Document and email
similarity threshold

| 65 | % |

☑ Themes

Max number of themes

| 100 |

☐ Include numbers in themes

☑ Adjust maximum number of themes dynamically

☑ Automatically create a query named "For Review" after running analytics on a review set

Min number of words

| 10 |

Max number of words

| 500000 |

Ignore Text (0) ✎ Edit

Optical Character Recognition

☐ Enable OCR

Max image size

| 24576 | KB |

◉ Low accuracy (fastest speed)

FIGURE 3-44 Advanced case Search & Analytics settings

8. Click the **Review Set** tab. Then click **Add Review Set**.

9. Type a name for the review set and click **Add**.

10. Click the review set to open its query page. Then click **New Query**.

11. Add a condition to the query and click **Save**.

12. On the review set's page, click **Manage Review Set**.

13. In the **Analytics** section, click **Run Analytics for the Review Set**. (See Figure 3-45.)

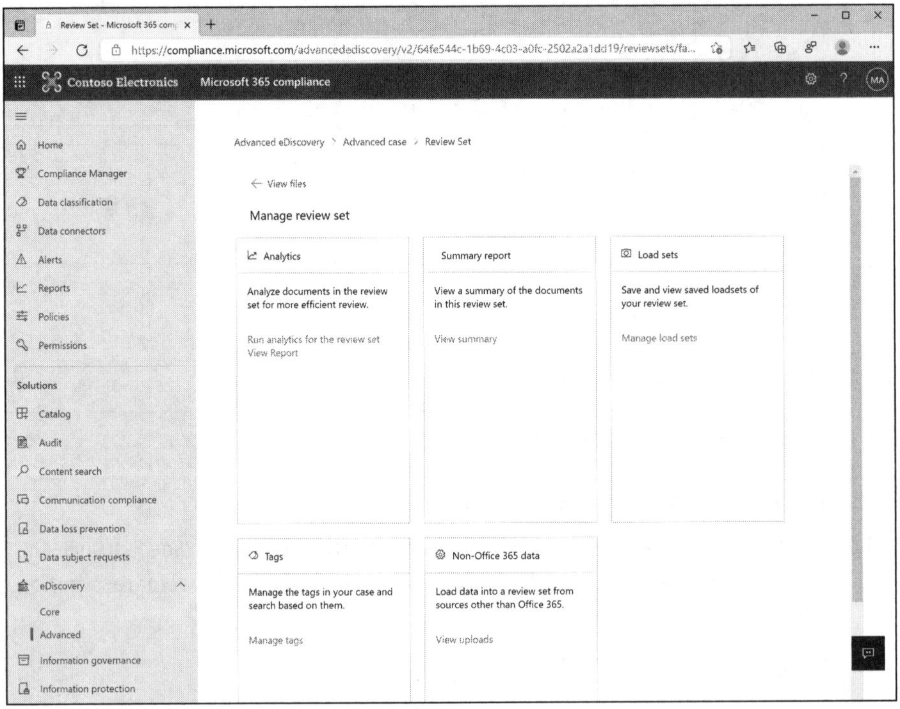

FIGURE 3-45 The Manage Review Set page

14. Click **Yes** to confirm that the analytics run could take some time to process.

NEED MORE REVIEW?   EXPRESS ANALYSIS SETTINGS

You have the option to run an express analysis. To find out more, see *https://docs.microsoft.com/en-us/microsoft-365/compliance/analyzing-data-in-review-set?view=o365-worldwide.*

Implement insider risk management

Insider risk management is another component of the Microsoft 365 compliance center that targets internal policies and alerts for the organization. Insider risk management is a part of the Microsoft 365 E5 compliance add-on, which is included with Microsoft 365 E5 or as an add-on to a variety of E3 subscription types.

Understand insider risk management roles

Insider risk management has five built-in roles to manage or audit risk-related policies. These roles are as follows:

- **Insider risk management**   This role provides a single group with all permissions. This is useful in small organizations where separation of roles or duties might not exist.
- **Insider risk management admin**   This role can be used to create and manage policies, global settings, and the roles for other users.
- **Insider risk management analyst**   This role has permission to access and view alerts, cases, analytics insights, and templates. However, the role cannot view the content explorer.
- **Insider risk management investigator**   This role has permission to access alerts, cases, templates, and the content explorer.
- **Insider risk management auditor**   This role can access the insider risk management audit log.

Change insider risk management global settings

After you have identified the appropriate role or roles for the administrators and users in your organization, the next aspects of insider risk to consider are the global settings. These settings apply to all policies created across several policy control components. As of this writing, many components are still in preview. The current global settings are:

- Privacy
- Indicators
- Policy timelines
- Intelligent detections
- Export alerts (preview)
- Priority user groups (preview)
- Priority physical assets (preview)
- Power Automate flows (preview)
- Microsoft Teams (preview)
- Analytics (preview)

To access these global settings for configuration purposes, follow these steps.

1. Use an administrator account to log in to the Microsoft 365 compliance center at *https://compliance.microsoft.com.*

2. In the navigation bar, click **Show All**, and then click **Insider Risk Management**.

3. At the top of the page, click **Insider Risk Settings**.

   Figure 3-46 shows the settings, including the settings still in preview at the time of this writing.

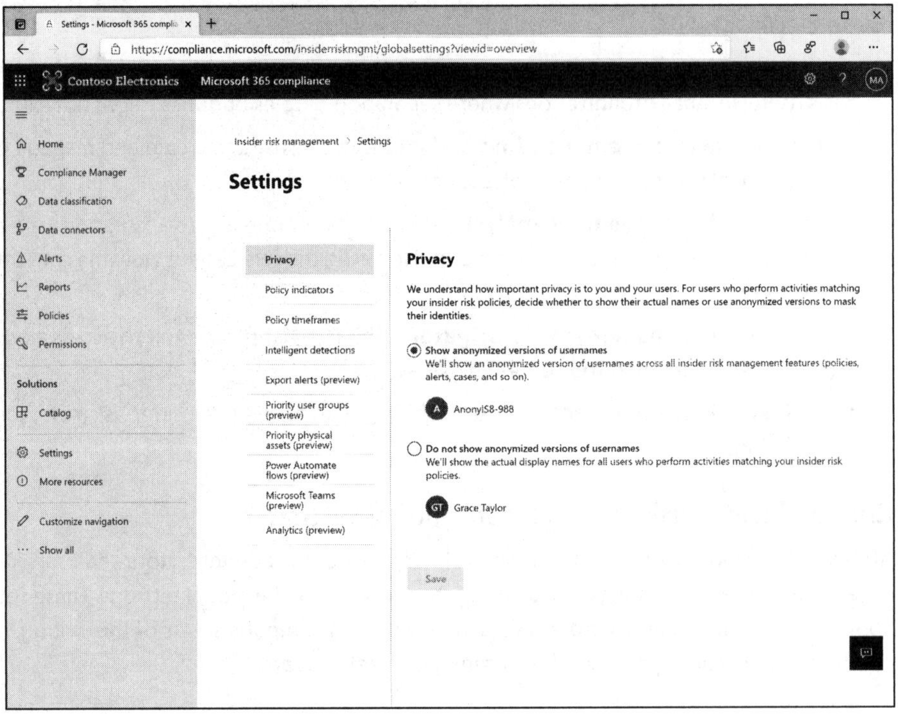

FIGURE 3-46   Insider risk management global settings

Create an insider risk management policy

After you have configured the desired global settings, your next step to implement insider risk management is to create policies. Insider risk management policies are divided into three categories:

- Data theft
- Security policy violations (preview)
- Data leaks

Each category has built-in templates that you can use to begin creating policies for your organization. Follow these steps to create an insider risk management policy:

1. Use an administrator account to log in to the Microsoft 365 compliance center at *https://compliance.microsoft.com*.

2. In the navigation bar, click **Show All**, and then click **Insider Risk Management**.

3. Click the **Policies** tab and click **Create Policy**.

4. Select the **Data Theft By Departing Users** template. Then click **Next**.

5. Type a display name for the policy and click **Next**.

6. Select specific users or groups to which the policy should apply. Alternatively, leave the default setting of all users and groups as is. Then click **Next**.

   Choosing specific users and groups is helpful in a global organization, where you might need individual policies for certain geographies or regions.

7. On the **Content to Prioritize** page, accept the default setting to specify content. (Alternatively, you can choose to specify content later.) Then click **Next**.

   You can prioritize SharePoint sites, sensitive info types, and sensitivity labels.

8. On the **Indicators and Triggering Event** page, specify what event should trigger the policy and what indicators might be associated with that event. Then click **Next**.

   The specific policy settings are as follows:

   - **Triggering Events**   The condition that causes the event to be triggered.
   - **Office Indicators**   Actions a user takes in Microsoft Office or Office 365 that trigger the policy.
   - **Device Indicators (preview)**   Actions a user takes on a monitored device that trigger the policy.
   - **Physical Access Indicators**   Attempts to access sensitive information after termination.
   - **Microsoft Cloud App Security Indicators**   Activities within connected cloud apps that trigger the policy.
   - **Sequence Detection**   When two or more activities are performed that suggest a higher risk of data leaks.
   - **Cumulative Exfiltration Detection**   A user appears to be sharing more data than the average user in the organization.
   - **Risk Score Boosters**   Activities that increase a user's risk score compared to normal day-to-day activities.

9. On the **Indicator Thresholds** page, specify whether to use default thresholds or set your own custom values, and click **Next**.

10. On the **Review Settings and Finish** page, click **Submit**.

Figure 3-47 shows all the settings configured for this policy.

> **NOTE** It can take as long as 24 hours for alerts to appear on the Alerts tab after you create the policy.

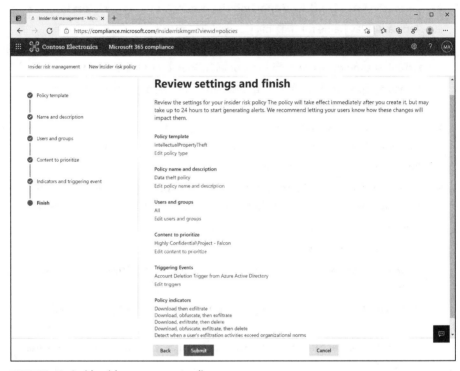

FIGURE 3-47 Insider risk management policy

Thought experiment

In this thought experiment, demonstrate your skills and knowledge of the topics covered in this chapter. You can find the answers in the section that follows.

You are the systems administrator for Contoso Electronics. Contoso Electronics runs several skiing and outdoor activity locations throughout the world.

The company has an on-premises environment with two data centers. The company has AD DS on-premises, along with some internal servers and Windows 10 clients. For email and collaboration, the company uses Office 365. Soon, the company will start using OneDrive for Business to store data that is currently stored on-premises file servers. The company recently created a dedicated IT team to handle IT security. The new team is responsible for compliance, data loss prevention, backups, and data governance.

The new team reviewed the existing implementation for data in Office 365 and found the following:

- The company is using Exchange Online retention tags and retention policies.
- The company is not using information rights management (IRM) with SharePoint Online.
- The company is not retaining SharePoint data.
- The company is not using OneDrive for Business.

The security management team has drafted new requirements for the organization:

1. The company must centralize the configuration of retention to ensure that retention settings are the same across as many Office 365 services as possible. What action must be taken to unify the data retention configuration?

2. The data in some SharePoint Online libraries must be encrypted, even if users do not opt to encrypt the data. What should be configured to encrypt data automatically?

You must reconfigure the environment to meet the new requirements.

Thought experiment answers

This section contains the solution to the thought experiment. Each answer explains why the answer choice is correct

In this scenario, there are multiple requirements. We will look at solutions for one requirement at a time.

The first requirement is to centralize the configuration of retention. The company currently uses retention, but it is configured in Exchange Online. This retention configuration cannot be used outside of Exchange Online. To centralize the retention configuration, you must configure retention in the Security & Compliance Center. In this scenario, you should configure retention to apply to Exchange Online, SharePoint Online, and OneDrive. This will ensure you meet the requirement to retain data across as many services as possible.

The second requirement is to encrypt SharePoint data in libraries. To meet this requirement, you must enable information rights management (IRM), which allows for the use of encryption throughout SharePoint Online. Thereafter, you must configure document libraries with IRM settings to make sure that documents are encrypted. This ensures you meet the requirement to encrypt data even if users do not opt to encrypt their files.

Chapter summary

- Retention policies enable you to retain data, delete data, or both. You can retain data across multiple Office 365 locations.

- Retention labels enable users to retain data by putting a label on their content. Labels can also be applied automatically, which strengthens your retention.

- Exchange Online has multiple data recovery methods built-in, including saving deleted items, archiving email with archive mailboxes, and holds (legal and in-place).

- SharePoint Online stores data for SharePoint and OneDrive. There are two Recycle Bins (site level and site collection level) that maintain deleted data for up to 93 days.

- SharePoint Online and OneDrive for Business offer document versioning. With document versioning, documents have a version number associated with them. When documents are changed, a new version number is created. Users can go back to previous versions if needed.

- By default, OneDrive for Business keeps deleted user data for 30 days.

- An administrator can restore email items out of the Purged Items folder. However, users can only restore deleted items that are in the Deleted Items folder.

- For some operations in Exchange Online and SharePoint Online, you must use PowerShell. Each service has a specific method to connect to PowerShell.

- Your Office 365 licensing dictates how long your audit logs are retained. For some subscriptions, you get up to 90 days of logs, while other subscriptions provide up to 365 days.

- Most admin activity is logged by default. Many user activities are also logged by default. User activity for Exchange Online is not logged by default, and some SharePoint site-specific information is not logged by default.

- You can search unified audit logs using the Microsoft 365 compliance center or using PowerShell.

- You can disable audit logging altogether, although this isn't recommended due to the lack of information that will be available for investigating security incidents.

- Unified audit logs cover Azure Active Directory, Exchange Online, SharePoint Online, OneDrive for Business, Dynamics 365, Microsoft Flow, Microsoft Stream, Microsoft Teams, Power BI, Sway, Yammer, and eDiscovery activities in the Microsoft 365 compliance center.

- Azure AD is a prerequisite of AIP. Additionally, a sync between your on-premises AD DS and Azure AD is required so you can license your users.

- WIP is a data protection technology that complements AIP and is focused on protecting data on client computers that run Windows 10.

- With WIP, an enlightened app is an app that can differentiate between personal data and corporate or organizational data.

- Labels in AIP help users easily see the sensitivity of data (such as with visual markings) and can automatically protect data based on the data as well as conditions.

- DLP uses dictionary matches, keyword matches, regular expression matches, and internal functions to detect sensitive data in DLP rules.

- DLP has a central policy store, where policies and rules are initially created and stored. From the central policy store, replication is used to replicate policies to Exchange Online, SharePoint Online, OneDrive for Business, and Office 2016 desktop apps.

- DLP offers a wide array of built-in policies for financial companies and medical and health companies, and with privacy settings applicable to just about all organizations.

- DLP offers a test mode for policies. In test mode, you can see whether the policy does what you expect before you turn it on for your production environment.

- Data retention policies can be used to retain data for a specified period. For example, you can retain data for five years. Users cannot bypass data retention policies.

- Data retention policies can be used to delete data when the data reaches a specified age. For example, all data older than seven years can be automatically deleted. You can combine policies to retain data with policies to delete data.

- Data retention for Exchange Online stores copies of original content in the Recoverable Items folder, while data retention for SharePoint Online stores copies of original content in the Preservation Hold library.

- You can use PowerShell to create, manage, and delete policies for DLP or data retention.

- AIP has three versions that you can license: Azure AIP for Office 365 (least features), Azure AIP P1 (standard features), and Azure AIP P2 (most features).

- You can use the built-in reports in the Security & Compliance Center to get an overview of your DLP incidents, DLP policy matches, and DLP overrides.

- Content Search and eDiscovery deliver the same results and leverage the same search query format. Content Search should be used for quick scenarios, while eDiscovery should be used for case tracking and in-place holds.

- To organize your searches, preserve content, and export data, you can use eDiscovery cases. Cases are especially beneficial if you have multiple administrators and perform many searches.

- You can enable more eDiscovery features by upgrading your Office 365 licenses. Office 365 E1 provides search capabilities; Office 365 E3 provides search, export, and holds; and Office 365 E5 provides search, export, holds, and advanced eDiscovery features such as analysis.

- An eDiscovery manager can work with cases that they create or are given access to. An eDiscovery administrator can gain access to any case.

Index

Microsoft Deployment Toolkit (MDT), 53

Microsoft Edge baseline, 21

Microsoft Endpoint Manager

  admin center, 3

  configuration profiles, 6–8

  Historical reports, 3

  Intune setup, 4–5

  Operational reports, 3

  Organizations reports, 3

  Specialist reports, 3

Microsoft Office 365, tenant security and Secure Score, 82–88

Microsoft Store for Business (MSfB). *See also* apps; mobile application management

  Benefits page, 32

  Billing & Payments page, 32

  client app types, 35

  configuring, 31–33

  creating and deploying apps with Intune, 36–40

  customization controls, 32–33

  Devices page, 32

  first time sign-in, 29

  getting apps, 30

  Home page, 31

  licensing models, 26–27

  Order History page, 32

  overview, 25

  Partners page, 32

  Permissions page, 32

  prerequisites, 25–27

  private store, 27–30

  Products & Services page, 31–32

  Quotes page, 31

  Settings page, 32

  Support page, 32

mobile application management, 40–44. *See also* apps; MSfB (Microsoft Store for Business)

MSfB (Microsoft Store for Business). *See also* apps; mobile application management

  Benefits page, 32

  Billing & Payments page, 32

  client app types, 35

  configuring, 31–33

  creating and deploying apps with Intune, 36–40

  customization controls, 32–33

  Devices page, 32

  first time sign-in, 29

  getting apps, 30

  Home page, 31

  licensing models, 26–27

  Order History page, 32

  overview, 25

  Partners page, 32

  Permissions page, 32

  prerequisites, 25–27

  private store, 27–30

  Products & Services page, 31–32

  Quotes page, 31

  Settings page, 32

  Support page, 32

N

NIST assessment templates, 152

security reports and alerts, 81–82. *See also*
Microsoft 365 security center

Sender Policy Framework (SPF), 116

sensitivity labeling, 155–158

ServiceNow, Microsoft Cloud App Security, 125

servicing plan, Windows 10 Enterprise deployment,
58–62

session policies, Microsoft Cloud App Security,
135–136

SetupDiag diagnostic tool, 58

SharePoint Online

backups, 166–171

and IRM (Information Rights Management), 186

legal holds, 216

restoring deleted data in, 161–162

snapshot reports, 139–143

Specialist reports, Microsoft Endpoint Manager, 3

SPF (Sender Policy Framework), 116

spoofing, preventing, 116

subscriptions, device compliance, 15

System Center Configuration Manager
(ConfigMgr), 53, 55–56, 61–62

T

telemetry settings, Windows 10 Enterprise
deployment, 63

threat protection, 68. *See also* Microsoft Defender
for Endpoint

traffic logs, managing, 139–143

True alerts, 88

U

UEFI and BIOS, 54

unified audit logs, searching, 210–211

Universal Windows Platform (UWP), 25

upgrade readiness, Windows 10 Enterprise
deployment, 62–67

users and groups, device compliance, 13

UWP (Universal Windows Platform), 25

V

VLSC (volume license service center), 55

W

WaaS (Windows as a Service)

deployment rings, 47

feature updates, 46

LTSB (Long-Term Servicing Branch) identifier, 48

overview, 45–46

quality updates, 46

semi-annual channel, 48

servicing channels, 46–48

Windows Insider, 47–50

WIM (Windows Imaging Format), 52–53

Windows, Microsoft Defender for Endpoint, 99

Windows 10. *See also* device services

deployment, 45–51

device compliance use cases, 12

in S mode, 68

WaaS (Windows as a Service), 45–51